Namoluk Beyond the Reef

Westview Case Studies in Anthropology

Series Editor

EDWARD F. FISCHER
Vanderbilt University

Advisory Board

Tecpán Guatemala: A Modern Maya Town in Global and Local Context
Edward F. Fischer (Vanderbilt University) and Carol Hendrickson (Marlboro College)

Daughters of Tunis: Women, Family, and Networks in a Muslim City
Paula Holmes-Eber (University of Washington)

Fulbe Voices: Marriage, Islam, and Medicine in Northern Cameroon
Helen A. Regis (Louisiana State University)

Magical Writing in Salasaca: Literacy and Power in Highland Ecuador
Peter Wogan (Willamette University)

The Lao: Gender, Power, and Livelihood
Carol Ireson-Doolittle (Willamette University) and Geraldine Moreno-Black (University of Oregon)

Namoluk Beyond the Reef: The Transformation of a Micronesian Community
Mac Marshall (University of Iowa)

Forthcoming

From Mukogodo to Maasai: Ethnicity and Cultural Change in Kenya
Lee Cronk (Rutgers University)

The Tanners of Taiwan: Life Strategies and National Culture
Scott Simon (University of Ottawa)

Urban China: Private Lives and Public Culture
William Jankowiak (University of Nevada, Las Vegas)

The Iraqw of Tanzania: Negotiating Rural Development
Katherine A. Snyder (Queens College, City University of New York)

Black Skins, French Voices: Caribbean Ethnicity and Activism in Urban France
David A. Beriss (University of New Orleans)

Namoluk
Beyond the Reef

*The Transformation of a
Micronesian Community*

MAC MARSHALL
University of Iowa

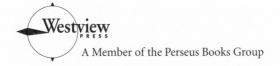

Westview
PRESS

A Member of the Perseus Books Group

An chon Namoluk monson, ren ttong fiti pwos.

Copyright © 2004 by Westview Press, A Member of the Perseus Books Group.

Published in the United States of America by Westview Press, A Member of the Perseus Books Group, 5500 Central Avenue, Boulder, Colorado 80301–2877, and in the United Kingdom by Westview Press, 12 Hid's Copse Road, Cumnor Hill, Oxford OX2 9JJ.

Find us on the world wide web at www.westviewpress.com

Westview Press books are available at special discounts for bulk purchases in the United States by corporations, institutions, and other organizations. For more information, please contact the Special Markets Department at the Perseus Books Group, 11 Cambridge Center, Cambridge, MA 02142, or call (617) 252–5298, (800) 255–1514, or e-mail special.markets@perseusbooks.com.

A Cataloging-in-Publication data record for this book is available from the Library of Congress.
ISBN 0-8133-4162-0 (paperback)
ISBN 0-8133-4163-9 (hardcover)

The paper used in this publication meets the requirements of the American National Standard for Permanence of Paper for Printed Library Materials Z39.48–1984.

10   9   8   7   6   5   4   3   2   1

Contents

List of Illustrations   ix

List of Abbreviations and Acronyms   xi

Series Editor Preface   xiii

Preface and Acknowledgments   xv

1 Openings   1
   OPENING DARK SEAS, 1
   OPENING A WIDER WORLD, 3
   OPENING THE FLOODGATES OF MIGRATION, 6
   OPENING MY ARGUMENT, 8
   OPENING MYSELF, 14

2 Namoluk Atoll, 1969   17
   LAGOON IN THE MIDDLE, 17
   THE OUTSIDE WORLD DISCOVERS NAMOLUK, 19
   COLONIALISM COMES TO NAMOLUK, 22
   DAY-TO-DAY LIFE AT THE END OF THE 1960S, 27
   THE FOUR E'S, 34
   PRIMORDIAL SENTIMENTS OF SHARED IDENTITY, 35

3 Journeyings   43
   ARRIVING AT THE REEF OF HONOLULU, 43
   WAVES, 44
   COLONIZING MERIKA, 53
   BAD TRIPS: BEER AND TURKEY TAILS, 55
   VENTURING, 58

4 Namoluk People, 2002   61
   GETTING THE LEAD OUT, 61
   THE MOTORBOAT REVOLUTION, 62
   TYPHOON PAMELA: MORE WINDS OF CHANGE, 65
   CHANGES IN INFRASTRUCTURE, 67
   CHANGES IN SOCIAL STRUCTURE, 68
   CONTINUITIES, 70
   EXODUS, 74

5 Heading Off to College   77
   THE LEGION OF THE COLLEGE-BOUND, 77
   CHON NAMOLUK AND COLLEGE EDUCATION, 79
   THE XAVIER CONNECTION, 86
   FROM COCONUTS TO COCONUTCHAT, 87

6 Heading Off to Collage   89
   IT'S A SURREAL WORLD OUT THERE, 89
   UNHERALDED, LARGELY FORGOTTEN JOBS, 90
   MOVIN' UP, 94
   LIVING IN A COLLAGE, 96

7 Reef Crossings   105
   MIGRANTS: THE NEW NAMOLUK, 105
   MIGRATION PATTERNS, 106

8 Four Locations Beyond the Reef   113
   ROAMING THE GLOBE, 113
   WÉÉNÉ: THE FIRST STEP, 114
   CHON GUAMOLUK: LIVING WHERE AMERICA'S DAY BEGINS, 117
   WILL DREAMS COME TRUE IN BLUE HAWAI'I?, 122
   EUREKA! I'VE FOUND IT!, 126

9 Closings: Points of Departure   133
   NO ISLAND IS AN ISLAND, 133
   POINTS OF ORIGIN, 135
   NESTED IDENTITIES, 137
   POINTS OF ENTANGLEMENT, 139
   YOUR PLACE OR MINE?, 141
   THE PERSPECTIVE OF FOLKS ON THE SHORE, 143
   CODA, 144

Glossary	*147*
Suggestions for Further Reading	*151*
References	*153*
Index	*161*

Illustrations

MAPS

1.1	Micronesia (Including the Caroline, Mariana, and Marshall Islands)	4
1.2	Chuuk State, Federated States of Micronesia	5
1.3	Namoluk Atoll, Eastern Caroline Islands	9

TABLES

2.1	Namoluk Clans by Number and Percent of *De Jure* Population, 7/13/2001	37
3.1	Number and Percent of Namoluk *De Jure* Population by Location and Year	53
4.1	Locations of *Chon* Namoluk by Ten-Year Age Cohorts, 7/13/2001	75

FIGURES

1.1	Three *Chon* Namoluk and a *Chon* Ettal in the Snow Outside the Author's House in Iowa City, Iowa, Thanksgiving 1975	12
2.1	A Typhoon House on Namoluk, March 1970, Constructed After Typhoon Phyllis in 1958	29
2.2	Namoluk Canoe House (*Fáál an Paros*), with Two Styles of Sailing Canoe, May 1970	30
2.3	The Protestant Church on Namoluk, April 1995	31
2.4	Namoluk Canoe House (*Fáál an Falukupat*), with a Day's Catch of Yellowfin Tuna, December 1969	33
3.1	A Second-Wave Namoluk Man Making Coconut Sennit Cord (*Lul*) in a Canoe House on the Atoll, May 1970	46

3.2   Fifth- and Sixth-Wave Namoluk Men at Chuuk International Airport,
      Wééné, June 1985   50
4.1   *Waaserik* Crossing Namoluk's Lagoon, Bound for Amwes,
      January 1970   63
4.2   Motorboat on Namoluk, April 1995   64
4.3   Damage Caused by Typhoon Pamela on Namoluk, May 1976   66
4.4   The Protestant Minister and Deacons Seated in the
      Namoluk Protestant Church on Easter Sunday 1995   72
5.1   College-Educated Namoluk Schoolteachers on the Dock on Wééné,
      Preparing to Sail to Namoluk, July 2001   81
5.2   Young Namoluk College Student in Great Smoky Mountains
      National Park, North Carolina, August 1977   83
6.1   *Chon* Namoluk in Honolulu Apartment, July 2001
      (Note Security Guard Uniform)   94
6.2   *Chon* Namoluk Dressed for the Sunday Service at
      Island Community Church, Portland, Oregon, June 2002   97
8.1   *Chon* Namoluk Outside One of Their Homes in Iras village on
      Wééné, July 2001   115
8.2   *Chon* Guamoluk in an Apartment on Guam, May 1995   119
8.3   Two Members of the Namoluk Contingent in Eureka, California,
      Outside Their House, July 2002   129

Abbreviations and Acronyms

ABCFM	American Board of Commissioners for Foreign Missions
ASAO	Association for Social Anthropology in Oceania
CMA	California Maritime Academy
CNA	Certified Nursing Assistant
CNMI	Commonwealth of the Northern Mariana Islands
COM	College of Micronesia
COR	College of the Redwoods
FSM	Federated States of Micronesia
HSU	Humboldt State University
ICC	Island Community Church
IBP	Iowa Beef Packers
MIPS	Micronesian Institute of Pastoral Studies [now PIBC]
MOC	Micronesian Occupational College
NIDDM	Non-insulin dependent diabetes mellitus
PATS	Pohnpei Agricultural and Technical School
PBMOTP	Pacific Basin Medical Officer Training Program
PCV	Peace Corps volunteer
PIBC	Pacific Islands Bible College [formerly MIPS]
PICS	Pacific Islands Central School
RMI	Republic of the Marshall Islands
SDA	Seventh-Day Adventist
UNI	University of Northern Iowa
UOG	University of Guam
UPS	United Parcel Service
USIU	U.S. International University
USTTPI	U.S. Trust Territory of the Pacific Islands
WHO	World Health Organization
WPC	Warner Pacific College

Series Editor Preface

The world is more connected now than ever before. In 1930 a three-minute telephone call between New York and London cost $300; today it can be had for less than 10¢ a minute. Airfares have likewise fallen, even as planes have gotten faster and travel times have shortened. What was once the luxury of the "jet set" has become commonplace for a large sector of the middle class in the world's more developed countries. In the words of geographer David Harvey, globalization has brought about a dramatic collapse in time/space distances.

Much has been written about how these processes have transformed Western societies. But, lest we forget, the West does not have a monopoly on mobility. Pacific Islanders have been voyaging for thousands of years, keeping in close contact with neighboring islands and regularly mounting long-distance trips. For them, air travel and the Internet are but new variations of a long-established theme.

Mac Marshall first traveled to Namoluk Atoll in the Federated States of Micronesia in 1969 as a young graduate student. At that time, only four *chon* Namoluk (people of Namoluk) lived abroad. The rest resided on the five small islets where their ancestors had lived for centuries. But much has changed over the last thirty-five years, and Marshall is in a unique position to comment on this change. One of anthropology's virtues is long-term fieldwork with a particular community, but even still the anthropological lens generally only captures a snapshot of a particular group at a given moment in their history. Marshall's decades of friendship with *chon* Namoluk adds rare depth to his analysis. For example, he can tell us not only how children were raised in the late 1960s and early 1970s, he can show us what those children are doing today as adults.

And more likely than not, those adult children do not live on Namoluk. In 2001 there were almost 900 *chon* Namoluk in the world. Of these, only 337 (39 percent) resided on Namoluk. The rest lived in Wééné (25 percent), Guam (18 percent), the United States (10 percent), and elsewhere around the world. Many of the *chon* Namoluk migrants have found work abroad at McDonald's and Pizza Hut outlets; others pursue university degrees, and others still go to be with their children who have left the islands.

This book focuses on the waves of Namoluk migration during the past thirty-five years and the ties that bind migrants to their home community. Although Namoluk lacks regular electricity, gas generators provide power for a few televisions and VCRs that are used to watch video postcards sent by friends and relatives living abroad. By looking at the networks that link Namoluk to Guam, Hawai'i, and Eureka, California (among other places), Marshall details the transnational connections in which not only *chon* Namoluk but many of the world's remote peoples are caught up.

This book looks at kinship and social structure, informal networks of sharing news and gossip (the so-called "coconut telegraph"), the rise in education for both men and women, and the impact of alcohol and tobacco on native society. Marshall conveys these and other anthropological facts with a deeply humanistic sensitivity. Through vignettes and biographical sketches, we get to know *chon* Namoluk not from abstract sets of cultural rules and social categories but rather as individuals, making the best of their lives as they see fit in a globalized world. We meet women such as Erewhon, who left Namoluk a poor single mother and now lives a life of relative luxury in Guam. We also meet young men such as Moses, who left Namoluk with great dreams only to find himself stuck in a series of low-wage jobs from which he cannot seem to escape.

Marshall's judicious mix of personalized ethnography and analysis of broader trends speaks to the world far beyond the reefs of Namoluk. In this way, *Namoluk Beyond the Reef* makes an important contribution to the Westview Case Studies in Anthropology series and to the discipline as a whole. This series presents works that recognize the peoples we study as active agents enmeshed in global as well as local systems of politics, economics, and cultural flows. There is a focus on contemporary ways of life, forces of social change, and creative responses to novel situations as well as to the more traditional concerns of classic ethnography. In presenting rich humanistic and social scientific data born of the dialectic engagement of fieldwork, the books in this series move toward realizing the full pedagogical potential of anthropology: imparting to the reader an empathetic understanding of alternative ways of viewing and acting in the world as well as a solid basis for critical thought regarding the historically contingent nature of ethnic boundaries and cultural knowledge.

Namoluk Beyond the Reef addresses current theoretical issues in anthropology as well as the realities of *chon* Namoluk living in a globalized world. Marshall writes in an engaging and accessible style, advancing our understanding of cultural diversity while uncovering the often hidden webs of global relations that affect us all.

EDWARD F. FISCHER
Nashville, Tennessee

Preface and Acknowledgments

The research that undergirds this book has been conducted off and on during a period of thirty-four years, and it was supported by a number of different funding sources. I am very grateful to all of them, and they are presented here in chronological order: for my doctoral research on Namoluk from 1969–1971, a predoctoral grant and fellowship from the National Institute of Mental Health (U.S. Public Health Service, MH 11871–01 and MH42666–01) and supplemental funds from the Department of Anthropology, University of Washington; for field research on Wééné during 1976, a grant from the American Philosophical Society (Johnson Fund) and a Faculty Developmental Assignment from the University of Iowa; for field research on Wééné during 1985, a grant from the National Science Foundation (BNS–8418908); for a brief visit to Wééné in 1993 following the FSM/WHO Joint Conference on Alcohol and Drug-Related Problems in Micronesia, held on Pohnpei, a short-term consultancy from the Western Pacific Regional Office of the World Health Organization; for field research on Namoluk and Wééné in 1995, a grant from the Center for International Rural and Environmental Health, University of Iowa; for field research with Namoluk people on Wééné, and in Hawai'i, Oregon, and California during 2001 and 2002, an Arts and Humanities Initiative Grant from the University of Iowa; and finally, for support in the initial preparation of this manuscript during fall 2001, a University of Iowa Career Development Award.

Writers always are beholden to many other people, and I am no exception. Numerous colleagues have stimulated my thoughts as I worked on this book, and I cannot list them all here. Some also have provided me with key bits of information, or assisted me in other ways. The following have been particularly helpful: David Akin, Jane Barnwell, Kate Dernbach, Larry Gabriel, Elizabeth Keating, James D. Nason, Sarah Ono, Joakim Peter, Jan Rensel, and Samantha Solimeo. Periods of field research up through 1985 were conducted jointly with Leslie B. Marshall, and her research skills and contributions of data have enriched this volume. It is Margery Wolf, however, to whom I owe my greatest debt. Her encouragement, critiques of my writing, and love made all of the difference as I completed this book.

Karl Yambert, senior editor of Westview Press who earned an anthropology Ph.D., and Ted Fischer, editor of the series in which this volume appears, met my original book prospectus with enthusiasm, and each of them provided helpful suggestions on a first draft that have improved the final manuscript.

My debt to Namoluk people is deep and abiding. Nearly all of the adults on the atoll helped me in myriad ways during my initial fieldwork there, but I have a special and continuing indebtedness to Sarel and Simako Agrippa and their family, who took us in, fed us, and taught us. I fear that in mentioning particular people by name, others might feel slighted, and that is certainly not my intent. But for assistance and communication that relates specifically to the content of this book, the following *chon* Namoluk have my profound gratitude: Santer Agrippa, Seis Arechy, Henry Asugar, Kandhi Elieisar, Amato and Jane Elymore, Miako and Chris Hengio, Nerleb Likisap, Esekiel Lippwe, Jeem Lippwe, Kiper Lippwe, Kipier Lippwe, Tiser Lippwe, Herbert Lodge, Nasako and Scott Madsen, Deuter Malon, Chiteuo Puas, Fierten Rain, Thelma Raynold, Koschy Reuney, Theophil Reuney, Fiuling Ruben, Jano Ruben, Kino Ruben, Noah Ruben, Randy Ruben, Retain Ruben, Stem Salle, Repeat and Cathy Samuel, Risauo Samuel, Kasda Sana, Kaster Sana, Jeff Seladier, Pruta Seladier, Rainlik and Maruko Seladier, Mac Setile, Max Setile, Mike Setile, Misael Setile, Speeder Setile, Termotis Wilson, and Rioichy Yechem. As friends such as these have sought to teach me about their community and their lives, I remain acutely aware of how much I still don't know. *Killisou chapur ngeni ami monson!*

A brief mention of the pronunciation of Mortlockese and Chuukese words is in order. In general I have followed the orthography laid out in Ward H. Goodenough and Hiroshi Sugita's (1980) dictionary, although I provide Mortlockese rather than Lagoon Chuukese pronunciations and spellings where appropriate. Readers may find the following of help:

a pronounced like the *a* of English 'father'

á pronounced like the *a* of English 'hat'

e pronounced like the *e* of English 'set'

é pronounced somewhat like the *u* in English 'but'

i pronounced between the *i* of English 'fit' and the *ee* of English 'feet'

o pronounced like the *o* of English 'note'

ó pronounced like the *aw* in English 'law'

u pronounced between the *u* of English 'put' and the *oo* of English 'boot' *ú* pronounced as a high central unrounded vowel not encountered in standard English

ch pronounced in Mortlockese like the English *sh* (hence, *chon* is pronounced like the English name Sean)

when a vowel is doubled, this indicates vowel length, which is phonemic in Mortlockese and Chuukese

Last, I have used pseudonyms throughout for *chon* Namoluk, except in the two instances where I cite publications authored by people from the atoll. I am well aware that this will not hide people's identity from those insiders who know the Namoluk community, but at least it offers a measure of privacy vis-à-vis outsiders.

I

Openings

Looking for the suitable time, Pukueu
Went to observe the break of day at the other end of the
    island.
A steering wind blew, it blew from the east,
His canoe would be pulled out from its headrests:
Yet suddenly came his asipwar
To stop Pukueu's voyage.
But he did not change his mind; his eager heart sought
    the satisfaction
To open up those dark seas.

Theophil Saret Reuney (1994, 254)

OPENING DARK SEAS

We lingered under the coconut palms at Leor to say our good-byes and shake everyone's hand before we left to return to Seattle. Quicker than we expected or wanted, it was time to leave Namoluk Atoll where Leslie and I had lived for the past two years. As we waded through the warm, crystal-clear water and clambered into the motorboat that would wend through the narrow reef channel to the open sea where the government ship waited, a few women began to keen as if we were dead. Others took up the cry, and as our boat moved away from shore, we were soon overcome by the emotion of a Pacific island parting. Sobbing along

1

with us was our fourteen-year-old "daughter," Maiyumi, who was feeling the sweet sadness of departure from her home island for the very first time.

We had composed ourselves somewhat before coming alongside the *Truk Islander*, and strong arms reached down to help Leslie and Maiyumi up the ladder and onto the ship's deck. After handing up our last bits of luggage, I followed them, and the three of us stood together at the railing as the ship moved slowly away. Small children ran along Namoluk's shoreline, and Maiyumi's mother, Sabrina, waved a palm frond back and forth in farewell. The ship gained speed, and before the island faded to a mere speck on the horizon, the flash of handheld mirrors sent the sun's rays to us in a final silent good-bye.

As Namoluk disappeared, Maiyumi's momentary sorrow was soon replaced by the anticipation of visiting our destination—the urban center in Chuuk, an overnight voyage away to the north. She had graduated from eighth grade on Namoluk a few months earlier, and we were about to finalize her enrollment in a Protestant-run high school that would begin classes later in the month. The captain decided to spend the night anchored in Losap's protected lagoon, and the next morning after off-loading some seedling coconuts and selling a few remaining goods, we set sail for the mountainous volcanic islands of Chuuk Lagoon. The passage from Losap Atoll to Chuuk is not far, and the ship bypassed the captain's own island, Nama, en route, making the journey shorter than usual. To Maiyumi's wonder, the tops of Chuuk's higher peaks came into view even before we steamed past the outer reef to reach the northeast pass. Once the *Truk Islander* slipped through the pass, she no longer rolled with the dark open ocean swells, and the captain made straight for the dock area on Wééné Island. As we drew closer, we could see homes scattered along the shoreline road below the rounded octopus head of Mt. Tonaachaw and then the miscellany of stores and government buildings concentrated in the "downtown" area and up on the elevated saddle called Nantakku.

When government field-trip ships come in from outer islands like Namoluk, they tie up at the main pier to unload. On this day, however, the pier was already occupied by the *Asterion*, a large freighter from overseas, so the *Truk Islander* had to drop anchor, and everyone and everything had to be lightered ashore on a 60-foot-long military surplus landing craft. The three of us gathered our belongings and were soon propelled shoreward to be greeted by a host of Namoluk people who had come to meet the ship. After chatting awhile, and eager to clean up and wash off the salt spray from our voyage, I hailed a taxi to carry us to the campus of Mizpah High School. We would stay there—in small guest rooms up on the hillside under the massive old mango trees planted by New England Congregationalist missionaries in the nineteenth century—until Leslie and I returned to the United States in a couple of weeks and Maiyumi moved into her dorm room almost next door to begin ninth grade.

The taxi I found was typical: a small Datsun pickup truck outfitted with wooden benches along each side of the bed for people to cling to as it jounced along Wééné's mostly unpaved roads at 5–10 mph. The driver helped me load our possessions into the back, and Leslie climbed up after them. Meanwhile Maiyumi just stood next to the truck, and Leslie urged her, "Come on, Maiyumi, get in!" She continued to stand there quietly, looking perplexed, and as I climbed up into the truck bed so she could ride comfortably in the cab, I said with a trace of irritation, "What's wrong, Maiyumi? Let's go!"

At that, she turned to us with a shy smile and asked, "How do I open it?"

OPENING A WIDER WORLD

Chon Namoluk, "the people or citizens of Namoluk Atoll," have been learning how to open new things for more than a century as the colonial powers in Micronesia have shifted from Spain to Germany to Japan to the United States, and now to their participation in the independent country of the Federated States of Micronesia (FSM).[1] Of course, like many other Pacific islanders, long before such external control was imposed, Namoluk people maintained contact with communities on numerous other islands via sailing canoe voyages using sophisticated celestial navigation techniques. Although such regular contacts introduced *chon* Namoluk to occasional new ideas and objects, for the most part the other Micronesians with whom they were in contact shared a common pool of information and materials.

Travel beyond the sphere of traditional voyages and encounters away from the atoll with foreigners from industrialized societies did not begin for Namoluk people until the Germans recruited labor for the phosphate mines on Nauru and Angaur after 1906 (see Map 1.1). None of the Namoluk men who worked in these mines during the German colonial era before the outbreak of World War I was still alive when I first went to the atoll in 1969. Although they had "opened" the door to wage labor and learned to live among people who spoke languages other than their own, their experiences occurred within a familiar geographic setting. The number of Namoluk men engaged in such labor increased markedly during the Japanese colonial period, especially prior to World War II when the Japanese conscripted island laborers to work the phosphate mines on Angaur and Fais and to help construct airfields, bomb shelters, roads, and military installations. Also during the Japanese time, some Namoluk people gained access to a few years of elementary education. Young women as well as young men left their island for school on Oneop in the Mortlocks[2] and (for some) on Tonowas in Chuuk Lagoon (see Map 1.2). A small number of *chon* Namoluk held paid jobs in the Japanese colony in Chuuk. More doors (and eyes) were opened by these experiences, but once again they were limited to familiar Micronesian locations.

Only well after World War II, with the advent of American colonialism in Micronesia, did Namoluk people begin to travel farther afield. On my first visit to the atoll in 1969, only four Namoluk persons resided outside of the U.S. Trust Territory of the Pacific Islands (USTTPI, or the Trust Territory), a jurisdiction set

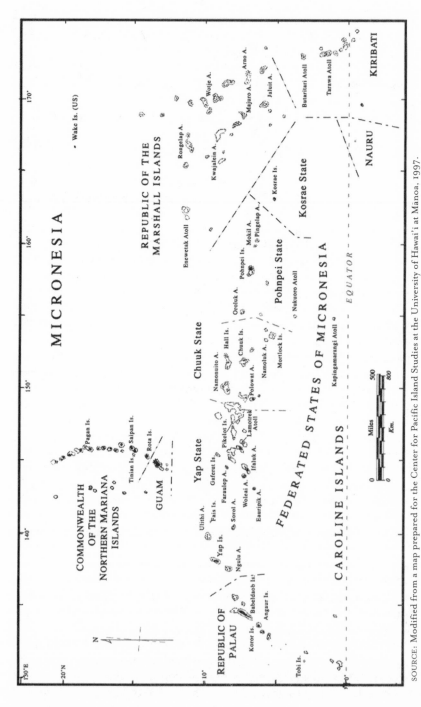

SOURCE: Modified from a map prepared for the Center for Pacific Island Studies at the University of Hawai'i at Manoa, 1997.

Map 1.1—Micronesia (Including the Caroline, Mariana, and Marshall Islands)

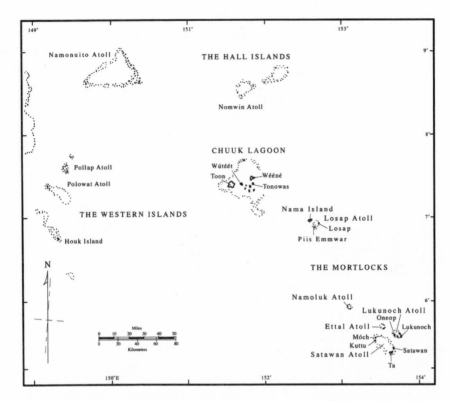

Map 1.2—Chuuk State, Federated States of Micronesia

up by the United Nations at the end of World War II under control of the United States after it defeated Japan (the previous administrative power). These included a middle-aged woman living on Guam with her second American husband, a young woman attending her final year of high school on Guam, a young man doing the same as an exchange student in Oregon, and another young woman enrolled at Honolulu Community College. At that time, a mere thirty-four years ago, only one Namoluk person had earned a college degree. As we shall see, these circumstances have changed markedly over the past three decades. The chapters to follow illustrate some of the experiences *chon* Namoluk have had as they embraced new places of residence, work, and school.

The remainder of this book focuses on migration from Namoluk and the openings it has provided for engagement with a wider world. Migration to Wééné beginning in the 1960s, movement to the United States from the early 1970s, the establishment of roots on Guam commencing in the late 1980s, and the buildup of a Namoluk network in Hawai'i over the last decade will receive attention, as will occasional migration to other more distant places.

OPENING THE FLOODGATES OF MIGRATION

From the dawn of history, human beings have moved around and migrated. Micronesians—especially the atoll dwellers with their sophisticated deep water sailing canoes and remarkably accurate star compass—not only migrated originally to their island homes via sea highways, but they also maintained a high degree of mobility through interisland voyages. Movement, migration, and voyaging beyond the horizon are nothing new to Micronesian people.

During the Japanese colonial period (1914–1945), active efforts were made to discourage and prevent interisland canoe voyages, although the numerous small ships that plied among the islands provided an alternative means of moving about. These efforts were not entirely successful—especially in the Western Islands of what is now Chuuk State and in the more remote atolls in Yap State, where the navigational arts continued to flourish (e.g., see Gladwin 1970)—but they did decrease the frequency of canoe voyaging and contributed to its demise on many islands such as Namoluk. When the United States replaced Japan as the colonial power in Micronesia following World War II, it continued the provision of small interisland "field-trip" ships to carry passengers and cargo back and forth between the urban centers and outer island communities. Overall, these interruptions to and reductions in direct voyaging among many of the islands, combined with the availability of field-trip ships, contributed to a center-and-periphery pattern of transportation and reduced the density of interisland networks. For example, in pre- and early colonial times Namoluk people sailed from their island to Polowat Atoll and back, without intermediate stops. By the post–World War II period, someone wishing to travel from Namoluk to Polowat had to catch a field-trip ship to Wééné, Chuuk, and then wait weeks or sometimes months until a different field-trip sailed for Polowat. Such shifts in transportation patterns served to strengthen the importance of the urban center.

Even so, the Trust Territory's urban centers grew very slowly until the advent of the Kennedy administration and much larger island budgets in the 1960s led to an expansion of infrastructure and wage employment. In Chuuk, this growth of the town center initially had only a modest impact on most outer island communities such as Namoluk, although it stimulated some limited population movement from the atolls to town in search of short-term employment. Such communities as Namoluk, then, remained largely "intact" through the mid-to-late 1960s, in the sense that the great majority of their members continued to reside "at home." The first significant factor that pulled *chon* Namoluk to the urban center on Wééné was what Francis X. Hezel (1979) has called "the education explosion," a phenomenon that he dates to 1965 and to Truk[3] High School's first graduating class.

With greater opportunities for a high school education from the late 1960s onward, the emigration of Namoluk's people—especially its young people—began in earnest. These opportunities were furthered by the establishment of junior high schools (ninth and tenth grade) in 1970, with the one for the Mortlocks located on Satawan Islet, Satawan Atoll (see Map 1.2). The tremendous increase in the number of high school graduates in Chuuk from 1965 to 1977 that Hezel (1979) documented was joined by an expansion of scholarships and other funds to pursue a college education in the United States.

These resources provided the financial wherewithal for hundreds of Chuukese high school graduates to enroll in colleges and universities in Hawai'i and on the U.S. mainland, beginning in the early 1970s. Namoluk students were prominent among these college migrants, as will be discussed in subsequent chapters.

The next big stimulus to migration from places like Namoluk to Wééné and beyond resulted from a combination of factors. Many of the college students who went to the States in the 1970s returned and found salaried jobs, particularly government jobs, in Micronesia's urban centers. Those who followed just a few years later, however, returned to find nearly all the available jobs taken, and they grew restive (Larson 1989 provides a sensitive account of their dilemma). Casting about for work, some of these young adults moved to Saipan during the early 1980s. Saipan, the capital of the Commonwealth of the Northern Mariana Islands (CNMI), had earlier been the capital of the USTTPI, and consequently people from elsewhere in Micronesia could freely immigrate there. The CNMI experienced a tourist boom during the 1980s as large numbers of high-end hotels were built by Japanese corporations to cater to a Japanese market. In addition to jobs in Saipan's tourist industry, numerous Micronesians, including a few from Namoluk, found employment in the two dozen garment factories that were set up there beginning in 1983 to exploit cheap labor and to find a way around U.S. import quotas of clothing from foreign countries.

At about the same time that hotel construction and tourism took off on Saipan, it also began to boom on Guam, notably after early 1984 (see Map 1.1). By this time job prospects in places like Wééné were poor to nonexistent, but immigration of Micronesians to Guam was still tightly controlled. Then things changed. With the implementation of the Compact of Free Association between the newly constituted Federated States of Micronesia (FSM) and the United States on November 3, 1986, "For the first time Micronesians were allowed free entry into the US and its possessions to live and work without restriction" (Hezel and McGrath 1989, 49). Not long thereafter, the number of Micronesians who moved to Guam grew by leaps and bounds, and by September 1988 approximately 1,100 people from Chuuk State were living there (Hezel and McGrath 1989). Most of this migration was in search of jobs, although better schools and health care also figured into people's decisions to move to Guam. At first only a few Namoluk people were part of this late-1980s flow, but within a very few years—by 1995—Guam had the third largest number of Namoluk people of any location (see especially Chapter 8).

In the late 1990s, Guam's economy began to sour, and Micronesians resident there—along with others from their home islands—went to Hawai'i and the U.S. mainland in growing numbers. There they joined some of their compatriots who had gone originally to the United States for college in the 1970s and had never left. Most such "long-timers" had married Americans and had children, so they were allowed to stay in the country before the Compact was signed for that reason. During the past thirty years, a number of places in the United States have attracted especially large numbers of people from Chuuk State, for example, Honolulu; Portland-Salem, Oregon; and Corsicana, Texas, to name but three. These beachheads in a new Micronesian archipelago now contain three- or four-generation families, workers, students, and spouses of varied ethnicities. Once again, as we shall see, *chon* Namoluk have been fully participant in all of these developments. By midsummer 2001, more than a quarter of Namoluk's population was resident in the United States or its territories, with 10 percent of them in the fifty states, and another almost 18 percent located on Guam. This book is about the implications of these profound shifts in population during the past forty years for individual Namoluk people and for the Namoluk community.

OPENING MY ARGUMENT

In the once-upon-a-time anthropology of an earlier generation, the world was divided into neatly demarcated sociocultural systems—usually called societies or cultures—that were located in particular geographic places. The quintessential examples of this way of ordering the ethnographic world were islands—clearly bounded mini-worlds such as the Andaman Islands, made famous by A. R. Radcliffe-Brown, or Raymond Firth's Tikopia. Times have changed, and concepts have also changed, and today's anthropologists think very differently about cultures, societies, places, and boundaries.

It is erroneous to label Namoluk as "a culture" per se. Culturally, socially, and linguistically, Namoluk is thoroughly intertwined with a number of other Carolinian communities. The atoll's closest connection is with Ettal, its nearest neighbor and the putative source of its present population following the eradication of Namoluk's "original" people. As the story is told, a canoe sailed from Ettal across the 35 miles of open sea to visit Namoluk, but when they arrived, they found no one there. After checking thoroughly for signs of life, they hurried back to Ettal to share the news. The result was that members of several Ettal lineages moved to Namoluk to recolonize the abandoned atoll. Ever since then, the ties between the two communities have been especially close, and this is expressed by stating that Ettal is the canoe's hull and Namoluk its outrigger.

But Namoluk has very strong ties with several other island communities in its vicinity as well, notably Oneop, Moch, Nama and Kuttu. As with Ettal, these connections are via the settlement of people and the establishment of lineage branches on another island: from Namoluk to Nama and Moch, and from Kuttu

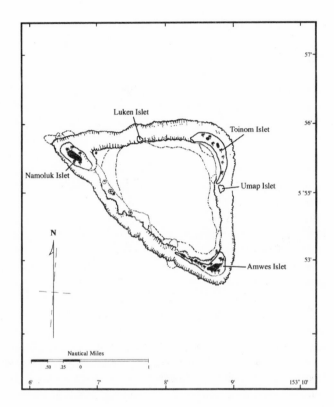

Map 1.3—Namoluk Atoll, Eastern Caroline Islands

and Oneop to Namoluk. So at a minimum, Namoluk is bound up socially and culturally with at least five other Mortlockese communities. But stopping here would ignore the numerous relatively recent marriages between *chon* Namoluk and spouses from Losap, Satawan, and Lukunoch, three more atoll communities in the Mortlocks, and it would also fail to account for colonially wrought changes during the twentieth century that increasingly have bound "the Mortlocks" together as a sociopolitical unit within what is now Chuuk State, FSM.

My point here is that as one expands outward from Namoluk Atoll, one discovers social, cultural, and linguistic connections that range far afield. For instance, Namoluk has historical trading ties to Peniyésene village on Wééné Island, Chuuk; links to Polowat Atoll via multiple marriages and a shared lineage; marital connections with the Mortlockese settlements on the island of Pohnpei; and linguistic relationships with the speakers of "Trukic" dialects who extend westward from Chuuk State through all the outer islands of Yap State, FSM, and the Southwest Islands of the Republic of Palau (Quackenbush 1968). Given such circumstances, where does one culture stop and another begin?

This question underscores the point that we live in a time when anthropologists no longer view cultures as discrete, bounded units attached to specific places in the old Murdockian sense. Instead, culture is not bound to place, and in an ever more mobile world it is carried with migrants as they cross national borders in search of new opportunities for education, employment, or safety from warfare and revolution. With this in mind, perhaps the best way to think of Namoluk culture is that it is one part of a cultural-linguistic gradient that stretches across much of the Caroline Islands.

That said, what of Namoluk as a "society" and the atoll as a "place"? I noted above that as a social entity Namoluk has been wrapped together for quite some time with several other island populations in a quasi-ethnic, quasi-linguistic grouping called "the Mortlocks." If we accept the widespread social science idea that societies are comprised of multiple communities, then I argue that Namoluk is one of the communities that make up Mortlockese society and that it is not a society unto itself. This leaves the matter of place to be addressed.

Namoluk is irrefutably a physical place, a coral atoll made up of five islets located at 5 degrees 55 minutes North, 153 degrees 08 minutes East, approximately 125 miles southeast of Chuuk in the Eastern Caroline Islands (see Map 1.3). But to state this is in some ways to state the obvious. What is more interesting is that humans imbue particular places with names, with a history, and with emotional attachment. Keith Basso observes that "what people make of their places is closely connected to what they make of themselves as members of society and inhabitants of the earth, and while the two activities may be separable in principle, they are deeply joined in practice. If place-making is a way of constructing the past, a venerable means of *doing* human history, it is also a way of constructing social traditions and, in the process, personal and social identities" (1996, 7). Places are not just locations; some places are *home*, and home is a key to personal and social identity. Namoluk is a place of this sort: it is home to the members of the named community from the atoll who have kinship ties and land rights there, and it is the primary source of identity for those who are called and call themselves *chon* Namoluk.

Critiques and discussions of place have been very much center stage in anthropology during recent years, but the significance of place for identity has sometimes gotten lost in the rush to discuss the powerful effects of globalization and transnational migration. Arjun Appadurai (1988) set this recent discussion in motion, and his work was followed soon thereafter by two much-cited articles by Margaret Rodman (1992) and by Akhil Gupta and James Ferguson (1997a).

Urging a reappraisal of the concept of place in anthropology, Rodman contends that places are socially constructed, and she argues that anthropologists should seek to understand how *others* constitute places out of their own interests and experiences. From this Rodman develops the idea of multilocality, in which places are to be seen from others' viewpoints, can be analyzed as parts of larger networks, can be used to highlight the contrasts between the known and the unfamiliar, and can have multiple meanings and be experienced differently by different people (1992, 647). She concludes that "By joining multilocality to multi-vocality, we can look 'through' these places, explore their links with others, consider why they are constructed as they are, see how places represent people, and begin to understand how people embody places" (1992, 652).

Following on Rodman's suggestions, as our story about Namoluk unfolds we will have occasion to see how different people from the island construct their images of home. Some of them maintain a passionate attachment to the land and surrounding sea, whereas others have all but dismissed their connection to their home atoll. How these differences relate to personal identities and the maintenance of a "Namoluk community" will be explored in later chapters. The ways Namoluk fits into larger social networks (e.g., "the Mortlocks," "Chuuk," and "Micronesia"), and the ways that the scattered locales of contemporary Namoluk people may be said to constitute a viable network also will be examined. Related to this discussion will be reflections on how unfamiliar places (e.g., Guam or Eureka) have been "colonized" by *chon* Namoluk, that is, made into known or now-familiar places. Through all of this, I will make the case for what Rodman calls "the inseparability of place and people," as shared home place (Namoluk) frames and defines the new transnational boundaries of what continues as a viable community despite its dispersal through migration. In other words, we will see how Namoluk as a place represents people, "and begin to understand how people embody places" (Rodman 1992, 652).

In their influential paper on "the field" as a place—as a location for anthropological studies—Gupta and Ferguson remark on an irony of these times: "that as actual places and localities become ever more blurred and indeterminate, *ideas* of culturally and ethnically distinct places become perhaps even more salient" (1997a, 39). Invoking Benedict Anderson's (1983) idea of "imagined communities," they picture "displaced peoples cluster[ed] around remembered or imagined homelands, places, or communities in a world that seems increasingly to deny such firm territorialized anchors in their actuality" (1997a, 39). They go on to state that "in such a world, it becomes ever more important to train an anthropological eye on processes of construction of place and homeland by mobile and displaced people" (1997a, 39). As we discuss the transformation of the Namoluk community during recent decades, our attention will be on the *idea* of the atoll as a distinct place that helps people to construct their personal and social identities. Although such a connection between people and place may be fairly straightforward and obvious for those who continue to reside on Namoluk, it is less so for *chon* Namoluk who have taken up extended residence abroad. It is for this latter group in particular that the *idea* of Namoluk as a community rooted in a place occupies a special prominence.

Gupta and Ferguson discuss anthropology's history of "the radical separation of 'the field' from 'home,' and the related creation of a hierarchy of purity of field sites," with exotic sites privileged over those "at home" (1997b, 12). Even though the primary field site on which this book is based is Namoluk

Three *Chon* Namoluk and a *Chon* Ettal in the Snow Outside the
Author's House in Iowa City, Iowa, Thanksgiving 1975

Atoll, my fieldwork with *chon* Namoluk has been multisited, in George E.
Marcus's (1998) sense of "multi-sited ethnography," from the very beginning.
In 1969, while awaiting a ship to carry us to the atoll, I began fieldwork with
Namoluk people then resident on Wééné. Over the years I have continued to
work on several occasions with this urban population of *chon* Namoluk, but
my "Namoluk field sites" also have expanded well beyond Chuuk State to
Pohnpei, Guam, Hawai'i, and the mainland USA. In a blurring of anthropology's traditional field versus home distinction, the "field" literally came home
to me in Iowa City, Iowa, or at my parent's homes in Kailua, Hawai'i, or
Coronado, California, as Namoluk friends came to visit or spend school holidays with me in these places. More recently, as part of the research for this
book, I have traveled to see *chon* Namoluk in such places as Pensacola, Florida,
and Honolulu, Hawai'i; Cedar Falls, Iowa, and Lincoln, Nebraska; Portland and
Salem, Oregon, and Eureka, California. Such visits have been richly and regularly supplemented by Internet and telephone communications with a host of
Namoluk folks scattered around the United States. Reflecting the dispersed nature of the contemporary Namoluk community, then, multisited ethnography
has been an essential research strategy from 1969 to the present.

Place and identity. Do multiple places then lead to multiple identities? Or is there a way in which common roots in a shared place reach deep into people's lives, entangling them in one another's affairs until they die? Questions such as these will occupy us in later chapters, but they are by no means unique to Namoluk. In describing the centrality of place for the Western Apache, Keith H. Basso comments that "places possess a marked capacity for triggering acts of self-reflection, inspiring thoughts about who one presently is, or memories of who one used to be, or musings on who one might become" (1996, 107). It seems certain that Namoluk as a place, and the other places across the sea in which Namoluk people have settled, have all likely inspired such thoughts and musings as the community has transformed and been redefined in the process.

Anthropologists' argument over and rethinking of the culture concept is part of a response to a congeries of intertwined processes variously called "globalism" or "transnationalism." These words represent efforts to find a language both to imagine and to investigate the profound transformations in world commerce, population movements, and the flow of images and ideas consequent on revolutions in transportation and communication. Much exciting ferment and many good ideas have resulted from anthropology's engagement with globalization and its effects on people's lives all over our planet. But at the same time, as James L. Watson reminds us, "local culture" persists in the face of transnational border crossings and global flows: "Local culture remains a powerful influence in daily life. People are tied to places, and those places continue to shape particular norms and values. The fact that residents of Moscow, Beijing, and New Delhi occasionally eat at McDonald's, watch Hollywood films, and wear Nike athletic shoes (or copies of them) does not make them 'global'" (2002, 137).

This book is an attempt to provide insight into how the carriers of one "local culture" (Mortlockese culture) from one small Pacific Island community (Namoluk Atoll) have moved with increased alacrity and adventuresomeness into a wider world. In the pages to follow I discuss how *chon* Namoluk have become architects of their own history, even as their personal and collective identities remain tied to a reef-girt set of islets in the far blue Pacific. My discussion is based upon ethnographic fieldwork with Namoluk people for more than three decades. During that time, both the conduct and the writing of ethnography have altered in various ways. Many—perhaps most—ethnographers now endeavor to show "how the region and beyond is present in the local and how the local can in turn be. . . in a transcending field of action" (Ulin 2001, 223). And many—perhaps most—ethnographers now seek new ways to present ethnography to what we hope will be wider audiences than in years past (e.g., Wolf 1992).

In this book I examine Namoluk as a local place whose people's lives are now woven into regional and transnational processes. As I write about the transformations I see in the Namoluk community, and wonder about its future, I am reminded that "the anthropologist as subject is encompassed within the same frame as the subjects of anthropological enquiry, is coeval with them, and is constituted through relations with them" (Moore 1999, 19). Elsewhere (Marshall in press) I have speculated on the ways this mutual involvement in each other's lives has affected my career as an anthropologist; I offer the pages to follow as a testimonial to what my Namoluk friends have taught me about their community and their lives.

OPENING MYSELF

In this final section of the introduction I address the matter of my connections to different members of the Namoluk community, and I reflect upon my positionality vis-à-vis *chon* Namoluk. This information allows you, the reader, to better assess what is to come, and it engages with the larger matter of representation and "who speaks for whom" posed by James Clifford: "How should differently positioned authorities (academic and nonacademic, Native and non-Native) represent a living tradition's combined and uneven processes of continuity, rupture, transformation, and revival?" (2001, 480). How indeed?

Prior to traveling to Micronesia in 1969, I wrote to the mayor and members of the island council to request permission to live among them and to conduct the research for my doctoral dissertation. They agreed to this request, and by the time Leslie and I first visited the atoll, there already had been a discussion of where we would live. Four Peace Corps volunteers (PCVs) had been stationed on Namoluk by that time, and in most cases the PCVs had occupied the municipal house adjacent to the island's dispensary and close to the Namoluk Elementary School where all of them had taught. It was thought that similar accommodation would work for the visiting anthropologist, but the problem was that a PCV couple was already living in the municipal house. After considerable negotiation, which had more political implications than I then realized, Leslie and I arranged to rent an as-yet not quite finished cement house owned by the island's health aide and his wife. In so doing we also gained a set of Namoluk kin, something we only came to understand upon becoming more familiar with life there.

Our Namoluk family is an extended family, and in principle it involves all members of the matrilineage on whose land we lived. These general ties have been reinforced in various specific ways. The health aide, Sergio, and I became *pwiipwi* "created siblings," as did his wife, Sabrina, and Leslie (a discussion of created siblings as a part of Chuukese kinship may be found in Marshall 1977). This tie gave each of us the clan identity of our "sibling"; hence Leslie was Wáánikar and I was Sór, connecting us to still other people. Later on, Leslie and I *muuti* ("adopted") their eldest daughter, Maiyumi, who we sponsored at Mizpah High School when the three of us sailed to Chuuk in 1971 (Namoluk adoption is explained in Marshall 1976). Three years after that, our own son, Kelsey, was born, and we spent the first summer following his birth living with my parents in Kailua, O'ahu, while we conducted archival research at the B. P. Bishop Museum in Honolulu. That summer we resolved to have him baptized at a ceremony held in my parent's home, followed by a big party. Sergio and Sabrina's firstborn, a young man named Butch, was a college student in Honolulu then, and he regularly visited my parent's home on weekends to relax, play music, and go to the beach. Butch consented to be Kelsey's godfather and to bear witness at the christening. Along with these formal ties, in the years since we first arranged to rent Sergio and Sabrina's house, various members of their family have visited us in the United States, and this family has unfailingly hosted us on our return visits to Chuuk. It is with them that I have my closest personal connections to the Namoluk community.

Through them, and their spouses and descendants, my Namoluk network ramifies into several other matrilineages. My network also encompasses many people from the community, my age or somewhat older, who befriended me and resolved to teach me what they could while I lived among them. Several of these people, and some younger than I as well, have become special friends with whom I routinely communicate by card, letter, e-mail, or occasional phone call. A few of them, including Theophil Reuney (author of the epigraph that opens this chapter), have earned advanced degrees and comprise a brain trust of men and women intensely interested in their own community and its place in a larger world. Some of them, and alas, Theophil among them, are now deceased.

There is a broader sense in which my connection to Namoluk extends to the entire population. I met and knew nearly everyone in the *de jure* population between 1969 and 1971, missing only a few people who already lived abroad or on a distant island that I was unable to visit. Some of those whom I did not get to know personally during my original fieldwork I met subsequently, whereas many of the atoll's younger children are known to me today only by their names. All of us are bound together through our connection to Namoluk as a place, although I am keenly aware that my connection is categorically different from that of someone born into a Namoluk lineage. I have been fortunate to be entrusted with certain kinds of information about the atoll, the genealogies I gathered from old people now long dead, the land tenure histories in my files with all their contradictions, the ethnographic data that fill my notebooks, and the photographs of people and places dating back to 1969. This information forms a small part of the community's history, and I bear a responsibility to preserve it carefully and to write about it wisely. This book is a conscious attempt to address my Namoluk friends and to repay in one small way the friendship, knowledge, and many kindnesses they have so generously given me over the years.

When I arrived on Namoluk the first time, I was not quite twenty-six years old; a husband, but not a father; a graduate student, but not a professor. From a Mortlockese perspective I was an *aluel*, "young man," and I had to work to construct a persona as a *mwáán*, "an adult man." I believe that I succeeded in this, in part because I am a foreigner, and it meant that both my questions and my opinions were taken more seriously than they otherwise might have been. I have maintained more or less continuous contact with Namoluk people from 1969 to the present, when I am now sixty years old, a father, and a full professor who has taught at the university level for thirty-one years. Although still a *mwáán*, my white beard and bald head signal that soon I will be a *chielap*, "elderly person." As my years accumulated, as I became a father, as Leslie and I divorced and both re-married, these alterations in my roles have had repercussions on my relationships with *chon* Namoluk. Older, but probably no wiser, I am now accorded a measure of the respect given to old men in Chuuk who remain physically and mentally vigorous. And so I am presently positioned as an intimate outsider, as someone who has demonstrated a long-term commitment to the community and who seeks actively to keep in touch. In this, I resemble a few of the Namoluk migrants who have been away for twenty years or more, who remain committed to the place of their birth and connected to other *chon* Namoluk via the Internet or the phone, but who are unlikely to take up residence on the atoll again. The differ-ence, of course, is that they are intimate *insiders*.

This brings us back to Clifford's question about how an academic, non-Native "authority" should "represent a living tradition's combined processes of continu-ity, rupture, transformation, and revival?" (2001, 480). I do not pretend to speak for *chon* Namoluk about themselves, their history, and their personal experi-ences. Instead, I try to provide what has been called "the 101st account."[4] What is meant by this is that if an imaginary anthropologist worked with a community of one hundred people, each of them would have a slightly different story to tell based upon their age, gender, marital status, and the like. It is the anthropologist's job, according to this idea, to abstract from conversations with and observations of these one hundred people, to synthesize, dissect, and organize this information into a separate distinct version of events: in other words, the 101st account. What follows is such an account, written with respect and affection and intended both to record and to edify experience.

Notes

1. The FSM is made up of four states: Chuuk, Kosrae, Pohnpei, and Yap, covering most of the Caroline Islands in the western Pacific (see Map 1.1).

2. The Mortlocks collectively refers to the atolls and islands stretching southeast from Chuuk Lagoon and including Nama, Losap, Namoluk, Ettal, Lukunoch, and Satawan. Losap comprises two distinct communities (Losap and Piis-Emmwar), Lukunoch has two communities (Lukunoch and Oneop), and Satawan consists in four inhabited communi-ties (Satawan, Ta, Kuttu, and Moch). See Chapter 2 for further information about the Mortlocks.

3. Truk is an older name for Chuuk, representing a mispronunciation and misspelling of the Chuukese word. Chuuk means "mountain" in the Chuukese language, and the name was reclaimed following the establishment of the FSM in 1986.

4. I associate this idea with Roger Keesing, but neither I nor others familiar with his ex-tensive publications have been able to locate an appropriate citation.

2

Namoluk Atoll, 1969

Today is a great day to fish. On my island, we usually go
fishing when the rain is really falling hard. The fish go
tame under the rain. That's why I want to be on my island
just for today. I want to be with the boys of my island
school because I know some of them are fishing this
morning for meat for the school's dining hall. They always go out in the rain in the morning to fish.

Kino S. Ruben (1973, 89)

LAGOON IN THE MIDDLE

The name Namoluk (pronounced "Nah-mow-luke") means "lagoon in the middle." This refers to Namoluk's position midway between the other two islands
that make up what is known as Lukeisel[1]—Losap and Nama to the north—and
the three atolls that lie to the south, called Nomoi—Ettal, Lukunoch, and
Satawan (see Map 1.2). From 1795, when the English sea captain James Mortlock
sailed past Nomoi in the good ship *Young William* and humbly bestowed his
name on this atoll cluster, Nomoi has been known to westerners as "the
Mortlocks."[2] In the post–World War II era this name was extended by American
colonial officials to the islands of Lukeisel as well. Lukeisel was called "the Upper
Mortlocks" in contrast to "the Lower Mortlocks" south of Namoluk. Transmuting
"Mortlocks" into the sound pattern of their own language, the denizens of these
islands today refer to themselves as *chon Morschlok*, or "Mortlockese."

Although today the Mortlocks share a loose sense of connection or togetherness, prior to European control Namoluk and the southern atolls were divided into two warring alliances. Namoluk was allied with Ettal, Oneop (in Lukunoch Atoll), and Moch (in Satawan Atoll) in the *marau* against Lukunoch (in Lukunoch Atoll), Satawan, Kuttu, and Ta (all in Satawan Atoll) in the *chin* (see Map 1.2). Losap and Nama were not usually involved in battles to the south, although they occasionally fought against each other. When they did so, Ettal and Namoluk joined together with Nama against Losap. These precolonial alliances continue to shape relative feelings of closeness among the different communities, and they are reflected in the history of intermarriages and the level of mutual visiting.

Linguists recognize Mortlockese as a distinct language and not just a dialect of Chuukese (Goodenough and Sugita 1980), and this shared language further bolsters the idea of a Mortlockese unity. But during the past half-century, as Mortlockese migrants to Chuuk Lagoon have accommodated their speech to that of the numerically dominant population there, much traditional Mortlockese vocabulary has fallen into disuse. For most purposes today the Mortlockese and Chuukese languages are mutually intelligible, and a clear linguistic convergence is underway. Nevertheless, as with the Deep South of the United States, there is an immediately identifiable Mortlockese accent, and when Mortlockese speakers venture to Chuuk proper, they must learn new words, new stress patterns, and new paralinguistic cues. Having learned Mortlockese on Namoluk before I conducted fieldwork in Chuuk, I became keenly aware of these language differences. Whenever I spoke in Chuuk, people would ask me where in the Mortlocks I had lived, and I found that I had to learn many new words to substitute for the Mortlockese ones I had so painstakingly memorized. To this day, my speech is deeply inflected by a Mortlockese accent.

Namoluk's name may have been bestowed by ancient Carolinian navigators in reference to the atoll's position midway between the Lower Mortlocks and the Nama-Losap cluster. This idea gains support from Jan S. Kubary (1880), who observed that Namoluk was sighted or visited without fail on voyages from the Lower Mortlocks to Chuuk. On the other hand, Max Girschner (1912) claimed that Namoluk is the European name, and another name by which Namoluk once was known to its people—Nomoilam, "deep place in the sea" (from *nom*, "lagoon," and *lam*, a contraction of *le mataw*, "the open sea")—is the atoll's native name. This is quite conceivable because Namoluk is the name for the atoll's largest islet. Early foreign visitors may have put ashore and asked the name of the place, only to be given the name of the islet they were on. But it may be significant that the first anthropologist to work in the Mortlocks doesn't mention Nomoilam at all, making reference only to Namoluk (Kubary 1880). Although the name Nomoilam is no longer in regular use today, the delegates to the Namoluk Constitutional Convention included it on the official seal of the Namoluk Municipal Government. One knowledgeable *chon* Namoluk told me

that "'Loilam' and 'Nomoilam' are the same. The root word is 'lam', which means:
1) light or bright[,] 2) deep thoughts of good nature. The prefix 'lo' means a calm
body of open water encircled by a continuous reef. It also means 'body oil' (usually thought of as coconut oil). The other prefix 'nom' means the same as 'lo'.
They are both referred to as 'deep lagoon'. 'Loi' and 'Nomoi' are the possessive
forms of the two words. 'Lo' (or oil) has another connotation in traditional
Namoluk. It also means 'peace', 'calm', and 'harmony'. . . . Nomoilam—'The deep
lagoon of good thoughts and wishes for a flourishing people, the land, and the
sea'" (e-mail message from Kendrick, 19 March 2003, pseudonym substituted).

Located across 35 miles of open sea from the Lower Mortlocks, Namoluk
stands alone in the sea, with Losap Atoll another 65 miles to the north. No matter
in which direction one looks from Namoluk, nothing but the wide, heaving ex-
panse of the Pacific stretches to the horizon. Along with this relative isolation,
Namoluk is the smallest—after Nama Island—permanently inhabited island in
Chuuk and Pohnpei States of the FSM. Its five islets have a combined total land
area roughly equivalent to a nine-hole golf course (only .322 square miles, or approximately 206 acres), and the lagoon these islets encircle covers just under 3
square miles (Manchester 1951, 237). Measuring 42 fathoms at its center,
Namoluk's lagoon is among the deepest in the Pacific, and the dark seas surrounding the atoll plunge quickly to depths of more than 400 fathoms only a
mile offshore. Typical of coral atolls wherever they occur, the highest point of
land on Namoluk is no more than 8 feet above sea level, although the coconut
palms and other trees, when fully grown, may reach 100 feet in height.

Long before foreign intrusion, Namoluk voyaging canoes sailed as far away as
Nukuoro to the east and Polowat to the west (Riesenberg 1965, 158). Open ocean
voyages from Namoluk are now largely a thing of the past, although trips are
made back and forth to Ettal in outboard motorboats using a Western-style compass. The last canoe voyage from Namoluk to Chuuk was more than eighty years
ago, and no Namoluk canoe (or motorboat) has traveled to the Upper Mortlocks
since a canoe was lost on such a trip in 1950.

THE OUTSIDE WORLD DISCOVERS NAMOLUK

Perhaps due to its small size, its relative isolation from other islands, and the dif-
ficulty of spotting an atoll from the sea until one is quite close, it was not until
1827 that the first documented sighting by a westerner appeared. In that year,
Captain Richard Macy, of the Nantucket whaleship *Henry*, sailed past, although
from his account it is certain that he made no contact with *chon* Namoluk (Day
1966, 171; Sharp 1960, 217).

It was only a year later, however, that Namoluk people had their first direct
contact with foreigners. Early in 1828, Fedor (Frédéric) Lütke visited Namoluk
aboard the *Senyavin* while on a Russian scientific cruise around the world.
Having just spent several weeks in the Lower Mortlocks, Lütke stopped outside

Namoluk's reef for a few hours, there being no deep water passage into the lagoon. Lütke's own words convey his impressions of *chon* Namoluk: "We traveled to the northeast of the Etal group, when the islands that we were searching for appeared right in front of us. . . . We then hove to in order to receive visitors who were already coming toward us in their canoes. . . . All of them asked to come aboard to explore the ship; none of them undertook on his own to go anywhere without permission, even less to touch anything. We could but find them very nice people, even after having seen the people of Lukunor [Lukunoch]. . . . After exchanging gifts, we parted in friendly fashion, and set our course to the north" (1835, 88–91). Given the unhappy initial contacts with Europeans of many other Pacific Islanders, this amicable first meeting was an auspicious beginning for *chon* Namoluk in their encounters with the outside world.

An interesting sequel to this early Russian contact with Namoluk occurred exactly 140 years later. In 1968, a Russian oceanographic research vessel from Vladivostok arrived off Namoluk at night. Seeing the lights, the men of Namoluk, who were out of cigarettes, thought that it was a Japanese fishing boat and despite a high wind, resolved to paddle out to the ship and ask for tobacco. Upon approaching the vessel, their anticipation turned to fear when they recognized the flag of the USSR. Unable to return to Namoluk because of the wind, the men hesitantly climbed the rope ladder let over the side for them. Once aboard they were treated to a feast, vodka, and a warm dry place to spend the night. The next morning the ship again came close to the reef, and after exchanging gifts and good wishes, the men paddled back to Namoluk, and the Russians continued on their expedition.

Whalers and traders began to frequent Micronesian waters soon after Lütke's visit, and several of them have left records of contact with Namoluk and its people. In 1830, Captain Benjamin Morrell, aboard the *Antarctic* out of Stonington, Connecticut, sailed past the atoll and later published this brief account in a compendium of his voyages:

> May 14th [1830]—On the following day we discovered three small
> low islands, being each from three to five miles in circumference,
> and almost entirely covered with cocoanut [*sic*] and bread-fruit
> trees. They were well inhabited with much the same kind of people
> as the western part of Bergh's Group [Chuuk]; having also the
> same description of canoes, war implements, fishing utensils, and
> wearing apparel. The islands are all surrounded and connected by
> a coral reef. They furnish *biche-de-mer,* pearl and tortoiseshell, and
> many curious and beautiful shells, valuable for their rarity. These
> islands extend about ten miles east and west, and about five miles
> north and south; being situated in lat. 6° 4'north, long. 153° 21'
> east; and as we could not find them on any chart, or see them
> mentioned in any epitome of navigation, we concluded that they

were new discoveries, and gave them the name of Skiddy's Group,
in honour of that worthy and enterprising navigator. (Morrell
1832, 388–389)

In 1833, the American whaler *Hashmy*, under Captain Harwood, called at
Namoluk. An extract from the *Hashmy's* log that was printed in newspapers in
Australia and the United States makes it clear that members of Harwood's crew
went ashore. They were the first westerners to do so: "In coming down from
Japan, fell in with a group of islands, not laid down in the charts, in latitude 5° 45'
north, and 152° 35' east longitude,—about 50 miles N.W. of Young William's
Islands [the Lower Mortlocks]; the tops of the trees of the islands were visible a
considerable distance at sea. I had the crew of the *Hashmy* on them, refreshing,
who were treated with great kindness by the natives. The islands are very thickly
inhabited, with plenty of cocoa nuts, vegetables, and such refreshments as are
necessary for crews coming from Japan with the scurvy" (Ward 1967, 3–4).
Apparently, Lütke's kind treatment of *chon* Namoluk five years before was recip-
rocated by them when the first outsiders stepped ashore for "refreshment."

The available historical sources suggest that *chon* Namoluk's interactions with
westerners in the late 1820s and 1830s were friendly and profitable on both sides.
Both Lütke and Harwood specifically mentioned the kindness of Namoluk people, and both wrote of receiving gifts and refreshments, presumably in exchange
for articles they had to trade such as the axes discussed by Lütke (1835). More
traders ventured into the Mortlocks area by the 1840s, although the Lower
Mortlocks received much more contact from them because of the deep water
passes that allowed for safe anchorage in Lukunoch or Satawan lagoons. Andrew
Cheyne was one of these early traders, and in 1846 he visited Namoluk and jotted
the following short passage in his journal:

> Hashmy's Group [Namoluk] consists of five low islands, covered
> with cocoa-nuts and bread-fruit trees, and connected by coral
> reefs, forming a lagoon inside, to which there is no passage
> through the reef. The group is fifteen miles in circumference, of a
> circular form, and may be seen twelve miles from a ship's deck.
> The reef may be approached to within 300 yards, as no hidden
> dangers exist. These islands are thickly inhabited by a light com-
> plexioned race, who although wearing the mask of friendship, are
> by no means to be trusted. I touched at this group in July, 1846,
> and made the centre in lat. 5° 47' N., 153° 6' E., by two good
> chronometers measured from Hong Kong. (Cheyne 1852, 129)

On the basis of his account alone it is difficult to determine what sort of re-
ception Namoluk's inhabitants accorded Cheyne. Because he does not mention
open hostility, it appears that they were at least still somewhat friendly toward the

foreigners who intruded on their lives. Cheyne's suspicion that they were not to be trusted is one he held of many other Micronesian peoples and hence may reflect *his* suspicious nature as much as that of the islanders. But it may also reflect *chon* Namoluk's second thoughts about foreigners based upon a visit of which we have no record.

After Cheyne's visit, there is nearly a thirty-year gap in the historical record before Namoluk is mentioned again. We know that numerous outsiders were in the Carolines during this time, and it seems safe to assume that at least a few of them must have found their way to Namoluk during the 1850s and 1860s. Perhaps it is as a result of such a visit that the missionary Luther Gulick (1862) was able to offer the first recorded population estimate of 300 people for the atoll, although he did not cite the source of his information. Namoluk's historical thread was picked up again in 1874 by another Congregationalist missionary, E. T. Doane, who called at the atoll aboard the mission ship *Morning Star* from Pohnpei via the Lower Mortlocks. In striking contrast to earlier visits in which Namoluk canoes hurried out to greet visiting ships, Doane reported that no canoes came out, and "as the *Star* passed along to the lee shore, groups of natives were seen sitting beneath the trees, watching the approach of the vessel. . . . This cautiousness of the people not to launch a *proa* [canoe], and 'come off', indicated fear; and so it was, for here were found those who had been kidnapped by the *Carl,* and taken to a Fiji plantation" (Doane 1874, 204). This reference to kidnapping—blackbirding, as it was called in the Pacific—makes it obvious that *chon* Namoluk had lost their innocence in their contact with the West. Even so, "Perceiving their unwillingness to come to the *Star,* a boat was sent to them. Three friendly natives from Satoan [Satawan] accompanied, and going up to the group, told them who the strangers were—friendly missionaries. A few threw aside all fear, came to us and shook hands, heard a message, bartered a little, and then with a friendly 'good-bye,' were left" (Doane 1874, 204). Regrettably, Doane did not elaborate on whether the kidnapped men he found on Namoluk were themselves *chon* Namoluk or whether they were from another island, nor did he provide any information on how they reached Namoluk from Fiji. But on the basis of this cursory evidence it appears that the blackbirder, *Carl,* known to have taken men from Satawan and Lukunoch (Hezel 1973, 67–68), may also have raided "the lagoon in the middle" sometime in the late 1860s or early 1870s and carried a number of Namoluk men off to Fiji. If so, there was no recollection of this in Namoluk's oral history by 1969.

COLONIALISM COMES TO NAMOLUK

Protestant mission activity began in the Lower Mortlocks in 1873, the year before E. T. Doane stopped by Namoluk. Pohnpeian teachers, under the supervision of New England missionaries sponsored by the American Board of Commissioners for Foreign Missions (ABCFM)—the same mission that evangelized Hawai'i beginning in 1820—established congregations on Satawan and Lukunoch Atolls and were received with enthusiasm (*Missionary Herald* 1876, 309). It took more than another five years before a young Pohnpeian mission couple, Julius and Lora, landed on Namoluk on December 1, 1879 (*Missionary Herald* 1880a, 175).[3]

Perhaps colonized more than anyone else on our planet, Micronesians endured four different colonial powers over the space of one hundred years.[4] The parade began with the Spanish period in Micronesia (officially 1886–1899), a time that wrought few changes on outer islands like Namoluk. Save for the growth of Protestant mission activity described above, life on the atoll followed a relatively undisturbed pattern during the late nineteenth century. In some measure Namoluk's geography protected her people from the diseases that ravaged island populations elsewhere in the Pacific, such as smallpox, measles, and influenza. With no close neighbor islands, with no ship passage into the lagoon, and with natural surge channels in the reef difficult to maneuver even by boat, Namoluk was never a regular port of call for the whalers and traders who frequented the Carolines. Add to this the proximity of the spacious anchorages offered by Lukunoch and Satawan Atolls a mere 50 miles to the southeast, and it is little wonder that few ship captains bothered with Namoluk. For similar reasons the major commercial ventures in the Mortlocks during the late nineteenth century—notably the Jaluit Gesellschaft—concentrated on the Lower Mortlocks, and Namoluk escaped their direct influence relatively unscathed.

Following the initial period of conversion and success in the Mortlocks, the ABCFM encountered a period of decline there that coincided with a focus of mission activity on the much larger new field of Chuuk Lagoon beginning in the early 1880s, political hassles with the German colonial government, and depleted operating funds. Despite this reported downturn in mission attention to the Mortlocks, the Namoluk church was able to support its own pastor by 1901, although the church building was said to be in a dilapidated condition (*Missionary Herald* 1901, 413, 415). But shortly thereafter a religious revitalization movement swept Namoluk, and Christianity reached its low point following its introduction a quarter of a century earlier. With but one-third of the Mortlocks population numbered as church members by 1903, the pre-Christian religion remained very much alive and influential (*Missionary Herald* 1903, 159).[5]

During the German colonial period (1899–1914) a trader, remembered by *chon* Namoluk only as Jack, set up shop on the atoll, buying copra[6] in return for trade goods. It seems probable that Jack staffed the tradepost that the Jaluit Gesellschaft opened on Namoluk around 1904 (Hezel 1995, 103). By 1907, a Frenchman, Pierre Nedelic, actively plied the Mortlocks in his eight-ton schooner, making periodic stops at Namoluk to trade. The Germans encouraged men to sign on as contract laborers to mine phosphate on Nauru and Angaur, and quite a few Namoluk men did so. But while some men traveled far away to shovel petrified guano, and while contact with missionaries and colonial government officials increased, the atoll community continued to operate in much the same way as it had in the precolonial period. It was also during the German administration that the first anthropological research was carried out on the atoll (Girschner 1912; Krämer 1935).

In 1911, two German Capuchins arrived on Lukunoch Islet, Lukunoch Atoll (at the opposite end of the lagoon from Protestant mission headquarters in the Lower Mortlocks), thereby inaugurating Catholic mission activity in what is now Chuuk State (Hezel 1991, 123). Although the Catholics made substantial headway in many Mortlockese communities (e.g., Lukunoch, Ettal, and Moch), they were more or less shut out of many others for a long time. It was thus with a great deal of opposition from the Protestants, who did not have a full-time pastor at the time, that the Catholic Church finally was established on Namoluk in 1949.[7] By 1969, with a Namoluk man as catechist, approximately one-third of Namoluk's population had converted to Catholicism.[8] A nice cement block, A-frame style church building had been erected on the atoll in the early 1960s, and a priest visited periodically by ship to hold Mass and hear confession.

Right at the end of the German colonial period in Micronesia, the Namoluk church came under the influence of the Liebenzell Mission, a German Christian Endeavor organization that supplanted the ABCFM in Chuuk after 1907 (Kohl 1971). In 1914, a couple from the Protestant mission headquarters for the Mortlocks on Oneop (Lukunoch Atoll) went to lead the Namoluk church, and they remained there until their deaths around 1918. They were succeeded by another Oneop couple, Edgar and Louella, and Edgar headed the Namoluk church until he died in 1947.[9] Namoluk's church was then led on an interim basis for several years by a *chon* Namoluk who perished at sea in a sailing canoe accident while en route to Oneop in 1955 for ordination as a pastor. Two years later, in 1957, a man from Piis-Emmwar (Losap Atoll) and his wife from Wééné assumed pastoral duties on Namoluk, which they continued until the mid–1970s.

In sharp contrast to the two earlier colonial administrations, changes that came about during the Japanese period (1914–1945) were direct, rapid, numerous, and enduring. Regular shipping schedules were established, and a cash economy was introduced in place of barter. Travel throughout Micronesia accelerated for Namoluk men, with many of them sent to work for the Japanese on Angaur or Pohnpei. For the first time, non-Micronesian foreigners resided on the atoll for long periods of time, married Namoluk women, and produced offspring.[10] Access to material goods and store-bought foods dramatically increased, and such things as rice became dietary staples. The Japanese established an appointed chief to run the island's local government, ushering in the slow but steady decline of traditional leadership on the atoll. With the inauguration of a cash economy, the buying and selling of land for money appeared. Education—even though it was limited—was made available to substantial numbers of young men and women who left Namoluk to attend Japanese-run elementary schools on Oneop and on Tonowas Island, Chuuk, during the 1920s and 1930s. Two Namoluk men achieved the highest education attainable under the Japanese, graduating from the special carpentry school on Koror, Palau. In short, the Japanese began to introduce Namoluk to the modern world.

Following precedent, the Japanese concentrated their attention primarily on the Lower Mortlocks, and Namoluk remained a mere way station between those atolls and the more important center on Chuuk. Commercial activity remained negligible on Namoluk throughout the Japanese era, and it consisted only in a copra-buying concession and a small-scale lumber mill operated by Nanyō Bōeki employees who married on the atoll. No Japanese military garrison ever was stationed on Namoluk, nor were fortifications of any kind erected.[11]

Namoluk had only two direct contacts with World War II. In the first instance, in 1942, fifty men from a Japanese ship torpedoed near Kapingamarangi reached Namoluk and were cared for by the community until they could be picked up and returned to Chuuk. As a reward for their helpfulness, the community was presented with one of the steel lifeboats with oars, and this was used to haul copra until 1949 when rough seas broke it up on the reef. The second direct contact occurred when American fighter aircraft dropped three bombs on the reef and strafed a sailing canoe in the lagoon during the extensive aerial campaign against Chuuk and the Lower Mortlocks in June 1944. Although it frightened people badly, this unprovoked and unnecessary attack fortunately caused no deaths or injuries and only minor damage to property. The heaviest inroad of World War II on Namoluk was through conscript labor for the Japanese elsewhere than Namoluk. Constructing roads, airstrips, and bomb shelters and growing food crops for military garrisons, several Namoluk men died and others were debilitated by the long, extremely arduous physical labor required of them.

From a purely local perspective, the most significant event during the Japanese colonial period was the abandonment of Amwes Islet as a habitation site. Although no archaeological data are available, Namoluk oral history records that both Amwes and Namoluk Islets had been inhabited from first settlement of the atoll. These two islets are close in size (77 and 69 acres), and both have good-sized taro excavations.[12] Each islet's community boasted a church, two named villages, several canoe houses, and its own localized descent groups. Despite these similarities, Namoluk Islet has always had a larger population, and unlike Ettal Atoll (Nason 1970), Namoluk Atoll never has been divided into two political districts.

Over the short span of about two years (from 1937 to 1939), an infectious disease epidemic (probably tuberculosis) inexorably moved through the Amwes settlement, resulting in the deaths of fifty to sixty people comprising at least 80 percent of the Amwes population. The survivors, along with some who were to die soon afterward, straggled over to Namoluk Islet, bringing the infection with them. As a result, many people there became ill and died, although the disease did not run rampant through the entire settlement as it had done on Amwes. Salvaging what they could, the people of Amwes abandoned their home to the weeds, the birds, and the pigs. The large taro swamp fell into disuse until it filled with a thick, thriving stand of trees. As of 1969, Amwes had not been recolonized.

Commencing with the end of World War II, the American colonial period essentially followed the Japanese example on a reduced scale. The cash economy, with copra as its mainstay, was continued, as was government-provided shipping service to and from Chuuk to the outer islands, providing trade goods, passenger service, and copra buying. Christian mission activity received a new impetus in the postwar period, and educational opportunities increased sharply, including the establishment of an elementary school on Namoluk (first through eighth grade), staffed by trained Namoluk teachers. By the late 1960s, a few especially worthy students left the atoll to attend high school on Chuuk. A Namoluk man, trained as a Navy corpsman, was employed on the atoll as a health aide and supervised a dispensary in which he saw patients and dispensed a limited array of Western medicines. A government-trained midwife returned home to Namoluk to practice her skills in delivering babies. Namoluk had a municipal government modeled after local governments in the United States, with a mayor, an island council, and assorted other offices all democratically elected by the atoll's adult men and women.

Paralleling the epidemic on Amwes as the most significant local event of the Japanese colonial period, the typhoon that smashed Namoluk in 1958 occupied a similar place during the American administration. On May 24 and 25, 1958, Typhoon Phyllis, packing winds over 100 mph, passed just north of Namoluk and caused extensive damage. Information provided by the U.S. Navy indicated that approximately 90 percent of the coconut palms were destroyed on the atoll (Slusser and Hughes 1970). The physical destruction on Namoluk was as follows: "Practically 75% of all trees were completely uprooted. The remaining 25% were mere stumps sticking 15 or 20 feet into the air. The damage to homes and community buildings was complete. Fortunately, only one person was lost [died] during the storm. Destruction of the islands' canoes was complete" (Davis 1959, 13).

Prior to Phyllis, the last typhoon to strike Namoluk was sometime in the nineteenth century. In Phyllis's aftermath, almost 100 percent subsistence was provided to Namoluk's people by the USTTPI government in the form of rice, flour, and C-rations for well over a year. Soon after the typhoon, traditional ties and obligations brought canoes from Ettal and Oneop, laden with taro and coconuts. Moch and Kuttu in Satawan Atoll and Lukunoch Islet in Lukunoch Atoll also sent taro and breadfruit via the Catholic mission ship. At the behest of the late Petrus Mailo, then mayor of Wééné, several islands in Chuuk Lagoon shipped taro, pandanus, and preserved breadfruit down to Namoluk.

As restoration and recovery began, the Agriculture Department on Chuuk started a gardening and coconut replanting program on Namoluk, and the government provided materials to rebuild forty-three homes, a school, a government house, a community building, and an island office. A deeper boat channel was blasted in the reef, and Namoluk people had their first direct experience with

Americans living on their island. Several Agriculture Department employees, along with their families, spent up to six months on the atoll in 1958 assisting in reconstruction and replanting. Eight months after the typhoon, the following status report was issued: "Progress. . . at Namoluk has been extremely fast. . . . The replanting program is well under way and is ahead of schedule. The 'two year' rebuilding program will be completed in one year. The morale of the people. . . is extremely high—partly because they have made such excellent progress on their canoe rebuilding, which means so much to them. Namoluk has completed nine large sailing canoes" (Davis 1959, 14).

A severe cyclonic storm such as Typhoon Phyllis on Namoluk may be thought of as giving people a clean slate on which to redraw their lives. This idea of a typhoon providing a new beginning—of a storm accelerating the pace of changes already in motion—was explored in detail by William Lessa (1964) for Ulithi, an atoll in the Western Carolines much like Namoluk (see Map 1.1). The degree of physical damage on both atolls was very similar, but what is of real interest is that many of the social changes that occurred on Ulithi after the typhoon in 1960 had their exact counterparts in the immediate post-typhoon years on Namoluk.

On both islands women abandoned the traditional dress style—topless with a wraparound skirt—in favor of Western-style dresses that covered their breasts. On both islands imported lumber, corrugated metal, and cement replaced home-grown wood and thatch as the standard building materials for people's homes. On both islands the residence pattern for houses shifted from one of dispersed homesteads to settlements clustered together. On both islands the typhoon engendered greater reliance on store-bought foodstuffs, especially rice, flour, and canned meats, possibly as an outgrowth of the relief food that had been provided. On both islands the importance of cash increased strikingly in the local economy, and the number of small stores grew apace. On both islands a realignment of political power was set in motion, with younger men taking an increasingly active role in local politics. On both islands greater inequalities in wealth than hitherto had been present sprang up in conjunction with the rising importance of cash. Finally, on both islands a trend toward advancing the interests of the nuclear family over that of wider, extended kin groups was intensified. In sum: "The winds and waves of the. . . typhoon. . . not only caused widespread physical changes on the tiny atoll but also dramatically transformed the social organization and traditions of the islands. They swept away old ways as well as trees. In doing so they stimulated social changes already in progress before the storm and at the same time provided a more dynamic way of life to cope with the program of reconstruction" (Lessa 1964, 46).

DAY-TO-DAY LIFE AT THE END OF THE 1960S

By the time that Leslie and I first stepped ashore on Namoluk on October 5, 1969, the social changes that had been accelerated by Typhoon Phyllis a decade before had become the day-to-day norm. Even so, it must be remembered that the typhoon came on the heels of a much longer process of change stimulated by external events. By 1969, *chon* Namoluk had had direct experience of foreigners for more than 135 years. Occasional visits by whalers and traders early on, followed by resident mission teachers and the coming of Christianity, access to the first formal schooling, and the ever greater encroachment of colonial governments all contributed to the atoll's slow but inexorable involvement with the world beyond the Mortlocks and beyond Micronesia.

A paradox between dependency and self-sufficiency framed the Namoluk community in 1969. Although *chon* Namoluk depended upon a variety of services provided from the district center[13] port town on Chuuk, the atoll was in many ways still a self-contained unit. Namoluk could and did easily feed itself, and in this sense it was still in a subsistence economy. Known throughout Chuuk State as an island rich in fish and other seafood, the atoll also produced a lot of breadfruit and taro, the two staple crops. In addition to these basic foods, a miscellany of condiment foods was available, such as bananas, papaya, soursop, limes, bitter oranges, and pandanus fruit. For special feasts or notable meals, pigs or chickens were killed and eaten with gusto, and occasionally a large sea turtle would be captured and devoured. Despite this cornucopia of local foods, by 1969 Namoluk people also had come to rely on store-bought foods imported from abroad. First and foremost among these was rice, followed closely by enriched flour, and both of these were purchased in 25- to 50-pound bags. Along with these starches, *chon* Namoluk—like most other Pacific Islanders—were accustomed to tinned fish (especially mackerel), canned meats (notably Spam and corned beef), cooking oil, dried noodles (such as ramen), salt, sugar, canned soft drinks (consumed warm), powdered milk, soy sauce, and assorted crackers and cookies. For these foods they relied on visits from the government field-trip ship every one to two months.

The paradox of intertwined self-sufficiency and dependency in regard to food is well illustrated by a description of fishing. As Namoluk's Kino Ruben writes in the epigraph that begins this chapter, *chon* Namoluk love to fish, and they have numerous techniques to catch their quarry. However, the fishing paraphernalia that was in use on the atoll in 1969 was a mix of homemade and industrially manufactured gear. In October 1969, there were still no outboard motorboats on Namoluk, although that was soon to change (see Chapter 4). Drop-line fishing in the lagoon or off the outer reef face was done from small, one- or two-person paddling canoes called *waafatil*, whereas open-sea trolling for big game fish like yellowfin and skipjack tuna, jacks, wahoo, yellowtail, and barracuda was done by dragging handheld lines behind the large sailing canoes, or *waaserik*. But even though the canoes were made in the time-honored way from local trees, and held together by coconut sennit[14] cord and breadfruit sap caulk, the cloth sails, nylon fish lines, and metal fishhooks were bought from stores that had acquired them from overseas. Big nets were used to surround schools of fish in the lagoon, but

A Typhoon House on Namoluk, March 1970,
Constructed After Typhoon Phyllis in 1958

where these once were handwoven from local fiber, the nets in use by 1969 were made of nylon and manufactured in Japan, Taiwan, or South Korea.

Likapich, "spearfishing," had been practiced on Namoluk from time immemorial, but in the old days it was difficult and relatively inefficient, done without goggles and by thrusting with a long, multipronged wooden spear. Spearfishing gear in 1969 included imported swimmer's goggles, barbed thin metal spears made from reworked rebar and other scrap metal brought down from Chuuk, and a "shooter" made of heavy surgical tubing that powered the spear. From age eleven or twelve, Namoluk boys developed ever greater skill at *likapich,* and this technique provided most of the reef fish that people consumed. So even as basic a subsistence practice as fishing on a coral atoll contained a paradoxical mix of local ingenuity and knowledge and imported material goods.

By October 1969, Namoluk's population was consolidated fully on Namoluk Islet, clustered together in three named but otherwise indistinguishable village sections (Pukos, Lukelap, and Sópwonewel) on the northeastern end of the islet. The community had a thriving elementary school and was divided into both Protestant and Catholic church congregations. Most people slept in the neat, square wooden houses with corrugated metal roofs that were erected in the aftermath of the 1958 typhoon. These houses were raised about 3 feet off the ground

Namoluk Canoe House (*Fáál an Paros*),
with Two Styles of Sailing Canoe, May 1970

on wooden pilings, providing a dry storage place underneath for miscellaneous household goods. A few of the wealthier community members had built cement houses, some sporting linoleum floors and glass louver windows, but other families still lived comfortably in traditional thatch homes with coral-pebble floors. Everyone did their meal preparation in a separate *mosoro*, or "cookhouse," typically made of thatch and containing an earth oven, a fire pit, and a place where a small single-burner kerosene stove could be used. Chickens and cats, not to mention small children, wandered in and out of the *mosoro*, while women and teenaged girls assembled and cooked the family's food there.

Seven large, thatched A-frame *fáál*, or "canoe houses," lined the lagoon shore, each owned by one of the island's major clans or subclans (a discussion of the kinship system follows below). The *fáál* served as gathering and sleeping places for men and boys and as storage places for the atoll's canoes, keeping them protected from the strong tropical sun and frequent rains. The large cement churches were the most imposing structures on Namoluk, with the Protestant Church rebuilt after Typhoon Phyllis and the Catholic Church—modeled after a *fáál*—erected in 1968. Also reconstructed post-typhoon, the big cement community meeting house was the focal point for weekly island-wide meetings, island council meetings, and other community events.

The Protestant Church on Namoluk, April 1995

The dispensary and the "municipal house" that contained a shortwave radio transceiver for communication with Chuuk and other islands in the Mortlocks were in structures identical to people's wooden dwellings. These were located near the elementary school complex, an array of two wood and corrugated metal classroom buildings and two smaller cookhouses surrounding an open grassy playing field. Walking past when school was in session, one heard the children enthusiastically reciting their lessons in unison, while preschool kids and a few older adults lounged about outside, listening and watching. Namoluk had seven locally owned and operated general stores in 1969, most of which were run out of their proprietor's home. The owners of these stores purchased most of their stock from the field-trip ships and then sold it to community members at a small markup. Commonly, the stores carried canned foods, cloth, matches, flashlight batteries, candy, soap, kerosene, cigarettes, instant coffee, and other by-then essential items.

In 1969, copra was the mainstay of most Namoluk people's limited participation in a cash economy. At that time, nearly everyone on the atoll lived mainly in a subsistence economy, with money and the goods it could buy treated as a supplement rather than as the primary means of survival. All who were able regularly gathered, husked, and split coconuts, and then removed the oily meat with deft strokes of a sharp kitchen knife. The meat would then either be laid out to dry in the sun on pandanus mats or, preferably, would be heated over a slow fire in a copra-drying oven introduced during the Japanese period (and called by the Japanese name, *kansopa*). Once dried, the copra would be put in bags provided by the trading companies on Chuuk who bought all the copra when the field-trip ship came. It was then stored in a dry place until ship day. Much time and effort and approximately 300 ripe coconuts resulted in one 100-pound bag of copra that earned $5.50. No one on Namoluk ever got rich making copra.

The atoll's municipal government included an elected magistrate (or mayor), a secretary, a treasurer, a municipal court judge, three police officers, and a six-person council (see Marshall and Borthwick 1974 for a technical analysis of these political positions). In addition to these offices, three men served as elected village foremen, or "bosses," and in 1969, *chon* Namoluk still elected their own representative to the Truk District Legislature. Although traditional clan chiefs—*samol an ainang*—continued to command respect and to exercise a modicum of influence in island affairs, they possessed no effective decision-making or administrative power in the political arena.

Idle time—a certain monotony—poses a problem for communities like Namoluk, and the repetitive boredom of outer island existence is among the reasons young people give for their eagerness to experience the energy and entertainment offered by Wééné and other bigger places. On a typical day, one or two bingo games were in full swing at a nickel a card, while players listened as radio station WSZC in Chuuk blared American country-western music, alternating with Chuukese love songs[15] and local announcements. A group of men who'd just returned from an early-morning troll for tuna in the open sea divided and distributed their catch from one of the canoe houses. Looking tired, a man and his adult son lugged a basket of ripe breadfruit they had picked with long poles and dropped it off at their *mosoro* before going to bathe. In the *mosoro* women cooked the day's food—breadfruit, taro, or rice—for the major evening meal, while yet others hiked out on the reef flat at low tide in search of octopi or shellfish to accompany dinner. Two sisters and their husbands prepared to sail across the lagoon to Toinom Islet to gather and husk copra nuts, spend the night in a small thatch lean-to shelter, check to see if any breadfruit were ripe there, and catch some delicious land-dwelling coconut crabs to roast on the fire. Infants and toddlers, accompanied by slightly older siblings assigned by their mothers to child-care duty, wandered freely about, exploring their green world and playing at children's games. The pace of everything, work or play, was leisurely, slow, and relaxed. No one hurried.

Bars, pool halls, movie theaters, and the general hubbub of urban life all appear attractive when seen from a distance and when one has not yet tried them. Although illegal on Namoluk in 1969, the consumption of alcoholic beverages was comparatively common by men—particularly young men—and occasional fisticuffs and wrestling fights ensued. At that time, drinking and the challenge it posed to the local powers-that-be were very much caught up in a struggle be-

Namoluk Canoe House (*Fáál an Falukupat*),
with a Day's Catch of Yellowfin Tuna, December 1969

tween younger and older generations for control of the island's municipal government (Marshall 1975b). The usual drink was *yiis*, "yeast," a rather unpleasant
brew of sugar, baker's yeast, and water allowed to ferment for a day or so in a glass
container or a big tea kettle and sometimes flavored with coffee or canned fruit
syrup before it was consumed. The time on people's hands was a major reason
that the mindlessness of bingo was endured hour after hour by Namoluk adults,
even though most of them consistently lost money at this game. Bingo offered an
excuse to socialize, gossip, and while away the time.

This monotony was shattered whenever a ship or canoe visited the atoll.
Announced by a loud, "Waaa-Ho!"—called *akkapwas*—the arrival of a vessel
from outside produced a commotion: frenzied activity, anticipation over who
might be coming or going, possible new merchandise or visitors, money from copra sales, and mail and other news from the world beyond. Everyone rushed
down to Leor—the landing spot—to observe the proceedings. And then, in no
more than a day and usually after just a few hours, the ship gathered up its passengers and its copra and sailed on, and life on Namoluk resumed its slow repetitive pace.

THE FOUR E'S

Education, employment, entertainment, and excitement: these "four E's" already acted as significant "pull factors" in 1969, beginning to pull Namoluk people to the urban center on Wééné, Chuuk. Anyone who passed the competitive high school entrance examination, and who thus qualified for one of the limited number of spots then available to continue schooling beyond the eighth grade, had to move to Chuuk to do so. In those days there were three high schools in Chuuk: Truk High School, where most students enrolled; Mizpah High School, sponsored by the United Church of Christ-affiliated Protestant Church;[16] and Xavier High School, a highly selective Jesuit-run institution that drew students from all six of the USTTPI's districts. Both Mizpah and Xavier required their students to pay tuition, but Truk High was a free public school.

Beginning in July 1962, during the Kennedy administration, the U.S. government greatly increased the USTTPI's budget in response to United Nations criticism over U.S. neglect of its trusteeship. Soon thereafter, hundreds of PCVs were sent to Micronesia, and many new public works programs were initiated in the district centers. It became clear by the early 1970s that the combination of money and PCVs was a calculated way for binding the islands more closely to the United States (Hezel 1995), but the sudden infusion of funds created a rapid profusion of jobs, in other words, employment, the second "E." Some Namoluk men and women emigrated to Chuuk at that time to avail themselves of the new opportunities to earn a salary in the emergent wage economy.

Part of the lure for these people was the pull of entertainment of various sorts in the urban center and also the sheer excitement of living in the polyglot and semi-anonymous world that Wééné offered. Unlike the slow, repetitive day-to-day life back home, Wééné had automobiles, motorboats, jet aircraft landing several times a week, and huge freighters and oil tankers tying up at the main wharf. The town contained people from every community in Chuuk State, and from most other parts of Micronesia, plus dozens of foreign workers (principally Americans and Filipinos) and legions of tourists (many of them from Japan). The pace of life on Wééné seemed nearly the opposite of that back on Namoluk.

Those who remained on the atoll were not unaffected by the increased growth and development occurring on Chuuk. In addition to "the four E's," Namoluk people looked to the district center for health care services, particularly when hospitalization was required. For radio news, mail, shipping, a market for their copra, and a stream of material goods, the district center was the source to which *chon* Namoluk turned. When government field-trip ships were delayed, as they often were, felt needs on Namoluk became acute. Cigarette smokers had to skimp, hoard, or do without. Bottle-fed infants faced a threat of no powdered or canned milk. Underwater spearfishing at night halted for want of flashlight batteries. School was reduced to half-day sessions because there was no U.S. Department of Agriculture rice and flour to feed the children lunch.

Anthropologists fretted because there was no mail. Life on Namoluk, as it was lived in 1969, was predicated on regular contact by ship with the district center.

PRIMORDIAL SENTIMENTS OF SHARED IDENTITY

Anthropologists long have viewed kinship as the "primordial sentiments of shared identity," and this is an especially apt way to think about kinship on Namoluk because for most of its history, the atoll has been a genealogically inter-locked kin community (see Marshall 1972 for illustration of this). These numer-ous genealogical connections among Namoluk people, such that most of them have at least distant kin ties to each other, contribute to their strong sense of shared group identity and mutual solidarity. Although this book is not about the details of kinship relationships and organization, it is necessary to have a basic understanding of Namoluk ideas of kinship in order to understand fully much of what follows in later chapters about migration and identity. For the same reason, it is also pertinent to comprehend the nature of marital relationships and the prescriptive system of marriage that governed most spousal choices on the atoll until quite recently.

Kinship organization on Namoluk, and throughout Chuuk State, is quite dif-ferent from the way kinship is structured in the United States and other Western countries. Whereas most westerners have what anthropologists call a bilateral (two-sided) system of reckoning descent, and do not privilege one side over the other, *chon* Namoluk calculate descent unilineally. More specifically, Namoluk people have a matrilineal descent system, meaning that their strongest and closest kin ties come through their mother's side or "line." Unilineal kinship systems typ-ically organize people into named kin groups such as clans and lineages. In Namoluk's case these named matrilineal kin groups are called *ainang*, or "clan." The eight clans represented on Namoluk in 1969 are localized parts of widely dis-persed groupings found in much of Chuuk State and on many of the outer island atolls of Yap State. Some of them also exist in the century-old migrant Mortlockese communities that were established on Pohnpei in 1907 after a terri-ble typhoon ravaged the Lower Mortlocks and the Germans relocated Mortlockese people there. Clans are named and dispersed kin groups whose members should not marry or engage in sexual intercourse with each other (i.e., they are exogamous). Clans provide links of hospitality when people travel to other islands, even if the people involved have never met before. Members of the same clan consider themselves to be distant kin by virtue of their shared clan name, but they cannot trace genealogical connections to one another.

Typically, in specific communities such as Namoluk, large clans may be di-vided into a number of subclans whose members are known or believed to share closer genealogical connections with one another than to other members of the same clan, even if they cannot reconstruct the precise kinship links. Clans and subclans ultimately are composed of lineages whose members actually know how they are related genealogically. Large lineages, in turn, are made up of multiple descent lines, *tetel en aramas,* that usually consist in a set of brothers and sisters (a sibling-set) and the offspring of the sisters. The connections among siblings are considered to be the closest and most binding kinship relationships on Namoluk (see Marshall 1981 for details), and they figure into marriage, adoption, and fosterage patterns in ways that will be touched upon briefly below.

Even though clans, subclans, and lineages are unfamiliar to most Westerners, they provide the fundamental connections that organize and regulate Namoluk people's access to land, to sexual and marital partners, and to what David Schneider (1968) called "diffuse, enduring solidarity." Descent lines and lineage ties are much more likely to be associated with such solidarity than subclan or clan ties, although this depends on a host of contextual and individual factors. Diffuse, enduring solidarity on Namoluk must be *demonstrated* by loving, nurturant acts of mutual caring: *tumwunuu ffengen,* "take care of or look after one another"; *alillis ffengen,* "cooperate"; and *tipeuo ffengen,* "agree or be of one mind." Close kin who fail to demonstrate *ttong*— "love, pity"—for each other may cease to function as kin, although such a case would be highly unusual.

Lineages, subclans, and clans are headed by *samol an ainang,* "clan chiefs," who adjudicate disputes among their members, distribute use rights to shared property (especially land, taro patches, and sections of reef), and represent the group vis-à-vis others. Normally, the *samol an ainang* is a man—the eldest living son of the eldest female ancestor in the group—although on rare occasions a woman may occupy the chiefly role in the absence of any suitable adult male. Namoluk clans are ranked by order of their arrival on the atoll, with the first to arrive accorded *makal,* or "atoll chief," status. The highest ranked clan on Namoluk is Wáánikar, which is divided into five subclans, one of which holds the *makal* title. Namoluk's other seven clans are named Sór, Katamak, Fáánimey, Sópwunupi, Souwon, Inemaraw, and Imwo.[17] The overall population is divided roughly in half between Wáánikar people and the other clans, who are known collectively as *tola,* "all [the rest]" (see Table 2.1).

Wáánikar's five subclans vary in size and number of lineages. The largest, hereafter called W2, has three large lineages (a fourth died out in 1999), numbering slightly more than one-quarter of the community's total *de jure* population. A second Wáánikar subclan, W1, is made up of three lineages and almost seventy members; a third, W4, has nearly as many members, but all of them today are in a single lineage. The remaining two Wáánikar subclans, W3 and W5, effectively contain a single lineage each[18] and number between thirty and forty individuals.

People who have matrilineal descent give priority to the female line, but one should not thereby assume that patrilateral relationships, those with the father's side, count for nothing—quite the contrary. These relationships to father and his lineage, subclan, and clan are known as *afakúr* ties on Namoluk. People who are *afakúran eu ainang,* "descendants of a clan's men," are considered to be siblings by virtue of this shared relationship and as such they are

Table 2.1—Namoluk Clans by Number and Percent of
De Jure Population, 7/13/2001[a]

Name of Clan	No. Persons	Percent of Total
Wáánikar	434	50
Katamak	142	16.5
Sór	135	15.5
Fáánimey	72	8
Souwon	46	5
Sópwunupi	25	3
Imwo[b]	15	2
TOTAL	869	100

[a] Until the deaths of its last two members during the late 1990s, Namoluk's clans also included Inemaraw.

[b] Imwo clan is represented in the Namoluk population by some of the children and grandchildren of the wife of the atoll's Protestant minister, who served the Namoluk church from 1957 until the 1970s. He was from Piis-Emmwar and she was from Wééné. No members of Imwo resided on Namoluk in July 2001, although they are considered to be *chon* Namoluk.

enjoined from marrying or having sexual intercourse. On Namoluk and elsewhere in the Mortlocks, it is common for children to inherit land and other property from their father in individual ownership. Such patrilateral gifts are very highly valued and jealously guarded and add strength to the father-child relationship. An adult child who fails to show *ttong* toward her or his father may be cut off from such an expected inheritance when the old man dies, so the ability to grant or withhold the patrilateral gift serves as a kind of "social security" for men as they age.

At the time I lived on Namoluk between 1969 and 1971, most of the marriages I recorded in genealogies followed what anthropologists call "preferential rules," meaning that they were arranged between people in certain specific relationships to each other. For starters, 86 percent of the nearly 1,000 marriages were between members of Namoluk matrilineages, in other words, the community was highly endogamous—marriages took place *within* it, rather than with outsiders. Second, more than three-fourths of all marriages were sibling-set marriages, meaning that one set of brothers and sisters married another such set.[19] A third preferential rule that shaped Namoluk marriage choices is that nearly two-thirds of all Namoluk marriages through 1971 were between actual or classificatory cross-cousins, that is, the children of opposite-sex siblings (mother's brother and father's sister). Finally, in more than half of the cases where Namoluk persons married more than once, they married a "sister" or "brother" of their first spouse. Anthropologists refer to such marriages as the sororate and the levirate. Thus, historically, the Namoluk community operated largely as a "closed" marriage market, in which marriages were arranged between sibling-sets and their cross-cousins. This was done so as to keep resources in land and people circulating back and forth between matrilineages over time, as one generation and set of marriages was succeeded by the next (see Marshall 1972). So-called alliance systems of this sort were common to societies that practiced unilineal descent in many different parts of the world.

By 1972, this system had begun to alter in the sense that the post–World War II years had seen an increase in out-marriage, particularly with spouses from islands in Chuuk Lagoon. During the approximately 120 years represented in the 1972 genealogies, more than half of all out-marriages had been with other Mortlockese, and only a fifth had been with those from Chuuk proper. By the beginning of 1973, however, 40 percent of the then-current out-marriages were to partners from Chuuk Lagoon, and comparable marriages between *chon* Namoluk and spouses from the Mortlocks had declined to 32 percent. Largely, this shift in the primary location of off-island marriage partners was a result of "the four E's" migration to the urban center on Wééné by Namoluk people discussed above, notably by those of marriageable age who went there for high school or wage work.

The number of current off-island marriages at the end of December 1972 was one-third of *all* out-marriages recorded for Namoluk's population in the genealogies, and most of the then-current marriages had occurred since the end of World War II. Moreover, the total number of out-marriages—both current and past—by *chon* Namoluk alive on December 31, 1972, was nearly half of all such marriages known to have ever occurred. Off-island marriage from Namoluk was increasing by 1972, and increasingly such marriages occurred with spouses from Chuuk rather than the other Mortlocks. Generally speaking, marriages of this sort did not follow the preferential marriage system rules that were sketched above.

Namoluk kinship and marriage is grounded in land and related resources, which henceforth will simply be referred to as land.[20] To survive on an atoll one must have access to land, for it is the source of food. To have no land is to have no food and therefore to be destitute. This equation of land with food is explicit in the way *chon* Namoluk refer to land—these resources are often called *mwéngé*, "food; to eat." People have access to their shared lineage lands by virtue of birth into that matrilineage, and their use rights to particular plots are assigned by the *samol an ainang*. Most people also have lands that they control individually, which they have received from their father or father's lineage. Some people acquire land (especially such things as breadfruit trees or coconut palms) as compensation from others to right a wrong, for special care or favors, or as payment for such things as traditional medical treatment. As is common throughout Micronesia, and in many other parts of the Pacific, kinship is commingled with land. Just as with shared blood, to share land with someone is ipso facto to share kinship. This equation of "mud and blood"[21] is pertinent here because it helps us to understand the passionate attachment that most Namoluk people have to the atoll as a physical place—pieces of land—that in turn help define who they are as individuals and as a people.

Compared to Western societies, adoption and fosterage of children is extremely common throughout most of the Pacific Islands (Brady 1976; Carroll 1970). Namoluk is no exception to this pattern. More than two-thirds of the households on the atoll in 1971 contained at least one foster child, and there was at least one adopted child in 41 percent of the households (Marshall 1976). Nearly all adoptions are by close kin, and almost nine out of ten are by the child's parents' siblings—aunts and uncles. These adoptions reinforce lineage and *afakúr* ties among the adults involved, as well as for the children, and they also strengthen an adoptive child's "sibling" connections to people Americans would call cousins. Adoptions also occasionally convert distant kinship relationships into closer ones, and sometimes they are used to create kin out of non-kin. Another means for making distant kin into closer relatives, or for transforming unrelated people into relatives, is via the *pwiipwi,* or "created sibling," bond (see Marshall 1977 for details). The key thing to understand is that all kinship ties, including adoption and created siblingship, are founded on and maintained through acts of sharing, whether that sharing be of biogenetic substance, land, nurturant acts, or understandings about mutually chosen bonds of committed caring.

Notes

1. Lukeisel literally means "middle of the rope" in reference to the imaginary line that ties Chuuk together with Nomoi in traditional sailing directions. Girschner (1912) stated that only Nama and Losap were included in Lukeisel, but use of the term today includes Namoluk. Lukeisel may be referred to in local parlance as *Morschlok Soulong,* "the Upper Mortlocks," and Nomoi as *Morschlok Souou,* "the Lower Mortlocks."

2. Hezel (1983, 82) claims that Captain Raven, aboard the British merchantman *Britannia,* first sighted the Mortlocks in 1793, although pride of place generally is accorded Captain Mortlock of the *Young William* two years later.

3. By that time, *chon* Namoluk had erected a church building and had sought mission teachers for more than a year. Julius and Lora were hampered by ill health, but they had good success on Namoluk: the Protestant Church numbered thirty-six baptized members and four deacons by the end of 1880. A year later, church membership stood at fifty, but poor health forced Julius and Lora to return to Pohnpei at the end of 1881, to be replaced by another couple from the Pohnpei mission training school. By 1886, Joram from Pingelap Atoll (see Map 1.1) became the mission teacher on Namoluk, where he remained until 1888. After a year, a mission teacher from Satawan replaced him. (See *Missionary Herald* 1879, 218; 1880b, 265; 1881a, 18, 269, 271; 1882, 221; 1886a, 311, and 1886b, 337; 1888, 300; 1891, 370).

4. An excellent historical account of this is provided by Hezel (1995).

5. Further evidence for this comes from Girschner (1912), who carried out anthropological research on Namoluk circa 1910, during which time he collected considerable data on traditional religious beliefs. (See also Goodenough 2002 concerning traditional religion in Chuuk.)

6. Dried coconut meat.

7. Hezel (1991, 192) reports that the Namoluk Catholic Church was founded in "c. 1950," but *chon* Namoluk assert that this occurred in 1949.

8. In the 1950s a Namoluk man who had converted to Seventh-Day Adventism (SDA) on Chuuk mounted a futile effort to establish an SDA church on the atoll. When he failed to make inroads into either the ranks of the Catholics or the Protestants, he abandoned his attempt and subsequently returned to the Catholic Church.

9. This woman's matrilineage remains important on Namoluk to the present day, with some of its members considered *chon* Namoluk and others *chon* Oneop.

10. Two Japanese men employed by Nanyō Bōeki Kaisha (the South Seas Trading Company) married and fathered children on Namoluk in the 1920s and 1930s, and an Okinawan employee of Nanyō Bōeki married and lived on Namoluk for more than ten years. He and three of his five children by his Namoluk wife perished while trying to escape Chuuk aboard ship during the Allied bombardment of 1944.

11. Richards (1957, 17) erroneously reports that eighteen Japanese naval personnel were removed from Namoluk in October 1945 by a U.S. search and evacuation party. Conversations with numerous *chon* Namoluk present on the atoll at that time confirm that no Japanese military were on Namoluk when the Americans came ashore after the war's end.

12. Taro is a root crop grown in freshwater swamps and is a staple of the Namoluk diet (see below).

13. The USTTPI was divided into six administrative districts (Marianas, Marshalls, Palau, Ponape [Pohnpei], Truk [Chuuk], and Yap), each of which had a district center that was the headquarters for governmental and commercial establishments. Chuuk's district center in 1969 was on what was then called Moen Island. Moen was a mispronunciation of Mwáán, a primary village on the island that Chuukese know as Wééné. After the FSM came into being in 1986, the correct name of Wééné (often Anglicized as Weno) was reclaimed, and it continues as the capital and urban center of Chuuk State.

14. Sennit is a cordage made from coconut husk fibers that are rolled into strands called *lul* (see Figure 3.1).

15. Love songs and other forms of vocal and instrumental music in Chuuk, including Namoluk, are discussed by Marshall, Gabriel, and Peter (1998).

16. The United Church of Christ (UCC) is the Congregational church that originally sent missionaries to Micronesia under the ABCFM aegis beginning in 1852 on Pohnpei and 1873 in the Mortlocks. Mizpah High School was eventually taken over by the state government and operated as a public junior high school.

17. Some descendants of the wife of the atoll's protestant minister, who served the Namoluk church from 1957 until the 1970s, are considered to be *chon* Namoluk. They belong to Imwo clan and are originally from Wééné; none of them resided on Namoluk in July 2001. The Inemaraw clan became extinct on Namoluk in the 1990s for want of descendants in the female line. When Girschner did his fieldwork on Namoluk early in the twentieth century, Inemaraw had only six living members. At that time, the *ainang* named

Tum also was present on Namoluk, but it had died out completely by 1969. The Katamak clan was not yet established on the atoll when Girschner was there (1912, 128).

18. W5 has a second lineage that has only one living member, an elderly man, so it will die out upon his passing.

19. It is necessary to keep in mind that in Namoluk's kinship system, one has several kinds of siblings: "real" brothers and sisters who share the same mother and/or father, and "classificatory" brothers and sisters of different sorts—those in one's lineage/subclan/clan, those who are descended from men of the same lineage/subclan/clan, and those created through adoptive and *pwiipwi* ties (see Marshall 1976 and 1977 for further details).

20. In addition to dry land parcels, called *fanu,* such related resources include *pwól,* "taro swamp plots"; *set,* "named sections of the reef flat"; *mae,* "stone fish weirs constructed on the reef"; *mei,* "breadfruit trees"; and *nu,* "coconut palms."

21. For more on this, see Marshall (1999, 121–125).

3

Journeyings

Using the rising Orion we will sight Ochopwot
And then use Corvus to reach Kapitau.
Mesarew and Antares sleep in a lagoon west of Anpout.
We passed by west of Sau,
And by using the Southern star we will arrive at the reef
of Urouran.

Theophil Saret Reuney (1994, 257–258)

ARRIVING AT THE REEF OF HONOLULU

Three times a week the "Island Hopper" jet operated by Continental Air
Micronesia leaves Guam, and using a different form of navigation than the star
compass of Carolinian *palu*, touches down at Chuuk, Pohnpei, Kosrae, Kwajalein,
and Majuro, before arriving on the reef runway at Honolulu International
Airport at 2:30 AM. Although Honolulu is a very busy airport, with planes landing at all hours from many time zones, there isn't much happening at
2:30 AM, and hardly anyone is around. But on the nights that the Island Hopper
comes in, the baggage claim area outside the international immigration desks is
alive with people. The first hint that these might not be typical foreign tourists is
given by the baggage that begins to tumble out of the conveyor belt tunnel. It includes suitcases to be sure, but as much as half of it is composed of large plastic
ice chests and heavy-duty cardboard boxes, taped tightly, with people's names
written on them with Magic Markers. As these items drop onto the baggage

carousel, they are quickly grabbed up by muscular young men clad in slacks or jeans, T-shirts, and zori (thonged sandals).

Because nearly everyone who is "local" in Hawai'i wears such garb, the clothing doesn't necessarily distinguish these young men. But a glance at the young women in the waiting area suggests that *they* may not be local. Many of them wear brightly colored skirts with a scalloped fringe sewn along the bottom, while others are in dresses with fitted bodices and full skirts made of equally bright material. A few of these women sport jeans and shirt tops, and all have beautiful, long, shiny black hair. Some of these clues (like the clothing) *might* suggest that the young women are not local, but others don't particularly set them apart. For instance, most people in Hawai'i have black hair, and many women wear it long. The giveaway is when one stops looking and begins to listen. These young people aren't speaking Da Kine, Hawai'i's local pidgin. Instead, they're chatting in soft-sounding, almost musical, and decidedly unfamiliar languages. Pohnpeian. Marshallese. Chuukese. Kosraen. Honolulu's Micronesian community is there to meet the Island Hopper and welcome their relatives and friends to Merika, "America." Once the new arrivals and their baggage have been cleared and collected, they are spirited away to Micronesian households spread around Honolulu and its suburbs.

Although one can fly to the U.S. mainland via Guam and Tokyo, bypassing Hawai'i entirely, most Micronesians bound for the mainland first reach "Merika" on the Island Hopper in the middle of the night. Even though Hawai'i is somewhat cooler and considerably less humid than Micronesia, the warm tropical breeze, the scents of plumeria and ginger, and the surrounding dark sea breaking on the reef are all familiar. But whizzing traffic on the H–1 freeway, the high rises of downtown Honolulu, and the wealth everywhere apparent are not, reminding new Micronesian arrivals that they are definitely somewhere other than home.

WAVES

Ocean waves are always moving to and fro. Whereas Westerners see one wave as pretty much like the next, Micronesians are much more keenly attuned to the sea. Islanders identify different *kinds* of waves that reveal such information as an approaching storm or the proximity to land. One kind of wave *chon* Namoluk recognize—large, rounded ocean swells seen as one approaches land—is named *nóó popo*, literally "pregnant wave." The waves of Namoluk people who've left their island home are like *nóó popo*—they well up as *chon* Namoluk approach new lands, whether these be the high islands of Chuuk Lagoon or the flat prairies of the American Midwest. These waves also are pregnant with future prospects, both for the migrants themselves and for the children they bear far away from Namoluk's sandy shores.

Namoluk men, and much later Namoluk women, have left the atoll in a series of waves during the twentieth century. These waves of people grew in size and reach with each passing decade. As with all waves, they remain in constant flux, always moving, never ceasing, filled with promise. *Nóó popo.*

The First Wave
Prior to 1900, during Spain's nominal control of Micronesia, Namoluk navigators regularly ventured to other nearby islands in their sailing canoes, as they had from time immemorial. Nearly all of these destinations were inhabited by people who spoke the same or a closely related language. It was not until the German colonial period in the Carolines that the first Namoluk men traveled by ship beyond the traditional sailing routes of their forefathers. As was noted in Chapter 2, the Germans hired islanders to work in the phosphate mines on Nauru and Angaur. Interviews I had with elderly people on the atoll during my initial fieldwork indicated that only about a dozen *chon* Namoluk signed on for this work, and they were the first wave—the pioneers of travel abroad beyond the traditional voyaging network.

The Second Wave
When I arrived on Namoluk in October 1969, two dozen men were alive who were born before 1921. They comprised the second wave of migrants that emanated from the atoll, and they too worked in the phosphate mines on Angaur, but this time for the Japanese between the 1920s and the early 1940s. All had also visited the islands of Palau and Saipan on their journeys back and forth. About half of them were aboard ships that stopped en route at Woleai and Fais as well, and sixteen had worked as conscript laborers on Japanese military installations on Pohnpei during the 1930s (see Map 1.1). The experiences of these men were more widespread and of greater duration than was the case for those in the first wave. For instance, one worked on Angaur for a total of six years between 1930 and 1943 in five different trips, as well as more than a year on Tonowas during World War II. Another spent three years working on Angaur, a year and a half on Pohnpei, and a similar length of time on Tonowas. A third man went to Angaur four times for a total of twenty-six months, worked a year on Pohnpei, labored six months on Tonowas, and was employed for three months on Satawan. Four men in the second wave moved away from Namoluk in early adulthood to reside with women they'd married from other islands—Ettal, Oneop, Wééné, and Pohnpei.

Travel to work elsewhere in Micronesia during the Japanese colonial period was the norm for Namoluk men, but the situation was different for women. Very few Namoluk women of that generation had opportunities to travel beyond Chuuk. Of the twenty Namoluk women alive in 1969 and born before 1921, only two had traveled outside of Chuuk State (both to Pohnpei and one to Guam). So whereas the second wave affected more men than did the first wave, as with the latter it hardly involved women at all. People's destinations in both of these waves were limited to other Micronesian islands, and their primary reason for travel was wage employment in colonial enterprises.[1]

A Second-Wave Namoluk Man Making Coconut Sennit Cord (*Lul*)
in a Canoe House on the Atoll, May 1970

The Third Wave

Matters changed somewhat for those in the third wave. Most of the fifteen men and eleven women born between 1921 and 1931, who were alive in 1969, were children or teenagers at the outbreak of World War II. Consequently, the boys were too young for conscript labor, and the primary reason for travel away from Namoluk by third wavers was for schooling. After the League of Nations granted Japan a mandate over Micronesia following World War I, a limited elementary education system for Micronesians was put in place. The nearest such school that

Namoluk students could attend was located on Oneop. This was the first formal schooling available to *chon* Namoluk, other than the basic literacy taught by Protestant mission teachers in earlier years. Just more than half the third wave men and about a quarter of the women attended the Japanese school on Oneop. It was for a maximum of only three years, and the teachers chose very few Micronesians to proceed beyond that level. It is therefore significant that three Namoluk men went on to finish fifth grade on Tonowas, two of whom were then selected for the special carpentry school the Japanese ran in Palau. One man studied there for three years, and the other for a year and a half. Soon after World War II ended, three third wavers obtained vocational training from the U.S. Navy, as a teacher, a health assistant, and an agriculture agent. One of these men also finished ninth grade on Wééné following the war.

Third wavers differed from their predecessors in terms of off-island travel. All but one woman and a third of the men had only traveled elsewhere in Chuuk State as of 1969, and the eleventh woman had never left Namoluk. But at that time three third-wave men had visited Guam and Saipan; two each had been to Hawai'i, Palau, Yap, Nukuoro, and Kapingamarangi; one each had visited the U.S. mainland and Japan (as sailors aboard ships); and yet another had been to Pohnpei.[2] The two who worked as sailors had traveled widely throughout the USTTPI. Thus some men of this generation ventured much farther afield than anyone from Namoluk had ever done before. Another difference was that some of these trips were made on airplanes rather than by ship. Still, by 1969, the primary off-island travel experiences of *chon* Namoluk then in their late thirties or older remained other destinations in Micronesia. Formal educational opportunities of any sort also continued to be very scarce. In the years since, both of these things altered dramatically for Namoluk people, especially for those born after 1931.

The Fourth Wave

The fourth wave from Namoluk—those born between 1932 and 1941—reached maturity early in the American colonial era after World War II, first under naval administration, and then under the Department of the Interior after June 1951. There were twenty-three men and twenty-three women alive in this age group when I began my fieldwork. All the men had finished sixth grade, and most had completed junior high school or more. About a fourth of them were graduates of the Pacific Islands Central School's (PICS) three-year high school program, three went through a full four years of high school, and in the mid–1960s one went on to obtain the first college degrees (an AA and a BA) to be earned by a Namoluk person.

That pathbreaking achievement heralded many other breakthroughs by members of the fourth wave. Several of these men acquired specialized training as teachers, nurses, radio broadcasters, or librarians at such places as the East-West Center and the College (now University) of Guam (UOG), and they have held jobs of high responsibility. For instance, the first college graduate has served as director of the Chuuk State Public Affairs Office, as state election commissioner, and was acting governor of the Truk District government before independence. Four men became school teachers, and two served as principal of Namoluk Elementary School (which covers first through eighth grade). Two worked in radio, and for many years one of them was FSM's broadcasting information specialist. Another was a stringer with the Micronesian News Service, and yet one more assumed major responsibilities for nursing administration at the Chuuk Hospital. Two of these men were elected to the Truk District legislature during the Trust Territory period, and two worked as language teachers for Peace Corps volunteers in Key West, Florida (1966), and in Hawai'i (1967). One worked as FSM liaison officer with the Guam Police Department, assisting in cases that involve FSM citizens on Guam. Finally, another fourth waver received a BA from the University of Hawai'i–Mānoa in 1985. Even though all of the fourth-wave women attended elementary school (usually through the sixth grade), only one went beyond that by completing midwifery training in Chuuk. Several of these women have worked in the wage economy on Wééné, and more recently on Guam, mostly as store clerks, cooks, and hotel maids.

Given all of this, it should come as no surprise that the fourth-wave men and women have traveled much more widely than any of their predecessors. Even though nine of the men have never left Chuuk State, the others expanded the travel horizon and worldly experience of Namoluk people in major ways. Taken collectively, members of this latter group have been all over the FSM, to the CNMI, Palau, the Republic of the Marshall Islands (RMI), Guam, and Hawai'i. But one or more of them also has visited other parts of the Pacific region and beyond, to include Nauru, Kiribati, Tuvalu, Tonga, Sāmoa, Fiji, Cook Islands, New Zealand, Australia, Japan, South Korea, the U.S. mainland, and Israel. A few of the fourth-wave women have been to Pohnpei and Pingelap (see Map 1.1), and during the 1990s, half a dozen of them have taken up residence on Guam or have stayed there for extended visits with their adult children and grandchildren. In recent years three fourth-wave women have traveled to Hawai'i and two to the U.S. mainland.

Expanded educational options provided the springboard, for fourth-wave men in particular, to go away to school and then find wage employment that let them explore the wider world well beyond Micronesia. Women of this generation did not have educational or employment opportunities equal to men's, so their travel has been more circumscribed. Despite this, in July 2001, four men and four women from the fourth wave resided outside of Chuuk State.[3]

The Fifth Wave

Namoluk's fifth wave includes those born between 1942 and 1951, in other words, during World War II and its aftermath. Even the oldest members of this group grew up under the U.S. colonial administration, and by the time they reached high school age in the 1960s, profound changes had begun to occur in Micronesia's educational system. Many in this group completed high school at a time when U.S. government loan programs first were extended to Micronesian students in 1972, giving them a chance to pursue postsecondary education.

In October 1969, this age group had thirty-nine men and thirty-one women. Their subsequent educational accomplishments are striking when compared to Namoluk's earlier generations. Twenty-five of the men are high school graduates, and sixteen of them attended college for at least a year, mostly in the United States. Nine have earned bachelor's degrees, and three hold master's degrees. Two (one of whom subsequently earned a BA) successfully completed the two-year nurse training program at the Trust Territory School of Nursing, which was then located on Saipan. Four others finished vocational training programs at the Micronesian Occupational College (MOC) in Palau, and one completed a computer school in Oregon. Nine of the women are high school graduates, and four went on to attend at least a year of college. Two have earned bachelor's degrees, and a third has an associate of arts degree and also graduated from Hawai'i Business College. Another completed her training at the Trust Territory School of Nursing.

Commensurate with the more advanced educational achievements of this age group, they have found a variety of important positions as well. Nine men have taught school in Chuuk State, two have been school principals, and two others have held administrative posts in the state's Department of Education. One has directed mental health services for Chuuk, another supervised the Medex program[4] in rural communities, and a third worked for years as the chief records clerk at Chuuk State Hospital. One was a journalist, became clerk of the FSM congress, and is now an FSM congressional representative. Another has been Chuuk's deputy chief of police, and a Namoluk age-mate has overseen the state government's computer operations. One college graduate has held several administrative jobs at the College of Micronesia (COM)–Chuuk Campus, while another has worked in the public defender's office. Two with master's degrees have held various important positions in national and state government, and in the private sector, including FSM health statistician, Chuuk State's finance officer, and the manager of Bank of Guam branches in several different parts of Micronesia. One fifth waver has been on active duty in the U.S. Army for twenty-two years and has yet to retire. And finally, one of these men served in the Chuuk State legislature. Fifth-wave women also have held responsible positions: five have been school teachers, one has worked as a nurse, and three have been employed in the private sector.

Members of the fifth wave have traveled widely, primarily in the Pacific region and in the United States. Three-fourths of the men have traveled beyond Chuuk State, at least to other parts of Micronesia. Two spent their senior year of high school on the U.S. mainland and graduated there. Several lived in Hawai'i or the U.S. mainland for four or more years while attending college or graduate school,

Fifth- and Sixth-Wave Namoluk Men at
Chuuk International Airport, Wééné, June 1985

and one attended law school in Papua New Guinea. Some have taken business trips to Japan, South Korea, and China, and two have served in the U.S. Army, with tours of duty in such places as Italy and Germany. Although about half of the fifth-wave women have not traveled beyond Chuuk State, fifteen of them have been elsewhere in Micronesia, mainly to Guam, where several have lived for more than a decade. Three have been to Hawai'i and to the U.S. mainland. One— married to an American—has lived for extended periods in Thailand and Switzerland and now resides in California. In July 2001, seven fifth-wave men and five women were located outside of Chuuk State.[5]

The Sixth Wave

The sixth wave of Namoluk migrants, born between 1952 and 1961, are now in their forties or very early fifties. Their group shows the continued effect of ever-greater educational opportunities for Micronesian students that prevailed during the 1970s and 1980s, especially for women. When I began tracking their progress in 1969, this wave numbered forty-nine males and forty-three females. They had some special advantages not shared by members of the earlier waves. For example, during elementary school, they were taught, in part, by American PCVs and by Leslie Marshall, so their English-language skills were honed by teachers who were native speakers. But they also benefited from a cornucopia of financial aid programs that became available to Micronesian high school graduates, allowing a great many of them to further their education in the United States beginning in the 1970s.

More than half of the men went to college for at least a year, primarily on the U.S. mainland. Three earned associate's degrees, seven obtained bachelor's degrees, and one completed a master's degree in Australia. Nearly all of those who attended college, whether or not they got a degree, found wage employment on their return to Chuuk, and some have moved into positions of major responsibility. Seven have become teachers, and one (a graduate of the Pacific Basin Medical Officers Training Program) is a doctor at Chuuk State Hospital. Two are Protestant ministers, and another is in training for that role. One has supervised nutrition programs for the state government and also has served as the state's election commissioner for recent national elections. One man is kept busy as a co-owner of a small private business; he also works as a legal assistant. Another member of the group is the state's fire chief, while his age-mate serves as Chuuk's senior land commissioner.

Eleven sixth-wave women attended at least a year of college at COM–Pohnpei, the UOG, or various schools in Hawai'i and on the U.S. mainland. One holds a bachelor's degree, four earned two-year associate's degrees, and one finished Hawai'i School of Business. Many women in this age group have been employed in the wage sector in Chuuk, on Guam, and in the United States.

Perhaps a stronger indicator of the impact of education and international travel is the fact that quite a few sixth-wave men have lived and worked outside of Chuuk State for most of their adult lives. For example, one was a noncommissioned officer in the U.S. Navy for twenty years and resided in Norfolk, Virginia, until 2001. Another met and married a Palauan woman while attending college in the States and worked at Palau Community College on Koror for many years. One man, who went away in the 1970s and has never returned to Chuuk, owned and operated a martial arts studio in Texas. Three of these men live and work on Guam, two in Hawai'i, and seven in the mainland United States.

Not to be outdone, many more sixth-wave women have lived and worked abroad than those who came before them. One left for college in the mid–1970s and has never returned to Chuuk; another did the same but has been back for a couple of brief visits over the years. Both of these women have been married twice to American men and have children who live in the States. As of July 2001, a total of five sixth-wave women were on Guam, three each were in Hawai'i and on the U.S. mainland, and two resided elsewhere in Micronesia.[6]

The Seventh Wave

The last wave to be discussed—the seventh—includes those born between 1962 and 1971. It is considerably larger than any of the previous waves. Forty-eight males and thirty-eight females had been born by October 1969; twenty-four more males and ten more females were born by the end of 1971.[7]

Nearly everyone in the seventh wave attended high school, and the great majority of them graduated. What is especially striking about these *chon* Namoluk—in their thirties in 2001—is how physically mobile they have been: at the time of my July 2001 census, three-fourths of the men (48/65) and two-thirds of the women (31/48) were located somewhere other than Namoluk. Taken together, thirty members of this age group were on Wééné, twenty-five on Guam, eleven in the mainland United States, eight in Hawai'i, three on Pohnpei, and two on Saipan. Fully 70 percent of the members of this wave were away from the atoll.

Not only do the seventh wavers demonstrate the emphatic off-island migration of large numbers of Namoluk people, but they also illustrate a fundamental shift in the reasons for such movement. Most of this group finished their schooling or graduated from high school in the mid- to late 1980s, by which time there were fewer funds available to attend college in the United States and fewer jobs available in Wééné's wage economy. Fortuitously, these changed conditions coincided with the implementation of the Compact of Free Association in November 1986, which allowed FSM citizens open access to the United States and its territories. Almost from that moment onward, emigration accelerated from the FSM, especially to Guam, where the economy was booming.

Relatively few seventh wavers have completed a college degree, if they've even gone to college at all. Part of the reason for this is that Pell and other grants became scarcer due to changes in the U.S. economy and related policies, but also many saw that several years of college education did not necessarily lead to a cushy job back on Wééné for those a few years their senior. Several men from this group got vocational Job Corps training in the United States and parlayed that into wage work there. Some seventh wavers went to the States to attend college, did so for a year or so, and then dropped out to work full-time. A lot of them have since married and had children and have remained outside Chuuk State, and it seems highly unlikely that they will return to school. On the other hand, five men and a woman from this wave finished baccalaureate degrees, and three of these men plus the one woman went on to earn master's degrees.

Those Namoluk people born after 1971—what would be the eighth, ninth, and tenth waves—have grown up in a very different world from that of their older siblings and their parents. A great number of them spent their childhood on Wééné or Guam, rather than on the atoll, because their parents were employed there in the wage economy. Whereas some of these children were fostered or adopted by grandparents or aunts and uncles and grew up and went to school back home, most of them became accustomed to the "bright lights" and found the atoll boring when they visited for any length of time. In more recent years, a substantial number of new *chon* Namoluk have been born away from their home island—in the hospital on Wééné, at Guam Memorial Hospital, or still farther afield in the United States. Some of these younger Namoluk people, born and

TABLE 3.1—Number and Percent of
Namoluk *De Jure* Population by Location and Year

| | Date of Namoluk Census | | | | | | | |
| | 1/1/1971 | | 1/19/1976 | | 4/1995 | | 7/13/2001 | |
Location	No.	%	No.	%	No.	%	No.	%
Namoluk	272	70.5	224	48.4	312	40.9	337	38.8
Wééné	69	17.9	132	28.5	204	26.7	213	24.5
Guam	4	1.0	1	0.2	121	15.9	155	17.8
U.S. Mainland	3	0.8	20	4.3	27	3.5	52	6.0
Hawai'i	1	0.25	3	0.7	7	0.9	45	5.2
Other Chuuk State	28	7.25	65	14.0	54	7.1	37	4.2
Other Micronesia	9	2.3	17	3.7	36	4.7	30	3.5
Other Countries	0	0	1	0.2	2	0.3	0	0
TOTAL	386	100	463	100	763	100	869	100

raised abroad, have never seen their native (is)land. But even those who *have* been to the atoll, or who have lived there for awhile as young children, are much more likely to seek schooling, jobs, adventure, and residence outside the FSM. They are part of the move to "colonize" America, and they can do this relatively easily because the Compact of Free Association between the FSM and the USA allows FSM citizens to enter the U.S. freely without a visa and to work there without a green card or other restrictions.

COLONIZING MERIKA

Less than thirty-five years ago, exceedingly few *chon* Namoluk had visited or lived in the United States, including the U.S. Territory of Guam. Not until the mid–1960s did a Namoluk person first reside on the U.S. mainland for an extended period (while attending his last two years of college in Illinois), although by that time perhaps half a dozen men from the atoll had taken some college classes on Guam. Still, when I completed my first census of the island's *de jure* population in early 1970, only four *chon* Namoluk were located on Guam and in the United States, all but one for schooling. At the beginning of 1971, there were still only eight Namoluk people—just 2 percent of the population—in these places (see Table 3.1). All of that was soon to change.

The number of *chon* Namoluk located in the United States and its territories tripled from 1971 to 1976, although the actual number of people involved back then was still quite small (only two dozen in 1976). During the next two decades, however, those who journeyed from Namoluk to America and its possessions grew dramatically, so that there were 155 of them—fully one-fifth of the atoll's citizens—by April 1995 (see Table 3.1). At that time, the primary site Namoluk people had "colonized" was Guam, which is where close to 80 percent of these migrants were then located. Although Guam has remained an important place for *chon* Namoluk to settle, it also has served as a stepping-stone to migration farther away—to Hawai'i and the U.S. mainland. Many of these migrants to Hawai'i and the mainland had lived for awhile on Guam, gaining important firsthand experience with American culture and institutions and improving their English-language skills in the process.

From the beginning of this migration to "Merika," a few people decided to cast their lot with the new world that had opened up before them. Marriage to an American provided one way for survival, especially if one wasn't enrolled in school. Quite a number of such marriages have occurred over the years, although most have ended in divorce because of fundamental differences in expectations about kinship obligations, spousal relationships, and child-rearing practices. Another means to survive, for those who decided to remain in the United States, was to enlist in the armed forces.[8] A half-dozen Namoluk men have followed this path.

In the early 1970s, one of them, Steemer, attended a prestigious private high school located on the Big Island of Hawai'i on a scholarship, after which he briefly enrolled at the University of Hawai'i before he gained admission to the California Maritime Academy (CMA). Approximately two years into his college studies at CMA, this man succumbed to a recruiter's siren song and decided to "join the Navy and see the world." He ended up making the Navy a career, rising through the noncommissioned ranks, serving for twenty years, including participation in the 1991 Gulf War. During this time, he married an American wife, by whom he fathered a child; divorced; and married another American, by whom he had another child and from whom he is also divorced. Now retired from the Navy, until recently he worked for a private firm in Virginia that handles Navy contracts. From his departure for high school, he did not return to Chuuk—let alone Namoluk—for twenty-three years, finally going back for a visit in 1994. As with a couple of others who've been away from Namoluk for a very long time, he found that he could still understand Mortlockese when spoken to, but that responding in his own language was difficult, at least at first.

This has become quite common among those *chon* Namoluk who've been away for a long time. Internet chat rooms such as "coconutchat" have provided one venue for refreshing language skills, as the following e-mail passage that I received that mixes Chuukese and English indicates: "Now I am a pro, I could speak Chuukese language just as good as they are. . . heheheheh. By the way do you still know how to speak Chuukese language or do you forget it too? *Iwe eli epwele pwal ina mo chok pun iei akan tam ach poraus nge* I have to go and check on who is in the chatroom today so I would keep up with what's going on on the islands.

Take care and I will *fos ngonuk* again next time" (e-mail from Kaylee, 28 December 2000; pseudonym substituted). In 2001, Steemer moved to Guam for some months, and in 2002 he married a woman from Chuuk whom he had met on the Internet. They have taken up residence on Pohnpei, where she is employed.

Another Namoluk man—Jasper—who went to Oregon for college in the late 1970s, also dropped out of school to join the Navy. Like Steemer, he fought in the 1991 Gulf War as an enlisted man aboard an aircraft carrier, but unlike his age-mate, he chose to leave the Navy after four years. Instead of returning home, however, he moved back to Oregon, resumed college, earned his BA degree, found a job, and recently married a fellow Mortlockese who has lived in Portland for eighteen years. Jasper sponsored or attracted a number of other *chon* Namoluk to the Portland-Salem area, and along with a multitude of other Mortlockese and Chuukese who reside there in 2003, they have established their own churches and social networks as they have begun to put down deep roots in the Pacific Northwest (see Chapter 6). Jasper has not been back to Namoluk since he left there in 1976, although he has made one or two short visits to Wééné over the years.

By July 2001, the number of *chon* Namoluk in Guam and the fifty states exceeded those on Wééné and elsewhere in Chuuk State for the first time, and this migration outside of Chuuk State is a growing trend. The implications of this for individual and group identity will be taken up in detail in subsequent chapters. Before doing so, however, we will explore another side of the journeyings of Namoluk people away from their home island—a side that doesn't have happy endings. These "bad trips" are caught up in broader processes of modernization that characterize the sites to which *chon* Namoluk have relocated.

BAD TRIPS: BEER AND TURKEY TAILS

In their long encounter with the outside world Namoluk people have been exposed to changes in diet, modes of transportation, levels of physical fitness and stress, and previously unavailable psychoactive substances. These lifestyle changes—taken singly and in combination—have produced new ways of dying, to accompany the infectious diseases and other sorrows that long have afflicted island peoples. Dietary changes are among the more dramatic alterations in lifestyle that have contributed to this process.

Before outside trade goods began to affect life on the atoll in the early twentieth century, *chon* Namoluk consumed a typical Pacific Islands diet of "fruits and roots," accompanied by many kinds of fish and other seafood products, such as clams, octopus, and spiny lobster. The main fruits were coconut, breadfruit, and banana, and the major root crop was taro in several varieties. Supplemented by the occasional consumption of pork, chicken, and sweet potato, this diet provided all of the major nutrients necessary for healthy growth and development.

Fatty foods—those that were *meyi iwi*, "greasy"—were relatively rare and highly prized. Because everyone did hard physical labor in food production and walked, swam, and paddled to get around the atoll, there was little, if any, obesity.

During the Japanese colonial era between the two world wars, polished rice and tinned fish entered and became staples of the Namoluk diet, and these are mainstays of contemporary meals. Nowadays, the "Calrose" rice comes from California's central valley, and the canned mackerel is caught in Micronesian waters, processed in Japan or Taiwan, and shipped back to line the shelves of Wééné's numerous stores where it sells for approximately a dollar a can. From a dietary point of view, these two new items are inferior to the foodstuffs they replace (breadfruit, taro, and fresh fish), but by themselves they aren't primarily responsible for the diet-related health problems that now beset *chon* Namoluk and other Micronesian peoples. Those problems derive from the heavy consumption of high-fat foods and much greater amounts of sugar and salt.

During the 1960s, Namoluk people, especially those in the urban center, began to consume more fatty meats, and this trend has continued and increased as the standard of living has risen during the latter forty years of the twentieth century. Canned corned beef; Spam; and similar high-salt, -fat, and -cholesterol tinned meats now compete with frozen beef, chicken, and pork for the consumer's dollar. Often these foods are fried, absorbing still more fat as they are cooked. When Namoluk people settle on Guam, Hawai'i, or the U.S. mainland, they seek out and are right at home in America's fast food restaurants, such as McDonald's or Kentucky Fried Chicken (see Chapter 6). However, a few introduced foods that are sought by Micronesians, including *chon* Namoluk, truly set them apart. The most notable of these is turkey tails.

By the 1960s, U.S. exporters already had discovered that they could sell what Americans deem less-desirable, fatty cuts of beef and pork to the islanders, and that Micronesians would pay top dollar for these. When, precisely, one of these exporters also discovered that Micronesians would pay good money for frozen turkey tails is not known, although it happened after the ready availability of frozen meats that began in the late 1960s on Wééné. In any case, turkey tails, those wonderful globlets of pure turkey fat—the ultimate "greasy" food—have been a part of Chuuk's cuisine for almost two generations.[9] Those in Merika periodically buy and eat them because, as one woman told me on the phone, "they remind me of back home." Most people cook these delicacies, but some actually make "sashimi" from the raw tails, such is the lust for fatty foods. Unfortunately, there is a price to be paid for this aside from the money at the supermarket.

During the past four decades, Micronesian people have undergone the "epidemiological transition." This technical phrase describes a major change in what people die from—the causes of death. Specifically, the shift is from infectious diseases as the primary cause to chronic, noncommunicable diseases, such as cancer, heart attacks, and non-insulin dependent diabetes mellitus (NIDDM).[10] A diet high in fat, sugar, and salt is a major risk factor that contributes to these "diseases of modernization." Such a diet and a lack of exercise typically produce excessive weight gain. The resultant obesity symbolizes the health problems that trigger new ways of dying. *Chon* Namoluk and other Micronesians have come to call these multiple new threats to their well-being "turkey tail disease."

Used in this generic sense, "turkey tail disease" already has taken a toll on Namoluk's population. Two-thirds of the deaths during the past thirty years[11] recorded for the group born between 1932 and 1971 have come from causes, many of which can be thought of as "turkey tail disease." For example, two men and a woman died in their early fifties from NIDDM,[12] and two other men—both also in their fifties—died of heart attacks. But the toll from noncommunicable diseases is exacerbated—especially for men—by sometimes heavy beer drinking and by regular cigarette smoking. Consumed to excess, alcoholic beverages are well-known contributors to heart disease and some cancers (not to mention obesity), and tobacco use also increases the likelihood that one will die of a heart attack, stroke, lung cancer, or other respiratory ailment such as emphysema. Drunkenness, and its associated disorientation, also significantly raises people's risk of death from road traffic crashes, brawls, and accidents.

When I look over my Namoluk data, it is striking that premature deaths have overwhelmingly affected males. A major reason for this disparity is that men are at much greater risk for alcohol-related and tobacco-related harms than are women, few of whom drink or smoke. At the end of 1971, Namoluk's population had 183 males and 145 females who were born between 1932 and 1971. Thirty years later, at the time of my July 2001 census, twenty-seven (15 percent) of these males had died, whereas only four (2.5 percent) of their female counterparts were deceased. Fully a third of the male deaths were alcohol-related, as was one of the three female deaths (she was killed in a drunk-driving crash on Guam). With a single exception, these were all people in their twenties and thirties. The deaths of three more men who died in their fifties were almost assuredly a consequence of heavy smoking.

Before foreign contact in the nineteenth century, and for much of the twentieth century, Namoluk people had little or no access to alcoholic beverages and tobacco. As with other Pacific Islanders, they did not manufacture alcoholic beverages traditionally, and colonially imposed prohibition laws kept most Namoluk people from experiencing the pleasures and sorrows of drink until the early 1960s. When drinking became legal in Chuuk approximately forty years ago, commercially manufactured alcoholic beverages were available in the urban center, but only very rarely did these make their way to such outer islands as Namoluk. Young men on the atoll would occasionally brew a pot of "yeast," but the quantity and the ethanol content was always limited. But as more Namoluk men frequented and then moved to the developing urban center on Wééné beginning in the 1960s, more of them experimented with alcohol. Binge drinking together in groups also occurred among some of the young men who went to the United States in the 1970s for college, and to Guam and the United States in the

1980s and 1990s in search of jobs. The drinking style was "drink to get drunk," and when money was available, men would often go on group binges that lasted two or three days.[13]

Beer—which is the overwhelming beverage of choice among Micronesian men—is related to Namoluk deaths in a variety of ways. Of the nine Namoluk men whose deaths can be linked to alcohol,[14] two were killed in drunk-driving crashes (at ages 23 and 34), two died in other alcohol-related accidents (at ages 23 and 33),[15] two were murdered by others who had been drinking (at ages 26 and 27), two died of an alcohol overdose (at ages 31 and 45), and one died from alcoholic cirrhosis (at age 51). As mentioned above, the sole alcohol-related woman's death (at age 31) was an unfortunate passenger in a car crash where the male driver was heavily intoxicated. The "bad trips" and events that precipitated all ten of these deaths happened to people who had journeyed away from Namoluk: five occurred on Wééné, three on Guam, one in outer island Yap State, and one on the U.S. mainland. Alcohol abuse—either by the victim or by someone else—is a new way of dying for *chon* Namoluk.

VENTURING

Kenneth and Micky were in their seventies, and until the 1990s neither had ever traveled outside of Chuuk State. Two of their five sons reside in Oregon, and when one son and his American wife sent them plane tickets begging them to come and visit their grandchildren whom they had never met, they decided to go. Hopping through Micronesia on the Island Hopper, they stayed but briefly in Honolulu and then continued on to Portland, where they were met by their family. Kenneth made everyone laugh when he told them he looked down from the jet between Chuuk and Pohnpei, after they had reached cruising altitude, and saw snow spread out below them. "That wasn't snow," said their son Kurt, "those were just fluffy clouds." But Kurt took his father to Mt. Hood a few days later, and the old man *did* get to see and feel snow. Best of all, once he did so, he could return to the less frigid temperatures of the Willamette Valley, relishing the experience and the stories he would tell his other grandchildren when he got back home to Namoluk.

Kurt and his wife, Sally, resided at the end of a cul-de-sac in a development of pleasant tract homes, all of which looked much alike. A few days after the old folks arrived, Kurt and Sally left for work, and Kenneth and Micky decided they would go out for a walk in the neighborhood. When they reached the connecting street, they noted a bright red car parked at the corner, which they agreed would provide them with a good marker to find their way back. They walked around for forty-five minutes or so, enjoying the sights, the fresh air, and the chance to stretch their limbs. Eventually, Micky said she was getting a bit tired, and they agreed it was time to return home. They walked and looked, and looked and walked, but the red car was nowhere to be seen. Getting somewhat worried, they continued to search for the right street, until it became clear that they were thoroughly lost. At that point, Micky began to cry. Soon thereafter, a friend of Kurt and Sally's happened by in her car. When she saw Micky weeping, she slammed on the brakes and asked what was wrong. That did little good because neither Kenneth nor Micky spoke English. The friend quickly concluded that they were lost, urged them into her car, and took them safely back to their son's house.

As this brief episode indicates, by 2002 Namoluk people—even Namoluk's elders—have ventured abroad as never before, and as later chapters will show, some have gotten lost in the process. This venturing beyond the reef raises the question of the conditions back on the atoll: Who remains there? What is life like for those who have stayed at home or have returned home? The next chapter describes everyday life on the atoll in 2002 for those who have remained there or who have returned home after living elsewhere. Specific things that have changed or that have stayed the same from 1969 to 2002 will be highlighted.

Notes

1. All twenty-four men and all twenty women of the second wave had died by July 2001.

2. Only four third-wave men and five women remained alive in July 2001.

3. Eight of the men and one woman in the fourth wave were deceased by July 2001.

4. Medex is the name given to graduates of a mid-level practitioner training program, similar to a physician assistant or a health officer. To expand and upgrade the skills of nurses and health assistants in the FSM and RMI, the Medex training program commenced in the mid- to late 1970s. The program was a collaboration between the World Health Organization (WHO) and the University of Hawai'i (WHO 2001). The program in Chuuk included two *chon* Namoluk among its trainees.

5. Ten fifth-wave men and one woman were deceased in July 2001.

6. Three sixth-wave men had died by July 2001, but all of the women were still alive then. One more man from this wave died in the spring of 2003.

7. At the time of my July 2001 census, six of the seventy-two males were dead, as was one of the forty-eight females. Half of the males died in their first year, whereas the other three, plus the woman, met untimely deaths in their twenties and early thirties. Their deaths—as with many members of the fifth and sixth waves—are part of a dark undertow associated with migration off the atoll that is discussed in more detail below.

8. An article in the Santa Rosa, California, *Press Democrat* (3 April 2003, p. A6) stated that "More than 37,000 noncitizens serve in the military; their numbers have grown about 30 percent since 2000." In a discussion on the listserv of the Association for Social Anthropology in Oceania (ASAO), commentators noted the significance of service in the British Army by Fijians, in the U.S. armed forces (especially the Marines) by American Sāmoans, and in the New Zealand military by men from the former New Zealand colony of Western Sāmoa (now just called Sāmoa). During this online discussion, participants mentioned Palauans from the Southwest Islands, *chon* Chuuk and Pohnpeians who have served in the U.S. military, and Craig Severance raised the question of whether Carolinians may have "seen this as an avenue of mobility, and access to [the] GI Bill."

9. E-mail correspondence with anthropological colleagues confirms that turkey tails are consumed throughout the FSM, in the RMI, and in the Republic of Palau (personal communication with Laurence M. Carucci, Suzanne Falgout, Karen Nero, and Alice Oleson, January 2002).

10. This list of diseases now also includes HIV/AIDS. One Namoluk man perished from AIDS during the 1990s when in his late thirties.

11. Twenty males and three females.

12. Quite a few *chon* Namoluk have been diagnosed with and are being treated for NIDDM, and access to proper healthcare for this disease has been a factor motivating migration for several of them. Another Namoluk man, age 66, died in early 2003 of NIDDM.

13. I have written extensively elsewhere about patterns of drinking in Chuuk State (e.g., Marshall 1975b, 1979a, 1990a, 1990b, 1990c; Marshall and Marshall 1990). As with all human behavior, the manner of drinking and how Chuukese men behave when intoxicated have changed over the years, and nowadays some have tempered the more rowdy and violent aspects of "weekend warfare," especially when drinking in the United States.

14. A tenth man from Namoluk, born in 1931 just ahead of the group under discussion, died in 1970 of an alcohol overdose at age 39.

15. While inebriated, one was struck and killed almost instantly by a locomotive in Florida in 1993, and the other was paralyzed completely by a several-story fall from a balcony while drinking on Guam in 1990. The second man lived for five more years before succumbing eventually to his injuries and debilitation.

4

Namoluk People, 2002

We, the people of Namoluk, the succeeding heirs and
guardians of the land of our ancestors by the blessings of
the Almighty God, do hereby pledge in these words our
solemn wish to make a more perfect community of peace
and harmony for all our peoples throughout the generations. . . .

With this Constitution, we affirm our desire to respect
and uphold our traditions and customs, protect and pro-
mote our natural heritage and the social bonds we have as
a people, now and forever.

Preamble to Namoluk Constitution 1991

GETTING THE LEAD OUT

The new boat with its 25-horsepower outboard motor was his pride and joy.
Only the second motorboat on the atoll, he had saved his money for a long time
before commissioning one of Chuuk's best-known boatbuilders to construct the
wooden hull. And the motor! A brand new Johnson that had cost him a pretty
penny. But there it was!

Although a boat and motor cost considerably more than a *waafatil* or
waaserik, a boat connoted prestige, modernity, and the power of the purse. A
man curious about the world around him and the world writ large, an innovator
who had brought the first personal radio to the atoll and the only one on the is-

land who owned and knew how to use a throw net, Sergio was immensely pleased
with his new boat. One major advantage that motorboats have over canoes is that
the former can be used to go out trolling for tuna and other delicious big fish of
the open sea even when there is no wind. And Sergio's boat was being used successfully to bring home *takou*, *angarap*, *póllai*, *serau*, and *ichich* on almost a daily
basis. Of course, this took quite a bit of gasoline, and gasoline was a limited and
prized commodity on Namoluk. It was imported in 55-gallon drums whenever
the field-trip ship came, and occasionally the smaller mission boats would carry a
drum. The boat's heavy use for fishing and trips across the lagoon to the uninhabited islets eventually meant that the engine began to act up for a lack of maintenance. In those early days of motorboat use men like Sergio were still gaining a
familiarity with how this new technology worked and what one had to do to keep
it going.

Somehow, in an attempt to clean the motor, the threads for the spark plug
were damaged. The plug began to leak oil around its base, and matters quickly
got worse. The motor was not producing full power, and it didn't seem safe to
take the boat out in the open ocean until it could be fixed. But Sergio the innovator hit upon an idea: he would repair the spark plug threads by melting some lead
fishing sinkers, carefully "puttying" the lead into the hole for the plug, and then
screwing in the plug before the lead fully hardened. Yes, that would solve the
problem!

The deed was done, the boat was launched, and I was asked to accompany him
on a test run across the lagoon. The motor roared, the boat zipped away from
shore at full throttle, and Sergio had a grin on his face from ear to ear. We
jounced across the lagoon's small waves for about 500 yards when there was a
loud, "Pop!" Looking aft, Sergio and I both watched the spark plug describe a
perfect arc as it blew out of the engine head and dropped into the depths below. It
was an ignominious paddle back to shore.

In the years since the first *chon* Namoluk purchased a motorboat and brought
it to the island in October 1970, life on the atoll has been transformed in a host of
ways. By 2002, new ideas, new products, new government, and new opportunities
to migrate all contributed to changing day-to-day life. But other, deeper rhythms
continued to frame these innovations, overpowering some, tempering others,
and embracing a few. This chapter provides a glimpse of what life on Namoluk
was like at the beginning of the twenty-first century.

THE MOTORBOAT REVOLUTION

Until October of 1970, paddling canoes—*waafatil*—and sailing canoes—
waaserik—were the atoll's sole means of transportation. These sleek and ingen-
iously designed craft were still made of local materials, with only the woven pandanus sails of old replaced by imported sail cloth or canvas. The first man to buy
and bring an outboard motorboat to Namoluk—Malcolm—inaugurated a "mo-

Waaserik Crossing Namoluk's Lagoon, Bound for Amwes, January 1970

torboat revolution"[1] that was complete in less than a generation. In just fifteen years the fleet grew to thirteen boats. Of the nine *waaserik* that sailed out to troll for tuna when I first lived on Namoluk, eight were completely gone by the time of my visit to the atoll in 1995. All that remained were their rotting hulls lying about near the old canoe houses, monuments to a hallowed past. No Namoluk man in 1995 could rightfully call himself a *palu*, "navigator," nor had anyone managed to learn canoe-building skills before the old men who had this mastery died, their knowledge dying with them.

Micronesian sailing canoes were technological masterpieces—they embodied the epitome of a nautical people's oneness with the sea. Fast, of shallow draft for skimming over submerged reefs, seaworthy, sailing canoes carried Micronesian peoples to their islands in voyages of initial settlement. Canoes were critical to the maintenance of interisland trade connections, visits among kin, and food procurement from open ocean trolling and visits to uninhabited islands and reefs. Among Micronesian atoll dwellers, the sea was a man's domain, and sailing canoes both symbolized and were vehicles of masculinity. They encoded skill, boldness, strength, and adventure. By comparison, a motorboat is a sorry substitute.

And yet today on Namoluk it is motorboats all the way down. Why should this be? Motorboats may not symbolize masculinity in the same way as *waaserik* did, but they do represent modernity and success in a monetized world. It takes money and the savvy to earn it to buy a boat and a motor. Outboards can be operated whether or not there is a wind, and they can carry somewhat larger loads than all but the largest sailing canoes. Although Micronesian sailing canoes amazed the first Europeans who saw them with their speed, motorboats are faster still. Islanders correctly saw them as the wave of the future.

And yet outboard motorboats have some serious drawbacks. Whereas sailing canoes were designed and built on islands like Namoluk by local men and out of local materials, motorboats are of foreign design and made of imported materials. Although Namoluk's first motorboats were wooden and crafted by boat-builders in Chuuk Lagoon, the boats in use today have fiberglass hulls that are molded overseas and shipped to stores on Chuuk. The outboard motors are manufactured in the United States or Japan, and when parts are needed they, too, must be imported. But the biggest weakness of the motorboat revolution is the dependency it has fostered on outside energy resources. Gasoline and oil must be brought to Chuuk in large tankers and then sent out to places like Namoluk in 55-gallon drums. The price of fossil fuels is fixed by market forces far beyond the control of Micronesian people, so once canoes have been forsaken, as on Namoluk, motorboat owners are at the mercy of transnational oil companies that exist only to make profits for their shareholders. And few, if any, Micronesians hold shares in Texaco, Mobil, or Chevron.

Belatedly, thoughtful sailors of Micronesia's younger generations realize that they have lost—or nearly lost—a thing that helped to distinguish them as a peo-

Motorboat on Namoluk, April 1995

ple. Aware of the revival in open ocean voyaging that has followed the riveting 1976 journey of the *Hōkūle'a* from Hawai'i to Tahiti (Finney 1979), Micronesians also have begun programs to resurrect sailing canoes and the star compass navigational techniques of their ancestors. Fortunately, in the Western Islands of Chuuk State and the outer islands of Yap State the requisite knowledge has survived, so the possibility of reintroducing *waaserik* to Namoluk is still there. Whether through the atoll's present and historical kinship ties to Polowat, or through a recent program begun through the Chuuk Campus of the College of Micronesia, it remains to be seen whether *chon* Namoluk may yet resurrect sailing canoes. Pukueu would be elated if they did.

TYPHOON PAMELA: MORE WINDS OF CHANGE

Just as the destruction caused by Typhoon Phyllis in 1958 spurred changes on Namoluk and led to new houses, public buildings, and the physical layout of the community, another major typhoon—Pamela—that struck in May 1976 was a literal force for change. After developing northeast of Chuuk on May 13th, the storm grew in intensity as it moved southwestward during the next two days. After curving back southeast of Chuuk in the vicinity of the Lower Mortlocks, Typhoon Pamela's winds reached full typhoon velocity of 75 mph as it passed between Namoluk and Losap on May 16th, after which it went on to hit Guam on May 21st.

All eleven communities in the Upper and Lower Mortlocks were damaged by Pamela, but not all to the same extent (see Marshall 1979b for details). Namoluk was among the six communities that suffered especially severe destruction—notably from the storm surge that pushed high waves ahead of the typhoon itself. Along with Ettal and Kuttu, Namoluk was submerged completely by ocean waves that swept across the islet for fifteen to eighteen hours. The salt water entered the taro swamps and killed all of the taro plants, and a high percentage of breadfruit, coconut, and banana trees perished outright from the combination of salt, wind, and wave. Equally devastating was the substantial damage to the atoll's reefs and reef organisms, many of which serve as a regular food source. Nearly all trees were denuded of vegetation, knocked down or snapped off in the typhoon, but the most startling rearrangements of the landscape were a result of wave action. Tons of coral rubble and sand were carried ashore to a depth of several feet on the ocean side of the islet. Much of this ended up in the taro swamp, requiring that it be re-excavated before it could again be planted after rain eventually neutralized the salt that taro plants cannot tolerate. A huge sandbar was deposited along a stretch of the outer reef shelf, comprised of material that had once been part of Namoluk Islet. And last, but certainly not least, a new islet was created by the storm. The long narrow tip of Amwes that points toward Namoluk Islet was cut across by waves, leaving a smallish new islet that local wags immediately named "Paméla."[2]

Damage Caused by Typhoon Pamela on Namoluk, May 1976

Typhoon Pamela knocked many houses off their foundations or badly damaged their roofs (ironically, a majority of these houses were built following Typhoon Phyllis eighteen years earlier). In the aftermath of the typhoon a relief effort was mounted by the USTTPI government and the International Red Cross for the affected communities. As a member of the initial damage assessment team, I visited all eleven communities in the Mortlocks—including Namoluk—very soon after the storm abated, and I made a second voyage in a similar capacity six weeks later. Between May 22 and July 7, 1976, Namoluk received 17,125 pounds of rice, 16,466 pounds of flour, and 3,464 pounds of canned meat (mostly chicken with some corned beef and a small amount of mackerel) to support the then-resident population of about 275 people. The community also received tools, lumber and plywood, metal roofing, tents, cooking pots, utensils, plastic water jugs, and used clothing to help them begin to reconstruct their lives.

Pamela's winds and waves altered the atoll's physical appearance, as had Typhoon Phyllis in an earlier time. But perhaps more than Phyllis, Pamela accelerated processes already in train that further altered both Namoluk's infrastructure and its social structure. As a result, by 2002 a number of things on the island looked very different from before.

CHANGES IN INFRASTRUCTURE

Second Homes

One thing that Typhoon Pamela demonstrated to *chon* Namoluk was that cement houses withstood such storms much better than wooden ones. Consequently, even though not everyone could afford to build a more substantial dwelling post-typhoon, many people did or resolved to do so in the future once they had the money. Thus Pamela stimulated further migration to Wééné as men went in search of wage work so they could purchase cement, rebar, lumber, and the other materials necessary to build a stronger house. Many of these migrants, then in their thirties, forties, and early fifties, worked for a year or two in Chuuk and then returned to the atoll. But others—particularly young men and women in their twenties or early thirties who did not qualify for high school or did not have the resources for postsecondary training once they graduated from high school—found the faster pace of life and the things money could buy on Wééné more to their liking, so they took jobs there and stayed.

While Pamela's devastation to Namoluk's housing triggered construction of larger and more substantial homes in the late 1970s and early 1980s, the continued emigration of *chon* Namoluk for education and employment produced yet another interesting consequence "back home." By the mid- to late 1980s, an ever-growing number of Namoluk people had found wage work in town and in the new FSM government headquarters on Pohnpei. By then a small number of Namoluk citizens also had settled in such places as Saipan, Guam, Yap, Palau, Majuro, and the U.S. mainland. Some of these salaried workers decided to erect new homes back on the atoll too, even though they themselves would not live in them regularly.

Most such homes, built from the mid–1980s onward, are of cement and have numerous amenities not found on Namoluk before. Several have two stories, with cement staircases to the upper floor. Most have glass louvered windows, linoleum floors, a place to cook inside the house, and consumer goods never before seen on the island. Some people on the atoll own private radio transceivers, allowing them to communicate directly with kin on Wééné. A couple of these homes boast solar panels with battery arrays to run lights and an assortment of small D/C electric appliances.

Many of the new houses built by nonresident *chon* Namoluk are occupied by the owner's elderly parents or by a sibling and her or his family who have remained on the atoll. These homes mark social status, are a physical symbol of claim on and commitment to the island, and are a place to stay when those who paid for them go home for a visit. Amazingly, a few of these "fancy" houses lie vacant for much of the year, serving only as vacation homes for their owners when they come back for a short visit.

Failed Projects

Two substantial efforts to alter the physical landscape of Namoluk during the 1980s and 1990s ended in failure, each for different reasons. The first of these was the reconstruction of a cement and coral rock seawall along a major portion of the lagoon shore of Namoluk Islet that had been erected as a community development project just a few years before Typhoon Pamela hit. The purpose of the seawall was to prevent erosion of the land there, although Typhoon Pamela demolished the wall and ate the land anyway. But the result of this effort to control nature—as so often happens in human affairs—was an unintended consequence: what had always been a wide, sandy beach that sloped gently into the lagoon was turned into a "non-beach" with a rocky bottom. The seawall and its post-typhoon replacement altered wave and current patterns, which then swept away the lovely sandy beach on which generations of Namoluk children had romped.

The second major effort to alter the landscape collapsed before it was finished. In the early 1990s, $100,000 out of what was to be a $300,000 government project was appropriated to build a small airstrip on Amwes. In order to orient the strip correctly to the prevailing winds, the consulting engineer said that it would have to cut diagonally across the islet, right through the old, overgrown taro swamp. Not only were the taro plots highly prized, but the middle part of the islet also harbored numerous giant old breadfruit trees, coconut palms, and other *mwéngé*. Almost all of the $100,000 was paid to landowners to free their property for the airstrip. Many trees were felled, and the site was partially cleared. Then, facing a combination of bickering over land rights and a lack of additional financial appropriations, the project was put on hold in late 1994 and has languished ever since. Moreover, the small airline that served the outer islands of Chuuk State during the 1990s, and which would have used the airstrip, has ceased operation, and no replacement is in sight. By 2002, the scar from the clearing that occurred had finally begun to heal.

CHANGES IN SOCIAL STRUCTURE

The physical structures built in Namoluk's recent housing boom—including the local variants of "trophy houses"—reveal a profound shift in the community's social structure. Namoluk today is ever more affected by social class differences, resulting in a split between the haves and the have-nots. This class division comes to a society that was profoundly egalitarian as recently as the 1960s.

Before large numbers of *chon* Namoluk gained access to a high school education, and before they began to emigrate to paid work in the district center and destinations beyond, the main economic difference among the island's people was in the amount of land and related resources they controlled. Kin obligations and the myriad crosscutting ties among the atoll's citizens muted even these differences. When I first arrived on Namoluk in 1969, there was only a handful of cement houses, and most people continued to occupy the wooden homes erected as part of the reconstruction following Typhoon Phyllis a decade before. A household survey of material possessions that I conducted at that time showed relatively few differences in what various people owned, although those with salaried jobs as teachers, health aide, and agriculture agent were somewhat better off than most. Still, the similarities in accommodation and possessions were far more striking than any variability. This is no longer the case.

The Namoluk community in 2002 is crosscut by social class differences. These are based primarily upon differences in monetary wealth that result, in turn, mainly from greater or lesser educational achievement. Nearly all of those in what I call Namoluk's new elite have a stable wage job in a skilled occupation, and most of them have at least an associate's degree or its equivalent in vocational training. With very few exceptions, these men and women do not reside on the atoll, even if they have built a nice new house there. With even fewer exceptions, these people see themselves as modern, forward-looking, even cosmopolitan is-land citizens. Even though they cling tenaciously—even fervently—to their Namoluk identity (and to their land rights on the atoll), they see themselves as part of other emergent, more encompassing identities as well. In later chapters we will explore these nested identities in greater detail.

As is true the world over, social class differences often become self-perpetuat-ing, and the Namoluk situation seems no different. When once the atoll's school led all of its competitors in Chuuk State in the number of its students who passed the high school qualifying examination, by 2002 this was no longer the case. Indeed, to the consternation of the former principal and several former teachers, Namoluk elementary school's eighth-grade graduates had fallen to near the bot-tom of the pack in qualifying for high school.[3] But a moment's reflection helps explain the major reason for this: Namoluk experienced a "brain drain." During the past thirty-five years, the atoll's most able young people went on to high school and then postsecondary training in goodly numbers. With a few excep-tions who took teaching jobs back home, these were precisely those people who led the migration to Wééné and other destinations. As they completed their training, found jobs, married, and had children, most of their children attended school where their parents lived.

Beyond this, during the 1980s and 1990s, there was a proliferation of new private, church-based schools on Wééné. These schools had a reputation for of-fering a more rigorous education than the public schools, but they charged tu-ition for each student. The new elite had the money to send their children to these private schools, and they did so. Namoluk's have-nots continued to send their kids to the free public schools, whether on the atoll or in town. As the mi-gration destinations of *chon* Namoluk shifted to Guam in the early– to mid–1990s, and then to Hawai'i and the U.S. mainland in the late 1990s and early 2000s, it was especially the children of Namoluk's elite who entered these U.S. public schools.

CONTINUITIES

The sun, the sea, the cycle of plants—natural rhythms continue to shape, even dominate, the daily round on Namoluk. These rhythms echo back through the generations, connecting people with their past even as they live in the present and the future. Roosters still herald the first light in the eastern sky, awakening sleepy Namoluk children and urging their parents to greet and meet the new day. People stir before sunup and carry out their morning ablutions in little bathhouses next to their homes, at freshwater wells in the island's woodsy interior, or at the lagoon-side beach. In a timeless pattern, older children shepherd their younger siblings, gently keeping them on task. Families gather around the bowl of leftover taro or rice from the previous evening's meal, and adults clutch cups of lukewarm instant coffee to which they have added copious amounts of sugar. Despite typhoons and heavy out-migration, the daily round on the atoll begins and proceeds much as it always has.

As their forefathers did with sailing canoes, half a dozen men right at daybreak wade out to two motorboats anchored in the shallows off the lagoon shore. Instead of a sail, they carry two full tanks of gasoline, along with heavy nylon fishline, and lures they have made from white chicken feathers and carefully attached to 2-inch-long double hooks purchased on Chuuk. Full of anticipation, but with muted voices, the men hike themselves into the boats, arrange their gear, and pull up anchor. One stands astern clutching a 10-foot pole with which he smoothly pushes the boat through the shallows until they reach the channel that has been dynamited in the reef to provide access to the open sea. The water is deep enough there to position the motor, rev it up, and snake slowly through the channel to the dark seas that lie just beyond the barely visible white line of breakers striking the outer reef face.

Once free of the channel, the throttle is opened up and practiced eyes search for *pwá*, the telltale flocks of noddy terns and other seabirds swarming over and diving into schools of *til*—"small minnows." Spotting a *pwá*, the helmsman steers in that direction while the other two men play out their lines, one on either side of the boat. Shortly, they approach the *pwá*, and the excitement mounts. Scores of terns swirl and dive in a ballet of movement, creating a frenzy on the sea's surface. The men know what lies beneath. While the birds feed on the *til* from above, the tuna and other big game fish dash in to gobble the *til* from below. The boat runs right through the flock of birds, momentarily swallowed up and surrounded by silent wings dipping and soaring.

Then it's past the *pwá*, and the fishermen begin jerking their feather lures to imitate *til* as the lines are pulled through the school of minnows. *Chiurume!* The shout goes up as the man on the left sets his hook and begins pulling in the line, hand over hand. *Chiurume!* Now the man on the right has a bite! Soon the first glistening, 20-pound *takou* is flopping in the bottom of the boat, while the second man continues to bring in his line. They can see this one as it draws close to the boat, and it's a big *ngel*, the most delicious fish of all. Just before the *ngel* is flung into the boat, a swift, dark shadow passes close astern. The man on the right heaves his line, and all that is left is the head of the *ngel*, hook still protruding from its mouth. Sharks have to eat too.

Back on the island, before the morning sun gets too high, a few men and women set out to weed their taro plots, knee-deep in wet mud, and to harvest some corms for the big meal that will come in late afternoon or early evening. Finding a taro of the right size, they uproot it with a digging stick, cut the leafy top off with a machete, and leave a small portion of the corm attached. This they replant in the rich muck to grow another root for another meal six-to-twelve months later. By this time the island's kids from approximately six years and older have assembled in the schoolyard, tummies full and minds open to the day's lessons. The cacophony of shouts and laughter settles down as the teachers arrive and call them into their classrooms. Younger children poke about close to their homes, watched over by their mother or an aunt. One woman sweeps leaf litter from her yard with a stiff broom made of coconut leaf midribs, and the sound attracts a mother hen and her chicks, who hope for a beetle or a food scrap. The chicks discover a coconut that had its top cut off for drinking, and one or two crawl right inside to peck at the soft flesh—*benunu*—that drinking nuts contain. Mid-morning, a bingo game gets underway, spiced with gossip and accompanied by music from WSZC, broadcast from Wééné. As always on Namoluk, the pace is slow and easy.

Behind this activity is a steady dull roar. Like white noise for atoll dwellers, this sound is so much a regular part of life as to disappear from consciousness. It is the bass note struck by the continuous army of huge ocean swells that rise up and pound on the outer reef. Life on an atoll is lived amid the perpetual sound of breakers always breaking. Most days it is also lived in heat, and as the sun rises higher in the sky, people seek shade in the *fáál*, under breadfruit trees, or beneath the gnarly old *kul* and *amoleset* trees that line the lagoon shore above the high-water mark. Normally, a tradewind makes the heat tolerable, and occasional quick downpours cool things off momentarily before the raindrops warm up and add to the omnipresent high humidity. Wind and rain can actually make it chilly on Namoluk, especially during the rainy season—from August to December—when as much as 5 inches might pour down in a single day.[4]

As the afternoon advances, the children are let out of school, and with whoops of glee the younger ones race for the lagoon-side beach to frolic and splash and burn off their pent-up energy. Teenaged boys gather up their spears and goggles and head for the reef edge to *likapich*, hoping to bring home a fat sea bass or a snapper for dinner. Old men sit in the canoe houses, telling stories while making sennit cord by rubbing strands of coconut husk fiber on their inner thighs. Around 4:00 PM the empty steel oxygen tank gongs sound for the daily service, and women pick up their bibles and shuffle respectfully toward church. Christianity is an active presence on the atoll every day—the two churches,

Catholic and Protestant, remain the most compelling social institutions in the community. As if to underscore this point, Resolution Number 3, passed during the second meeting of the Namoluk Constitutional Convention in March 1992, specifies that "Christianity has become part of Namoluk's culture" and that "Namoluk Municipality shall be recognized as a Christian Municipality" (Namoluk Constitution 1991).

By 2002, Namoluk's churches were thoroughly indigenized and deeply rooted. A sixth waver, Sampson, the Protestant minister, was born into the community, graduated from high school on Wééné, spent about a year in college on the West Coast during the 1970s,[5] and then returned to Chuuk. He married a distant cross-cousin from the atoll, became a schoolteacher on the island, and continued his education during summers via college extension courses, eventually earning a bachelor's degree. Meanwhile he devoted himself to Bible study and rose in the church hierarchy, a most appropriate path for the grandson of Edgar and Louella, the Oneop couple who headed Namoluk's Protestant church throughout most of the Japanese colonial period. Moreover, when he became minister, he succeeded his own father in that role. During the summer of 2001, a jubilee was held to celebrate the centennial of Christianity on the atoll.

The Protestant Minister and Deacons Seated in the
Namoluk Protestant Church on Easter Sunday 1995

The Catholic church on Namoluk is headed by a *katekista*, a lay leader from the community who oversees regular services but cannot hear confession or say Mass. Those latter tasks are handled by Mortlockese or Chuukese priests who visit the atoll periodically for that express purpose. The bishop of the Diocese of the Caroline and Marshall Islands is now a man from Moch, and priests are able to reach outer island communities such as Namoluk to give Mass more frequently because of an increase in the number of small interisland ships.

Back in 1969–1971, only two nongovernment vessels, neither of which was very large, visited the Mortlocks: the Catholic mission's *Star of the Sea* and the Protestant mission's *Chen*. One or the other of these church-operated boats, along with the more sizeable government field-trip ships, averaged a visit to Namoluk approximately every six weeks in those days. Even so, Leslie and I experienced two stretches while we lived on Namoluk when the atoll was without a ship for nearly three months. Uncertainty about ships to the outer islands—when they will sail and where they will go—provides a continuity from the past into the twenty-first century. But on the positive side there are now many more nongovernment vessels that ply the waters from Chuuk Lagoon, down through Lukeisel and Namoluk to *Morschlok Souou*.

In 2001, one of these, a former South Korean longliner that was confiscated by the FSM's Maritime Authority for illegally fishing in the FSM's territorial waters and auctioned off, belonged to Horatio, one of Namoluk's more distinguished citizens. Part of the fifth wave, this man graduated from high school on Wééné, worked several years as a journalist, married a fellow Mortlockese, became clerk of the FSM Congress, and was later elected to the congress itself. He acquired the 65-foot fishing boat for a song and operated it on the cheap. The same pattern obtained with most of the other small private ships: they were acquired already used, run for a few years with minimal maintenance, and then abandoned when they finally broke down. But for Catholic priests and other passengers alike, their presence has made circular migration from the outer islands to Chuuk's urban center much easier in the 2000s than it was in the 1960s and 1970s.

Along with the more frequent movement of people back and forth from the outer islands to the administrative center, products, ideas, and visitors all now move more frequently as well. How else to explain the fact that at least three *chon* Namoluk now use Grecian Formula to keep their hair black? How else can *chon* Namoluk get the parts and the fuel so that they can rely totally on outboard motorboats for open ocean fishing and for moving about the atoll? How else do those children who reside on Namoluk and only visit Wééné briefly learn firsthand about automobiles, cable television, telephones, ATMs, and the noise made by commercial jetliners? And how else do members of Namoluk's new elite find it possible to visit their home atoll for short vacations from their jobs in Oregon, Guam, or Pohnpei?

EXODUS

The exodus from Namoluk that occurred during the last decades of the twentieth century has had different destinations. Between 1971 and 2001 Namoluk's *de jure* population more than doubled, but its geographic distribution shifted markedly. Back at the beginning of 1971, nearly 96 percent of the atoll's population was located in Chuuk State, with 70.5 percent still living on Namoluk itself (see Table 3.1). Five years later, 91 percent of *chon* Namoluk were still to be found in Chuuk State, but the percentage residing on the atoll had dropped to less than half of the *de jure* population. At that time most migrants had moved to Satawan or especially Wééné, either to attend school beyond the eighth grade or to find wage employment in the urban center. Only two dozen Namoluk people were outside the USTTPI in January 1976, most of them attending college in the United States (see Table 3.1).

In the mid–1990s, the exodus from Namoluk took a dramatically different turn. Although the actual number of people on the atoll was greater in April 1995 than it had been in 1971 or 1976,[6] the *proportion* of the total population that was resident on the atoll had dropped to 41 percent (Table 3.1). *Chon* Namoluk who were located in Chuuk State—including Namoluk—had dropped to 75 percent, whereas the number who had moved to Guam had exploded to 121 people—16 percent of the *de jure* population. When I took my midsummer 2001 census, yet another change in the exodus from the atoll was revealed. At that time fewer than 40 percent of Namoluk citizens were to be found on the atoll, and the number located on Guam had grown to 155. But what was most notable in 2001 was that the number of Namoluk people in the United States had shot upward from just six years earlier.

By July 2001, more than 11 percent of the atoll's population was to be found in the fifty states. Although the number on the U.S. mainland had almost doubled during that time over what it was in 1995, the primary new destination of choice had become Hawai'i. As Table 3.1 shows, from 1995 to 2001 there was a six-fold increase in the number of Namoluk people in Hawai'i, and their total nearly matched the number in the other forty-nine states combined. Meanwhile, only two-thirds of all *chon* Namoluk remained in Chuuk State in July 2001.

The vignette at the end of Chapter 3 illustrates that the establishment of Namoluk families on Guam, in Hawai'i, and on the U.S. mainland has opened the travel horizons of even the atoll's senior citizens. While most of those over age 70 continue to reside on the atoll, many of them now take trips far afield to visit their children and grandchildren. Indeed, the exodus from the atoll has affected different age groups in different ways.

The easiest way to describe this is to talk in general terms about the geographic distribution of ten-year age cohorts as of July 2001 (see Table 4.1). More than two-thirds of Namoluk people between the ages of 20 and 59 were somewhere other than the atoll at that time. A glance at Table 4.1 shows that the high-

TABLE 4.1—Locations of Chon Namoluk by
Ten-Year Age Cohorts, 7/13/2001

Age Cohort	Top Five Locations from Highest Number to Lowest Number in Cohort[a]					
	1	2	3	4	5	Percent of Cohort Off Namoluk
0–9	N	G	W	H	C	51
10–19	N	W	G	C	H	55
20–29	N	W	G	M	H	70
30–39	N	W	G	M	H	68
40–49	W	N	M	G	H/C[b]	74
50–59	W	N	C	G/M[c]	G/M[c]	69
60–69	N	W	G	H	C/M/O[d]	60
70+	N	C/M/G[e]	C/M/G[e]	C/M/G[e]		18

[a] N=Namoluk; W=Wééné; G=Guam; H=Hawai'i; M=U.S. mainland; C=other Chuuk State; O=other Micronesia (FSM, RMI, CNMI, and Palau).

[b] Hawai'i and Other Chuuk State have the same number of persons from this cohort.

[c] Guam and the U.S. mainland have the same number of persons from this cohort.

[d] Other Chuuk State, U.S. mainland, and other Micronesia all have the same number of persons from this cohort.

[e] Other Chuuk State, U.S. mainland, and Guam all have the same number of persons from this cohort.

est percentage of those adults ages 40 to 59 resides on Wééné. For the most part, these are people who found government jobs after they returned from a few years of college in the States, or who met and married a spouse from Chuuk Lagoon or elsewhere in Chuuk State and settled in the town. Even though the second highest percentage of *chon* Namoluk ages 20 to 39 is located on Wééné, the most striking thing about people in these cohorts is that substantial percentages of them are on Guam (20 percent), the U.S. mainland (10 percent), and Hawai'i (7 percent). Thus more than one-third of these young adults resides in the United States and in Guam.

This, in turn, helps to explain the relatively high proportion of *chon* Namoluk under age 20 found on Guam in 2001 (and in the States to a lesser extent). A full 25 percent of the 0–9 age cohort lived on Guam in 2001, and another 5 percent were to be found in the fifty states. Sixteen percent of those ages 10 to 19 were on Guam, and 6 percent were in Hawai'i or on the U.S. mainland. Most of these children or teenagers—especially those under age 15—live in these places with their parents, attend American schools, and experience a lifestyle similar in many respects to that of someone growing up in Long Beach or Dallas. They watch TV, eat fast food, play computer games, listen to America's top hit songs, and speak English like someone from Des Moines. They shoot hoops, dance hip-hop, complain about homework, and yearn for a set of wheels. Some of these children have been sent to live with aunts, uncles, or older cousins so that they can attend free public schools in places where their parents expect they will receive a better education than if they remained on the atoll or on Wééné.

Notes

1. This phrase is a takeoff of Pelto's book title, *The Snowmobile Revolution* (1973).

2. This islet subsequently has reconnected to Amwes and is no longer a separate entity.

3. In 1970, there were openings for only one in five eighth graders in Chuuk State to attend Truk High School, and Xavier and Mizpah—the other two high schools at that time—could only enroll a few additional students. Hence competition for high school was very keen, and Namoluk's consistent success in moving its pupils on to high school speaks very well of the quality of its teachers and its student body.

4. Sergio and I maintained a rain gauge and a min-max thermometer on Namoluk from January 1, 1970, through July 31, 1971. The atoll received almost 140 inches of rain during 1970 and 108 inches during the first seven months of 1971. On three occasions the 24-hour rainfall exceeded 4 inches. The average high temperature during those nineteen months was 91 degrees Fahrenheit, with an average low of 78 degrees.

5. In May 1970, Sampson found a bottle containing a note that had washed ashore on the ocean side of Toinom, about fourteen months after a passenger threw it overboard as the *S. S. Monterey* crossed the equator at 158 degrees West. The note contained an address, and I helped Sampson prepare and mail a letter to the person who had set the note adrift. That initiative began a correspondence that eventually led Sampson to enroll in a community college near the note-dropper, with the latter and his wife serving as Sampson's host family while he was in California.

6. *De facto* population counts on Namoluk date back to 1900, and from then until 1971 the eight actual head counts fluctuated between 238 (in 1946) and 341 (in 1925). (See Marshall 1975a, 169.)

5
Heading Off to College

Towards the end of August each year, the Truk [Chuuk]
airport regularly overflows with swarms of young people,
decked out in their Sunday best and heaped with
mwaramwars, bidding a tearful goodbye to their parents
and friends before they leave Truk, most of them for the
first time. They are the latest crop of the college-bound
and their number has become legion of late.

Francis X. Hezel (1979, 172)

THE LEGION OF THE COLLEGE-BOUND

The two young women made a striking pair as they exited the plane and stepped
down the ramp to the tarmac at the Cedar Rapids Airport in eastern Iowa.
Wearing matching *holokū* in a bright lavender, green, and white tropical print,
their shiny waist-length black hair blowing in the breeze, each walked self-con-
sciously in unfamiliar high-heeled sandals. They had just journeyed nearly
halfway around the world to begin college classes in Michigan. Getting to Iowa
was not without mishap.

Maiyumi and Luanne graduated from high school in Chuuk in June 1975, and
each was admitted to a community college in Michigan. Leslie and I had finished
our PhDs a few years before and had accepted positions at the University of Iowa
in Iowa City, about 30 miles south of Cedar Rapids. Knowing that Maiyumi and
Luanne would be traveling abroad for the first time, we helped them arrange way
stations en route to Michigan. When they arrived at Honolulu International

Airport, my parents and youngest sister were there to meet them, and they stayed at my parents' home in Kailua for a couple of days. Mom and Dad put them on a flight to Denver, with an intermittent stop in Los Angeles. Because they didn't have to change planes in L.A., my parents emphasized that they should simply remain on board, if possible, during the layover. Then, when they arrived in Denver, Eldon Flowers, a college classmate who had been best man in our wedding ten years before, placated Leslie and me by agreeing to make sure they got onto the correct flight bound for Cedar Rapids.

As Eldon related it to us, Luanne and Maiyumi were easy to spot when they got off the plane from L.A., and he immediately identified himself and mentioned our names to reassure them. They had almost a two-hour wait before the Iowa flight, and he asked if they were hungry. Both nodded in assent, so they sat down in one of Stapleton Airport's restaurants to get a bite to eat. The young women found the menu somewhat puzzling, so Eldon inquired whether they liked Mexican food. They said they did, and he ordered a mix of tacos, enchiladas, and chile rellenos, plus soft drinks for three. The food came—piping hot and spicy, neither of which characterized food back home in Chuuk. Luanne took a tentative taste and made a face; Maiyumi poked at her enchilada but didn't really want to eat it. Eldon ended up eating for three.

After walking around the airport a bit, Eldon escorted them to the gate for their flight to Cedar Rapids via Des Moines, reminding them that "Mac and Leslie will meet you in Iowa." In those early days of Namoluk people's contact with the United States, "Merika" was conceived of as a single place, not unlike such big islands as Pohnpei or Guam or Hawai'i. When you got there, you were there. The same was true of named places in Merika, like Iowa; they were imagined to be single locations, perhaps comparable to the districts on Wééné like Iras or Peniyésene. Again, once you'd arrived, you'd arrived. So when Maiyumi and Luanne had flown for an hour and a half, and the flight attendant announced that they were beginning their descent into Des Moines, *IOWA,* it was "Iowa" that rang a bell for them. After all, Eldon had made clear to them that Mac and Leslie would be waiting for them in Iowa. So they hatched a plan. They decided to try to hide from us after they got off the plane, and then sneak up behind us and surprise us.

The plane landed in Des Moines and taxied to the gate. Luanne and Maiyumi gathered their small hand-carry bags and entered the corridor to the terminal after the aircraft had docked. Peering out, and not seeing us, they headed for the baggage claim area, slipping behind pillars as they approached, so we wouldn't see them and spoil the surprise. Other passengers gathered, and the luggage came off, but Mac and Leslie were nowhere to be seen. They watched for their bags, but they didn't appear either. Finally, getting a bit nervous, Maiyumi screwed up her courage and asked a uniformed airline employee about their missing luggage. The employee asked to see their tickets, and said, "You're in the wrong place—this is Des Moines, and you're supposed to be on the flight for Cedar Rapids, which is about to leave."

Laughing about it later, they said that they just looked at each other and pan-icked. They took off their high-heeled sandals, hitched up their *holokū* to just above the knee, and took off running barefoot as fast as they could go back to the gate where they had arrived. The door to the corridor was closed, and their hearts sank. With tears in their eyes, they approached the check-in staff at the counter, who were busy with their final tallies in preparation for the flight's departure. The staff looked at these clearly distressed and exotic young women, phoned the plane, and reopened the corridor and the plane's door to let them back aboard. Sheepishly, they returned to their seats. Half an hour later when they arrived in Cedar Rapids, the two young women made a striking pair as they exited the plane and stepped down the ramp onto the tarmac. Mac and Leslie were there to meet them, and this time they made no attempt to hide. Welcome to Merika!

CHON NAMOLUK AND COLLEGE EDUCATION

The very first *chon* Namoluk to enroll in college did so with a Trust Territory scholarship at what was then the Territorial College of Guam (later to become the University of Guam) in June, 1961, majoring in social science. Now in his late six-ties, this man earned an AA degree there and then transferred to a small college in Illinois, from which he received a bachelor's degree in political science two years later. Upon graduation, he returned to Chuuk, married a woman from Wééné, and entered a series of state government jobs before he retired recently after approximately thirty years of public service. Including this man, only three men born before 1942 attended college; two earned bachelor's degrees and one an associate's degree via extension classes offered on Wééné.[1]

At the beginning of the 1970s, four Namoluk young people were selected as foreign exchange students to attend their senior year of high school in the United States. One went to Wisconsin, two to Oregon, and the fourth to Minnesota. Returning home when they finished high school, all four of these students subse-quently attended college in the States, two of them in Oregon. One drowned while back in Chuuk, one dropped out after a year or so and enrolled in a business school to learn computer skills, and two eventually earned bachelor's degrees.

It was not until the early– to mid–1970s that more than a handful of *chon* Namoluk came to America. The extension of U.S. government financial aid pro-grams for needy college students to those from the USTTPI opened the door of educational opportunity, and people now in their forties and fifties like Luanne and Maiyumi were the first ones to walk through it. A few came as early as 1972, and by January 1976 twenty *chon* Namoluk were attending colleges on the U.S. mainland, with another two enrolled in Hawai'i. Half of these students matricu-lated at colleges in Oregon and California, but Maiyumi and Luanne were among five who attended schools in Michigan. Most of these students were male: Maiyumi and Luanne were among the first young women from Namoluk to study at U.S. colleges.

From the educational journey of the atoll's initial college graduate in the 1960s to that of the *chon* Namoluk enrolled in college in 2003, a surprising variety of institutions has contributed to the atoll's knowledge pool. Namoluk students have enrolled in schools in nineteen different states, on Guam, in the CNMI, at the College of Micronesia campuses on Pohnpei and Chuuk, in Australia, and in three South Pacific countries (Fiji, Papua New Guinea, and Sāmoa). Many of these schools are community colleges, but they also include such well-regarded institutions as Gonzaga University, the University of California–Berkeley, the University of Hawai'i–Mānoa, and the University of Iowa. My records indicate that *chon* Namoluk have matriculated in more than fifty different institutions of higher learning in the United States, five in Micronesia (including Guam), and four in other Pacific countries (including Australia).

For a community numbering fewer than 900 people, Namoluk has had remarkable educational success. During approximately fifteen years from the late 1960s to the early 1980s, Namoluk Elementary School led all others in Chuuk State in the percentage of its graduates who passed the competitive examinations for admission to high school. Three different *chon* Namoluk have been valedictorians of their high school classes. But perhaps the most impressive statistic is the number who have earned college degrees. Drawing upon my records and fieldnotes, and brainstorming with Malcolm and several other informed Namoluk people, members of the community have earned more than thirty-five associate's degrees, almost fifty baccalaureate degrees, and ten master's degrees. Given that 36 percent of the atoll's *de jure* population in 2001 were under age fifteen, and that another 6 percent were over age sixty, and therefore mostly did not have the opportunity to attend college, these degrees were earned by the remaining 58 percent, or around 500 people. Thus 10 percent of those from the age groups that have had the opportunity, and from a population that only had its first college graduate in the mid–1960s, now hold bachelor's degrees, and 2 percent hold an advanced degree. Easily a third of those *chon* Namoluk between the ages of sixteen and fifty-nine have at least a semester or more of college education, and quite a number have attended classes for several years, accumulating many credits but never graduating.

A majority of Namoluk people who attended college in the United States during the 1970s eventually returned to Micronesia, some with degrees, and others without. At that time relatively few *chon* Chuuk had college degrees, and as a consequence many of those who gained experience in the States were able to parlay it into wage employment—mostly government jobs—back home. This is reflected by the fact that the highest percentages of those *chon* Namoluk in their forties and fifties as of July 2001 were located in Chuuk's locus of state government and urban center on Wééné (see Table 4.1).

But not all those who came to America in the 1970s returned home to jobs in the islands. The journey provided some with a different kind of opening—a chance to marry and live and work abroad. Six of the twenty-two Namoluk stu-

College-Educated Namoluk Schoolteachers on the Dock on Wééné,
Preparing to Sail to Namoluk, July 2001

dents who were in the States in January 1976 were still there twenty-five years
later. Four of them had remained in the United States for nearly that entire period, marrying Americans (or a German, in one case); two have had careers in the
U.S. armed forces that span more than twenty years of service. During the late
1970s and 1980s, quite a few members of the sixth and seventh waves joined their
older brothers and sisters in the States, and many have remained there to bolster
the number of Namoluk people who have settled in the States. They will receive
explicit attention in the next three chapters.

Case 1: Hans
Hans's birthday falls right in the middle of the decade covered by the sixth wave.
A graduate of Xavier High School on Chuuk in the late 1970s, he pursued a
rather peripatetic but typical path as he combined academics with adventure.
Initially, Hans attended two different community colleges in Iowa, rooming for
awhile with another *chon* Namoluk a few years his senior. He did well in his
courses at these schools, which allowed him to transfer his credits and enroll in
the University of Iowa. While there, he lived in a dormitory and spent quite a bit
of time with my family and me, living with us during the summer of 1979.

Perhaps in part because we left for a two-year stint in Papua New Guinea, and in part because of loneliness for more familiar surroundings, Hans went first to Kansas City—a major mecca for Micronesian college students over the years—and then back to Chuuk and Namoluk for more than a year, hoping to find a job. He managed to land a teaching position at a Catholic elementary school, and a year later, in May 1982, he flew to Honolulu and enrolled at the University of Hawai'i for summer session. He shared an apartment with another *chon* Namoluk (and his Hawaiian girlfriend), and two young women from Namoluk—in Hawai'i for school—also lived in the same building.

By fall term, Hans switched schools again, this time to Hawai'i Pacific College, then located in Honolulu. His roommate had moved in with a Mortlockese woman (whom he subsequently married), so Hans was on his own briefly. But as so often happens among Micronesians in the United States, he soon found others from back home with whom to share expenses and company. By mid–October he was rooming with two other *chon* Namoluk also in Honolulu for schooling. And by then he could write that "I'm doing pretty good in my studies here. I think because the college I'm going at is not as tough as U. of Iowa. It's pretty easy. Besides, I eat lots of *angarap, takou, mon* and *likeriker* [all fish species] from the sea, not from rivers." By January 1983, Hans told me on the phone that he hoped to graduate with an accounting major in the fall, go back to Chuuk for a year or so to save money, and then return to Honolulu to finish a master's degree. Four months later, he was still rooming with one of his Namoluk relatives, and they'd added two more roomies from other islands in Chuuk State.

But when fall 1983 rolled around, Hans was still in Honolulu, still taking classes, and now rooming with several other Mortlockese. By March 1984, he had accumulated additional classes at Hawai'i Pacific in business, economics, and computer science, but he still didn't have a degree. That June he told me on the phone that he just needed a couple of more classes to earn a business degree. But he also told me that he didn't really want to return to Chuuk since he really liked Hawai'i. At that time he shared an apartment with three other Mortlockese, and they divided the monthly rent of $415. Within a year he was back on Wééné, still sans degree.

In the fall of 1985, Hans went to Guam and enrolled at UOG, and that same fall he married a woman from Chuuk Lagoon whom he met on Guam. Six years later, after teaching elementary school on Saipan for several years, he was still chasing the elusive baccalaureate degree—this time via the UOG extension program on Saipan. By then he also had three children to support. Hans eventually moved back to Guam, and by 1995, he had finally earned his degree in education from UOG. He has been gainfully employed on Guam ever since.

Case 2: Maiyumi

Having finished high school in 1975, Maiyumi—a sixth waver—was among the first ten Namoluk women to venture to the States for college. She enrolled at a community college in Michigan that had a number of other Micronesian students, and she was close enough to Iowa City, where Leslie and I lived, that she could spend her school holidays with us. Studying hard, playing volleyball hard, and traveling through parts of the midwestern and southeastern United States with us during summer break, Maiyumi saw the Great Smoky Mountains, Charleston, the Atlantic Ocean, and the wonders and monuments of Washington, D.C. In May 1977 she received her AA degree in Michigan, and the following fall she enrolled at Eastern Oregon State College (EOSC) in LaGrande, Oregon. EOSC probably has awarded more bachelor's degrees to students from Chuuk State than any other college. Not only did a great many *chon* Chuuk enroll in courses on its campus at the foot of the Blue Mountains, but EOSC also ran a college extension program on Wééné for several years during the 1980s. The extension program allowed many who had not finished school in the States to complete their degrees while working back home. At least half a dozen *chon* Namoluk have been EOSC students, and three hold degrees from that institution.

Maiyumi continued to apply herself in class, and she accumulated three more semesters of coursework—just one or two semesters shy of finishing her BA degree. She also met her Mortlockese husband at EOSC, and their son was born in LaGrande. Soon thereafter, word came that her father had died, and the three of

Young Namoluk College Student in Great Smoky Mountains National Park, North Carolina, August 1977

them flew home for the funeral. This unexpected expense left them financially unable to return to college immediately, so they remained on Wééné for about a year, where her daughter was born. Once they had saved up sufficient funds, they returned to LaGrande with both of their children in hopes that they could complete their college degrees. Not long thereafter, another family crisis required their presence back in Chuuk, and once again they scraped airfares together and island-hopped home. This expense, and the burden of two young children, proved too much of a financial obstacle, and they never returned to LaGrande.

Maiyumi spent about six months looking for work before she began a very responsible position with the state judiciary. Her husband, also just a few credits away from his BA, obtained a teaching job on Wééné for the 1982–1983 school year, and they settled into town life as a dual-career, two-income family. Maiyumi's husband enrolled in the EOSC extension program during the next three years and finally earned his bachelor's degree. Unfortunately, the press of work and family obligations prevented Maiyumi from doing the same. They have lived on Wééné ever since, although she travels quite a bit in connection with her work to such places as Saipan, Guam, Pohnpei, and Hawai'i, and she spent a couple of months in the U.S. mainland in the late 1990s while being treated for a medical condition.

Case 3: Moses

Moses represents the seventh wave who headed off for college in the United States. Actually, upon graduating from high school in 1985, he enrolled for a year at the COM campus on Pohnpei because—despite his sterling academic record—he had not yet received the state government scholarship he'd been promised. In January 1987, however, he sent me a letter from Corsicana, Texas, where he was then a student at Navarro College, along with more than eighty others from Micronesia. Like many community colleges in the States, Navarro actively recruited Micronesian students, who were eligible for Pell grants and similar U.S. federal funding, because the colleges received matching funds for each such student they enrolled. Navarro College continues to have a substantial Micronesian enrollment, and Corsicana has become an "island" in the "archipelago" of Micronesian settlements in America. In fact, Corsicana hosts a major week-long Fourth of July celebration every year, to which other Micronesians come from as far away as Oregon and North Carolina. Competitions are held in baseball and basketball, much fish is eaten, much beer is quaffed, and many stories are told.

Moses was still in Corsicana when I visited him there in February 1988, by which time he claimed that more than 100 Micronesians were enrolled or living there, mostly from the FSM, but also including some from Palau and the RMI.[2] He told me that Navarro College had only accepted about half the hours he had accumulated at COM as transfer credits, and consequently he would not complete his AA degree in pre-law until May 1988. While he attended Navarro

College, Moses sent application forms to two of his age-mates from Namoluk, both of whom enrolled there the following fall.

By then Moses had applied to Cleveland State University, Northeast Missouri State University, and Southeast Missouri State University as possible places to continue his studies. During my visit, I suggested that he also look into the University of Northern Iowa (UNI), and I gave him the relevant contact information. As it happened, he moved to Cedar Falls, Iowa, in August and occupied a dorm room with an American roommate who had never heard of Chuuk, and who didn't have a clue where Guam was either. That fall, as a first semester junior, Moses took Spanish, Quantitative Methods of Business, Humanities I, Elements of Physics, and Judo—a total of sixteen credit hours. He also rode the Greyhound bus down to Iowa City to spend Thanksgiving with me.

A year later Moses continued to plug away at his degree, although he had moved out of the dorm and into an apartment by himself. His academic performance was good, and he had become involved in a local Baptist Church, which provided most of his social interactions. In conversations with me he complained that he'd gotten very few letters from home, although he was in contact via telephone (and at least one visit to Washington State) with *chon* Namoluk who were elsewhere in the States. He had switched from judo to *tae kwan do* and prided himself on his developing martial arts skills.[3] By May 1990, he had changed his major to business, and he was looking forward to a trip down to Corsicana once school was out. At that time he saw himself as on schedule to graduate in August 1991. And then things fell apart.

Moses took a full load of classes during fall semester 1990, but the financial aid promised him from the Chuuk State government was delayed once again, and he was not allowed to enroll for spring term until this funding issue was clarified. Classes had begun, and Moses was in limbo, awaiting word on his combination of scholarship, Pell grant, and work-study. He resided again in a UNI dorm, where he watched TV with three other foreign students on the evening of February 4, 1991. One of those students was a Palauan whom Moses had known and had some run-ins with at Navarro College.[4] Moses and the Palauan had both been drinking. Words were exchanged. The two men grappled with each other, and to the horror of the Indonesian and Chinese students looking on, the Palauan stabbed Moses four times with a large folding knife he had hidden in his pocket. When Moses reached the hospital emergency room that, fortunately, was but a five-minute ambulance ride away, his blood pressure was in the 70s, he was in shock, he was unresponsive to pain, and he had lost an enormous amount of blood. The most serious stab wound—to the abdomen—severed his bowel and led to surgical removal of a kidney. Recovery took months and several more operations, including a major one later in the year to reinsert his colon and remove a colostomy. Needless to say, Moses never enrolled that semester, although he did continue to take classes at UNI and via University of Iowa correspondence courses over the next year or so.

The sad thing is that after amassing more than 120 college credits, this high school valedictorian has never completed his studies and obtained a bachelor's degree. Showing the efficiency of the "coconut wireless," right after Moses was stabbed, two of his first cousins—both married to American women and living in Oregon and Washington—caught a bus and rode all the way across country to visit him in the hospital. Another close relative phoned him long distance from Pohnpei, full of concern. I drove up to visit several times, and once Moses was finally released, he moved in to recuperate with a nurse and her family in Cedar Falls whom Leslie knew via her teaching in the University of Iowa College of Nursing. Eventually, he moved into his own apartment and began a series of jobs far beneath his education and his strong intellect: a minimum wage cook at Hardee's in 1993; a busboy and dishwasher at a Village Inn restaurant at $4.95/hour in early 1994; a nonunion hog butcher on the killing floor at Iowa Beef Packers (IBP) beginning in January 1995, starting at $6.00/hour (see Chapter 6). Seventeen years after coming to the States for college, Moses has yet to go back to Namoluk, let alone Wééné, for a visit. His one-time dream of earning a master's degree and working as a diplomat seems far away, indeed.

THE XAVIER CONNECTION

Beginning in the 1950s, Xavier High School on Wééné, operated by the Jesuits, drew students from all over the USTTPI, many of whom went on to assume major leadership positions in the CNMI, FSM, RMI, and Republic of Palau.[5] Referred to only half in jest as "the Harvard of Micronesia," Xavier accepted "the best and the brightest" and challenged them with a demanding curriculum. Not surprisingly, a high percentage of Xavier High School graduates went on to college. Eleven *chon* Namoluk have graduated from Xavier over the years, and it is instructive to look at what they have accomplished in their postsecondary education, where they reside, and whom they have married.

All eleven went off to college. One stopped after earning an AS degree, but the other ten all completed bachelor's degrees. Of those ten, three went on to finish master's degrees. In July 2002, five lived in the States (four on the mainland and one in Hawai'i), one each was resident in Guam, Pohnpei, Toon Island, Chuuk, and Wééné, and one was deceased (he worked and died on Wééné). Only one was back on Namoluk, teaching in the elementary school there. Nine of the eleven were or had been married, whereas two had never married. All nine were married to spouses from Chuuk State, but only one spouse was from Namoluk (five were from the Lower Mortlocks, and three from islands in Chuuk Lagoon).[6] These marriage patterns are highly pertinent to new, emerging identities among Mortlockese and Chuuk State migrants living abroad. "Mixed" marriages create connections to more than one home community and foster "mixed" identities among their resultant offspring. In the contexts of places outside of Chuuk State, for example, Pohnpei, Guam, and the United States, such identities as "Mortlockese" or "Chuukese" come more to the fore.

FROM COCONUTS TO COCONUTCHAT

Most Micronesian students who went to Guam, Hawai'i, or the U.S. mainland for college from the late 1980s onward were introduced to computers, the Internet, and the World Wide Web as a part of their education. As with most other college students in America, they received free access to e-mail and the Web so long as they were enrolled. These students soon taught their siblings and their friends how to log on, and for those who weren't in school, word spread rapidly about the free e-mail service provided by hotmail.com and yahoo.com. Rather quickly then, in the 1990s, *chon* Namoluk and other Micronesians in the States and on Guam began to communicate regularly using the Internet. For example, "Paulina" posted the following note on Microislands.com:

> I'm trying to contact my best friend, Berekita Walter. We went to High School together and last time I saw her was August of 94 which was the month after our graduation. She is probably 24 or 25 yrs. old now. She was born in Oct. second week of Oct. She's around 5'2" and she has a very pretty smile. I missed her and I want to contact her as soon as possible and I would like to say Happy B-day to her. She lives in Guam (Guahan) and that all I know [*sic*]. She is from the Island of Namoluk (Namoilam) in the State of Chuuk. Please email Paulina should you have any helpful information that might help her find her friend. (http://www.microislands.com/loslov.htm; 2/13/2000)

Beginning in 1996, the Internet arrived in the FSM and the RMI, and the number of local subscribers continues to grow. Gene Ashby and Giff Johnson (2001) report that by the end of 2000, there were nearly 1,500 users in the FSM and 545 in the RMI. Both countries have upgraded their links in terms of speed, new modems, and greater bandwidth, and the Internet's advent has provided islanders living abroad with inexpensive and instantaneous news from home. More significantly, however, "Internet chat rooms on Web sites devised especially for Marshallese and Federated States of Micronesian citizens link hundreds of people daily from every corner of the United States and the islands for mere pennies" (Ashby and Johnson 2001, 27). Among the best-known and most heavily used of these chat rooms for a number of years was coconutchat.

Conducted in a free-wheeling, multilingual format, coconutchat mixed English with several different Micronesian languages in a rapid flow of "conversation," contributed to by many aficionados, while others (myself included) simply logged on, lurked, and tried to keep track of the players without a program. Although serious matters having to do with island politics or life in the United States periodically surfaced, coconutchat served primarily as a place to find other Micronesians in the booming, buzzing confusion that is America. It also was a wonderful place to flirt. Because such flirtations were necessarily public—often occasioning comments by others—nearly everyone used a pseudonym when participating.[7] Part of the fun of the game was to try to guess who was hiding behind which name. Sometimes this could be clarified by signaling the other to exit the main chatroom and to enter a private chatroom together. Quite a few flirtations progressed in this way, and if the two people discovered via private chat that they were compatible and "interested," then the relationship might grow offline. Several recent Namoluk marriages involve couples who first met on the Internet, flirted (some might say, courted) online, and eventually arranged to meet in person. The Internet is rapidly becoming Micronesia's new marriage mart.

Notes

1. The other two bachelor's degree-earners received their degrees during the 1980s when they were in their late forties.

2. Hezel (2001, 150) reports "500 to 600" Micronesians to be living in Corsicana, and one assumes that this figure refers to the year 1999 or 2000.

3. Many, perhaps most, young men from Namoluk who've moved to the States have studied one or more of the martial arts, which have a Carolinian counterpart called *bwang* (see Lessa and Velez 1978). One Namoluk man, resident in Texas for more than twenty years without returning to the islands, was married to a Korean woman, and the two of them owned and operated a *tae kwan do* school there. Another Namoluk man, who has lived for more than fifteen years in California and who only returned home to visit for the first time in summer 2003, has risen to a very high rank in several martial arts and helps teach these skills to others.

4. Young men from Chuuk and Palau have a history of aggressive competition and often get into fights with each other. Essentially, young men from these two island groups both think that they're the best, the bravest, and the strongest, and they're forever challenging each other to prove it.

5. Wendel (1998) completed an anthropology doctoral dissertation about Xavier High School graduates that provides much more information about the impact of this remarkable institution.

6. This includes the deceased individual whose wife was from Chuuk Lagoon.

7. My moniker was Litopuler, or "wolf spider," a name I thought most appropriate for one who—like his namesake—just lurked in a corner and watched what happened.

6

Heading Off to Collage

. . . that we are living more and more in the midst of an
enormous collage, seems everywhere apparent.

Clifford Geertz (2000, 85)

. . . the men and women with hands and muscles are still
there, laying bricks, sweeping cafeteria floors, making
hotel beds. They are the army of manual workers doing
the unheralded, largely forgotten jobs that also make the
nation go. . . . In recent years immigrants. . . have filled
many of these manual jobs, especially the low-end, lowest-paying positions.

Steven Greenhouse (2002, 3)

IT'S A SURREAL WORLD OUT THERE

Clifford Geertz's observation that our world more and more resembles an enormous collage—a pastiche of tastes, patterns, ethnicities, languages, religions, and
the like—captures the plight and the promise in which *chon* Namoluk find themselves as they venture forth from their small atoll to ever-more cosmopolitan
places. A collage is a mixture of elements in incongruous relationship, originally

developed as a kind of surrealist art, a movement characterized by its irrational, noncontextual arrangement of material. For Namoluk people away from home, especially for those outside of the FSM, the world they encounter is a surreal place, filled with incongruity, irrationality, and diversity. They are just one more small piece in the collage.

In his stimulating essay "The Uses of Diversity," Geertz makes the further observation that "if it is in fact getting to be the case that rather than being sorted into framed units, social spaces with definite edges to them, seriously disparate approaches to life are becoming scrambled together in ill-defined expanses, social spaces whose edges are unfixed, irregular, and difficult to locate, the question of how to deal with the puzzles of judgment to which such disparities give rise takes on a rather different aspect" (2000, 85). How do *chon* Namoluk cope with the surreal experience of living in a collage? How do they navigate through the seriously disparate approaches to life they encounter every day in the United States? How have their own living patterns become scrambled into new, irregular social spaces? What puzzles of judgment must they confront daily in order to survive, or put otherwise, how do they make a living as new immigrants to a foreign land? These and related questions are explored in this chapter, with a particular focus on the movement to Guam and the United States during the past fifteen years in search of jobs. Most of these jobs are of the "unheralded, largely forgotten" variety—the "low-end, lowest-paying positions" of which Steven Greenhouse writes in the epigraph above. Save for those who have obtained college degrees, such employment is about all that is available to recent immigrants with minimal skills. Common bottom-end jobs taken by *chon* Namoluk have been as workers in the fast food industry, as housekeepers, as certified nursing assistants (CNAs), and as security guards. After a short discussion of each of these occupations, a description will be provided of some of the better-paying jobs that Namoluk immigrants have located.

Unheralded, Largely Forgotten Jobs

Whoppers and Big Macs

Where once America was thought of as "Mom and apple pie," today the more appropriate operative phrase might be "Coke and a Big Mac." Fast food has come to symbolize America internationally, with attacks on McDonald's serving as a surrogate for an attack on American culture.[1] In a compendium devoted to anthropological studies of McDonald's in East Asia, James L. Watson notes that "The Golden Arches have become. . . an icon of international business and popular culture, recognized nearly everywhere on the planet" (1997, vi). That said, it is certainly the case that fast food also is a part of nearly everyone's experience in the United States. One after another, fast food restaurants line urban and small-town strips, and they are also found in airports, university student unions, and some public buildings. They even pop up in what once were thought of as out-of-the-way places like national parks. McDonald's. Pizza Hut. Burger King. KFC. Hardee's. Denny's. Village Inn. Sizzler Steakhouse. These are among the firms where *chon* Namoluk and other Micronesians have found work on Guam and in the States. What could be more American?

What could be more American, indeed? In his exposé of this industry, Eric Schlosser comments that the fast food chains "rely upon a low-paid and unskilled workforce," and that "the vast majority lack full-time employment, receive no benefits, learn few skills, exercise little control over their workplace, quit after a few months, and float from job to job. The restaurant industry is now America's largest private employer, and it pays some of the lowest wages" (2002, 6). On Guam, in Honolulu, in Portland, and in Cedar Falls, Namoluk people and their Micronesian brethren slog away in this sort of work, with little hope of advancement under what might be called a "styrofoam ceiling." Finding work as new immigrants in these exploitative job circumstances, *chon* Namoluk are hardly alone. When fewer baby boom teenagers were available to hire, the fast food chains turned to "other marginalized workers: recent immigrants, the elderly, and the handicapped" (Schlosser 2002, 70). Schlosser makes it clear that obedient, docile, unskilled workers are exactly what the fast food industry seeks, and these unfortunates now comprise the largest group of low-wage employees in the United States—about 3.5 million strong.

Meat, Fish, But No Poultry

Beef is the ultimate "all-American" food, and the fast food restaurants that specialize in it—steak and burger joints—have had much to do with influencing basic changes in the cattle raising and meatpacking businesses. This influence results from their requirements for a uniform product that can be processed in assembly-line fashion and from the fast food industry's great purchasing power. Schlosser argues that "these changes have made meatpacking—once a highly skilled, highly paid occupation—into the most dangerous job in the United States, performed by armies of poor, transient immigrants whose injuries often go unrecorded and uncompensated" (2002, 9). At least two Namoluk young men have worked at such jobs for IBP,[2] and several others have worked in the fishing and fish processing industry, which has only a slightly better track record in terms of job-related injuries. Interestingly, unlike their Marshall Islands neighbors, no *chon* Namoluk, and few if any FSM nationals, have settled in Springdale, Arkansas, and nearby communities to work in Tyson Food's poultry processing plants.[3] Although this is also "dirty" meatpacking work, which often results in injuries, these facts have not discouraged as many as 4,000 RMI citizens from settling in the Ozark foothills. In Springdale, their children now make up 5 percent of the school district's students, and about one-third of the 460 production line workers at Tyson's Cornish hen plant are Marshallese (Roche and Mariano 2002a).

Making Beds, Emptying Bedpans

Although some have worked at these jobs in the States, it is especially in Guam's tourist-oriented economy that young and middle-aged Namoluk women have been hired as housekeepers by hotels and motels. They engage in such domestic cleaning tasks as changing bed linen and towels, vacuuming, and scrubbing toilets and shower stalls. Housekeeping jobs are notoriously poorly paid and usually do not include benefit packages of any sort. Similar to jobs in the fast food industry, such work is unskilled, often part-time, has a high rate of turnover, and additionally is typically performed by women, notably those at the bottom of the economic pecking order. Recent immigrants, such as those from Micronesia, fit this profile almost perfectly.

Related to housekeeper work is employment as a CNA in a nursing home for senior citizens. Like housekeepers, CNAs are involved in cleaning, with a notable difference that CNAs clean not only bed linens, dishes, and bathrooms but also the nursing home residents themselves. Lori Jervis, an anthropologist who has studied CNAs as part of her research in a U.S. nursing home, holds that such work is stigmatized because of its association with pollution via contact with elimination and bodily wastes. She concludes that "like other dirty work in America, aide [CNA] work remains for the most part devalued socially, if not downright invisible. The occupation's lowliness, however, is not only the result of its association with bodily waste, but also derives from the gender, race, and class backgrounds of its workers. That women, people of color, and those who are economically disadvantaged are overrepresented in nursing assistant work is hardly surprising. As a stigmatized occupation, aide work draws those with few alternatives" (2001, 94). Nursing home operators have great trouble finding Americans to take these low-paying jobs washing, grooming, feeding, and emptying the bedpans of elderly residents. Young women and men from the FSM and the RMI, including at least a dozen from Namoluk, are increasingly prominent among CNAs in the United States.

How did Micronesian young adults end up working as CNAs in American nursing homes? Beginning in 1998, several recruiting outfits—what Walter F. Roche Jr. and Willoughby Mariano call "body brokers"—contracted to provide nursing home companies that operate facilities all over the United States with Micronesian workers to take positions as CNAs.[4] Micronesians were selected because the Compact of Free Association allows them to enter the United States and work without a green card, making them easier to process through the Immigration and Naturalization Service. The recruiters received a fee of as much as $5,500 for each worker they provided. Most of these recruits had little idea of the obligation they were assuming, and many were still teenagers, often lacking even a high school diploma. With limited English-language skills, and with equally limited experience at living in a collage, they were told that they were going to work as nurses or could attend college, were signed up, and were flown from such places as Chuuk and Pohnpei to such places as Ashburn, Georgia, or Cynthiana, Kentucky. Typically, they found themselves "working the graveyard shift at a nursing home, [and] emptying bedpans for $5.50 an hour" (Roche and Mariano 2002b). According to a list I obtained from the FSM Embassy in New York, by the end of 1999, more than 250 FSM nationals had been recruited as CNAs, and in the years since, their numbers have grown considerably.

If even half of what Roche and Mariano report in their series of newspaper articles is accurate, it is clear that the young Micronesians recruited for U.S. nursing homes were misled about the work they would do and what their obligations would be. Once in the United States, many discovered that they were almost like indentured servants, tied by legal contracts that forced them to pay damages of up to half a year's wages if they left their job before the contract was up. A lot of them were cowed and felt trapped and served out their contracts, but others simply quit and fled. The "Micronesian archipelago," bound together via telephone and the Internet, offers numerous sanctuaries for such "castaways." I am aware of at least three women who left what they call their "slavery" and moved in with fellow islanders many states away from where they had worked as CNAs. Another way out of such bondage taken by some is to marry an American and cease working, a path followed by at least one young Namoluk woman. Roche reported in the *Orlando Sentinel* on April 3, 2003, that both the FSM and the RMI governments have taken formal steps "to regulate so-called 'body brokers'", following a proposal to that effect by the United States during negotiations to extend U.S. aid to the two countries.

Despite the stigmatized, difficult work, bad press, and low wages, some *chon* Namoluk continue to seek CNA certification. Kaylee, who came to the States for college more than twenty years ago, provides a case in point. She spent not quite a year at a community college in North Carolina, married an American, had two children, divorced her husband, married another American, worked part-time in a truck stop restaurant, and then divorced her second husband, who was abusive. She lived for a time with a third American man before she moved to a different state and began to share housing with a cluster of people from islands back home, most of whom had been her friends in high school. Needing work, and suffering from some chronic health problems, she has resolutely taken the necessary classes to qualify as a CNA. Her view is that, yes, it's hard work, but it's honest work, and it provides her with a modest income that can be stretched because she shares expenses with her housemates. So *some* Micronesian CNA workers have been in the States for quite awhile, have taken CNA jobs with their eyes wide open, and have learned to live in a collage.

Securing Premises

Yet another line of work pursued by numerous *chon* Namoluk—particularly men—is to hire on as a security guard. Although wages and benefits are not a

Chon Namoluk in Honolulu Apartment, July 2001
(note security guard uniform)

great deal better than in the occupations discussed above, the uniforms security guards wear and the possible element of danger should they have to apprehend someone appeal to a pan-Chuuk macho masculinity. Those who work as security guards on Guam do so mostly on the grounds of the big tourist hotels that line Tumon Bay. In Hawai'i, several work in shopping malls or for large chain clothing stores. In one group living arrangement of several Namoluk people in Honolulu during the summer of 2001, three different men held security guard jobs, pooling resources to pay the rent and utilities, buy food, and cover other shared expenses.

MOVIN' UP

Although the majority of Namoluk people who are employed on Guam and in the States work at low-end, low-paying jobs, not all of them do so. By dint of personal talent, diligent effort, some postsecondary education, a bit of luck, or a combination of these, a growing number of *chon* Namoluk have escaped the dulling trap of minimum-wage jobs with no benefits and no opportunity for advancement. The more experience they gain at living in a collage, the more they learn to deal with the disparities and the puzzles of judgment that such living entails. They may be said to develop a degree of "collagiality." As a result, they have moved up and into a host of better-paying and more responsible positions. Here is a sampler of some of these more desirable jobs.

Unsurprisingly, given the sorts of qualifications usually required for "middle-class jobs" in the United States, the more remunerative positions have gone to those who headed off to college and completed a degree before deciding to settle in the States. One seventh waver with a bachelor's degree is employed by the FSM Foreign Affairs Department and is stationed at the FSM Embassy in New York, and another—equally well educated—works as an adjuster for an insurance company in Honolulu. Two seventh wavers with master's degrees are employed in the States: one runs a small childcare business out of her home in Lincoln, Nebraska, whereas the other is an elementary school teacher in Honolulu. Others with bachelor's degrees have done quite well in the employment sweepstakes: one sixth waver works in a business management position in Flagstaff, Arizona; another sixth waver has a nursing career in Honolulu; yet a third is employed in a staff position by a small college in Portland, Oregon; a final sixth waver with a BA works for the Guam public schools. Associate's degrees also have helped some *chon* Namoluk land better-paying jobs. One such is a seventh waver in Eureka, California, who works as a unionized driver for United Parcel Service (UPS). His fellow seventh waver and Eureka resident manages an apartment building there and works in a well-paid job at a local lumber yard. A sixth waver with an AA degree used to own a small martial arts business and now works for Dell Computers in Texas.

Others with some college training but without degrees have managed to move up the economic ladder in spite of this handicap. As I mentioned in Chapter 3, two—a fifth waver and a sixth waver—enlisted in the U.S. armed forces and have had careers spanning more than twenty years each. One is now retired (and drawing his Navy retirement pay), while the other remains on active duty in the Army. Yet another seventh waver, resident in Eureka, along with a younger counterpart, both have good salaries from jobs in local lumber yards there. Another Namoluk man works part-time in a white-collar bank office job while he studies accounting at a community college in Salem, Oregon. A sixth waver held several responsible low-level business management positions on Guam before he immigrated to Hawai'i.

Finally, the Namoluk connection to Continental Micronesia bears mention. Six different *chon* Namoluk—four men and two women, none with college degrees—have worked for the airline (a subsidiary of Continental Airlines) in various capacities, and all of these have been well-salaried jobs with benefits. All but two of these "Air Mike" employees held their jobs on Guam (the others worked on Wééné, and one then shifted to Guam after several years).

LIVING IN A COLLAGE

Church at the Center

Christianity is an integral part of nearly all Pacific Islands societies, and Namoluk is no exception. Ever since initial missionization 124 years ago, the role of the church in people's lives has increased in significance. The Protestant and Catholic churches are central institutions in day-to-day life on the atoll, and religion figures importantly in the lives of migrants as well. On Wééné, for example, *chon* Namoluk have been especially active in the Berea Evangelical Church, affiliated with the Liebenzell Mission. A Namoluk man has served as one of Berea's ministers, and two have been deacons of the church. Another Namoluk man served for several years as the principal of Berea School (first through twelfth grades), and at least half-a-dozen college-educated *chon* Namoluk have taught there. Last, but not least, several Namoluk people have worked there in staff positions or on the construction of new church and school facilities.

Church involvement is important for most Namoluk people who migrate outside of Chuuk State. Half a dozen of them have been sponsored by missions for college and graduate theological training in the States (or, in one case, in Fiji). Some have helped to establish student church fellowships on Guam, and others have worked for the Catholic mission there. Church attendance remains an integral part of the lives of many *chon* Namoluk who live in the United States itself. Those who live by themselves—with no other people from Chuuk close by—often become deeply involved in a local church, as Moses did, for example. Typically, when there are small clusters of people from Chuuk State in the same community, they will all attend the same church together. But the true measure of "church at the center" is found in those locales where substantial numbers of Mortlockese or other *chon* Chuuk have settled.

Only a handful of places in the States have a sufficient "critical mass" of people from Chuuk State to support a church of their own, comparable to the Marshallese and Sāmoan church communities in America of which other anthropologists have written (e.g., Allen 2002; Janes 1990). In June 2002, I visited one such place—Portland, Oregon—and, along with close to 150 others, attended a Sunday service at the Island Community Church (ICC). The ICC rents a pleasant new assembly hall from Warner Pacific College (WPC), "an urban Christian liberal arts college dedicated to providing students from diverse backgrounds an education that prepares them for the spiritual, moral, social, vocational and technological challenges of the 21st century" (Warner Pacific College 2001, 5). Founded as Pacific Bible College in Spokane, Washington, in 1937, WPC moved to Portland three years later, where it remains affiliated with the Church of God.

The preponderance of worshippers and clergy at ICC during my visit were Mortlockese, especially people from Lukeisel, although a smattering of Lagoon Chuukese also were in attendance. Parishioners ranged in age from newborns, presented for confirmation, to elders in their sixties and seventies, and they arrived from all over the greater Portland metropolitan area and as far away as the state capital in Salem, an hour's drive to the south. Sunday church service at ICC is at once a religious experience, a social event, and an assertion of ethnic identity.

The assembly hall was filled with metal folding chairs on two sides of a central aisle, allowing for a "men's side" and a "women's side" as is typical of church services back home. One side of the hall was mostly glass, allowing cheerful morning sunshine to fill the space. The chairs all faced a speaker's podium, fitted with a microphone, and covered by a drape reading "Rejoice" in English. Familiar church music and related tunes came from an electronic keyboard and an amplified acoustic guitar. People began to assemble around 11:00 AM, although the service itself did not get underway until a little past noon. Most hymns were sung in Mortlockese, but a few were done in English. The prayers, sermons, and announcements were all in Mortlockese. When the formal service ended at 3:00 PM, the congregation ate a hearty meal together of rice, a beef-carrot-cabbage stew, fresh watermelon, and water to drink.

As is true of services back in Chuuk State, children wandered about during the proceedings, and teenagers and young adults made eyes at one another. Those in attendance arrived in some very nice late model vehicles (e.g., several new vans, a big Dodge sedan, and a shiny Chevy Suburban), underscoring the point that not

Chon Namoluk Dressed for the Sunday Service at Island Community Church, Portland, Oregon, June 2002

everyone in this growing community was a fast food worker or a CNA. The Portland-Salem area and corridor is now home to several thousand people from Chuuk State, a population that adds new immigrants almost weekly. In addition to ICC, which is thought of primarily as a Mortlockese church, the facilities for a second congregation are located just outside the small town of Aurora, Oregon, about two-thirds of the way from Salem to Portland. Known as "The Missionary Memorial Church Beyond the Reef," this congregation consists mostly of people from Chuuk Lagoon. Nestled in a rural setting, it occupies several acres of an old summer camp, with numerous cabins sheltered under big shade trees, several rather institutional one-story main buildings—one labeled "Tabernacle"—and some houses off on the periphery of the property. Along with the ICC, the Beyond the Reef Church provides a venue for people from Chuuk State to meet regularly in a familiar church setting, with services conducted in their own language. At the same time, people catch up on information from each other about others in their immigrant network, learn of new arrivals to the area, flirt with and court one another, and provide mutual emotional—and occasionally financial— support. Just like back home, church lies at the center of this dispersed immigrant community.

Virtual Kinship

As has been noted above, Namoluk is a face-to-face community in which everyone knows everyone else, and in which most people are related to each other. Historically, *chon* Namoluk either lived together on their own atoll, or they lived on nearby islands elsewhere in the Mortlocks or in Chuuk State. Those who lived away from the island didn't live so far away that they couldn't come home for a visit fairly often, so kinship ties and community bonds were reinforced regularly via direct interpersonal contact. But now that 60 percent of the populace reside somewhere *other than* Namoluk, with many of them located hundreds or even thousands of miles away, direct person-to-person visits are more difficult to arrange. It is in these circumstances that *chon* Namoluk have harnessed the wonders of the transportation-communication revolution to maintain their kinship connections.

Transportation, in the form of jet travel, has foreshortened time and distance across the Pacific, whether it be the 550 miles from Chuuk to Guam or the 5,500 miles from Chuuk to Los Angeles. If they can afford the airfare, relatives travel back and forth for visits from Wééné to Guam, or to Hawai'i and the U.S. mainland. Such visiting is the twenty-first century analogue to nineteenth century interisland voyaging in which, among other things, kin ties were reaffirmed. These days, as we saw in the vignette at the end of Chapter 3, it is not at all unusual for elderly grandparents from Namoluk to catch a small ship to Chuuk, board an Air Micronesia island-hopper to Honolulu, and then proceed to some location on the mainland where their adult children and grandchildren reside. Such travel by Namoluk seniors is increasingly common, as is the prospect that the old folks may settle down with their offspring in such places as Salem, Oregon, or Honolulu, Hawai'i.

But "virtual kinship" is something other than this. In our age of diasporas and large-scale transnational migrations, virtual kinship is practiced by many people around the world today. It is also relied upon by many Americans to maintain their family ties in such situations as they live and work in California, while their parents remain in Iowa, and their siblings are scattered in several other states. Virtual kinship is kinship of the "reach out and touch" sort that draws on communication breakthroughs. It makes use of satellite technology that permits direct-dial long distance telephone calls, and it thrives on e-mail messages. Arguably, it extends as well to two-way radio conversations.

Namoluk does not have telephones or computers; indeed, the atoll lacks electricity except for that produced by a few small gasoline-powered generators and some solar panels. Such generators allow a few people to operate VCRs and small radio transceivers. The former already had become quite the rage on Namoluk by 1985: there were four VCRs on the atoll by then. Videocassettes containing "family photos" are shipped to the atoll by *chon* Namoluk on Wééné, who either film them themselves or receive them by mail from relatives living elsewhere. Viewed over and over again, these images reinforce kinship at a distance by capturing important life events such as weddings, graduations, or funerals that may occur far from home.

Of course, the second largest concentration of Namoluk people after those on the island itself now live in the urban center, and most of them have regular access to telephones. In emergencies, and sometimes just for fun, phone calls come from *chon* Namoluk living outside Chuuk State for relatives on Wééné, and the essence of these conversations is then relayed via two-way radio to family members on the atoll. Relatively few *chon* Namoluk on Wééné have their own computers at work or at home, but there are two facilities there that make Internet access available for a fee. Unfortunately, that fee is beyond the reach of all but a few of the more prosperous Namoluk citizens. Students enrolled at COM's Chuuk campus have some limited access to the World Wide Web at little or no cost to them. So communication media of various sorts help sustain a certain amount of virtual kinship between Namoluk people abroad and those in Chuuk and back on the atoll.

It is *among* those Namoluk people who live on Guam or in the States, however, that virtual kinship really comes into its own. They may be separated by great distances, like the proverbial American family mentioned above, but they keep in touch with each other via phone calls and e-mail to a remarkable degree.[5] And news from one conversation or message is passed along in the next, so *chon* Namoluk who live apart continue to share a great deal of up-to-date information about each other. They know who's just had a baby, who's gotten married (and to whom), who's arrived from the islands, or who's gone back home. They hear quickly when someone from the atoll dies, and they gossip about one another's foibles and affairs as intimates everywhere do. For those who live on the U.S. mainland, communication via phone or e-mail allows them to set up periodic visits by car. Those attending college in Los Angeles may rent a car and drive to Portland for a long weekend. Those working in Louisville will hop in their jalopy and drive to western Iowa to visit kin. Others will take a Greyhound bus, as Moses's cousins did when he was stabbed (see Chapter 5). Those with the means will fly across country to see a sister or a son. Videocassettes are mailed back and forth among themselves, as well as back and forth to kin in Micronesia, including Guam. And cell phones have recently entered the picture as well. In this regard, the following e-mail message came to me from a *chon* Namoluk in the Los Angeles area: "Today I received an e-mail from my sister Beulah [on Wééné] and she said our folks are fine out there on Namoluk. After. . . I called Jed's cell-phone [in Honolulu] and we had a good time just reminiscence [*sic*] about Loilam [Namoluk]. Waioo was always our conclusion. I will give you his cell-phone # so you can ask him to locate Seraphim there in Hawaii. . . . Just yesterday he called me just to ask when will I be in Hawaii [for Easter]. I believe when Loilamese [*chon* Namoluk] meet there will always be new jokes from the Islands" (e-mail from Harold, 14 April 2003; pseudonyms substituted).

Long-Timers

Thirty years after the first substantial movement of Namoluk people to the United States, three patterns have emerged. In the first, typical of many in the fifth and sixth waves, migrants went to the States for college, stayed from one to six years, and then returned to take jobs somewhere in Micronesia, including Wééné and Guam. The case of Hans, discussed in Chapter 5, illustrates this. In the second pattern, migrants moved to the States and have lived there for at least seven years, but they return to Wééné or Namoluk every year or two for a visit. The final pattern forms the primary focus of this section: those *chon* Namoluk who left for college or work and have lived abroad—in some cases without ever coming back for a visit—for fourteen years or more. The vignette provided of Moses in Chapter 5 shows this way of being. Those who have been away from Namoluk and Chuuk for fourteen or more years are here called "long-timers," and three brief examples of their circumstances are provided below because this pattern becomes more common every year. Of eleven men and three women who qualify as "long-timers," eight of the men and all three of the women have married "foreigners." In most cases these have been American spouses, but one is German and one Korean. Clearly, marriage to someone "outside the system" makes it more difficult to sustain regular visits home. "Long-timers" resemble what *chon* Chuuk call *apeipei*, "drift logs." Like *apeipei*, "long-timers" float along far from the place they began, and no one knows exactly when or where they will wash up on the beach again.

Trina.   As of 2003, Trina holds the Namoluk record for having been away for the longest time: thirty-four years. She went to Honolulu for college in 1969, and after several years of school, she met and married an American physician. Due to his work with the World Health Organization, they lived for some years in Bangkok, and later in Geneva, Switzerland. Eventually, they moved their family to southern California—her husband's home—so that their two children could grow up and attend school in the States. Trina's son, now a college graduate, once accompanied her on a short visit to Namoluk when he was very young, but her daughter, a college senior in 2003, has never been to the atoll. Neither of Trina's offspring speaks or understands Mortlockese, although they are well aware of their island heritage and have met some of their Namoluk kin in the States. Trina and her college-aged daughter flew to Florida in summer 2002 to attend the wedding of her brother's daughter, an event that also was attended by several other Namoluk relatives.

Roxanne.   Roxanne came to the United States for college twenty-eight years ago and traveled all the way to Florida to enroll in a community college there with several other young Mortlockese women, including a close cousin from Namoluk. It is not clear whether she obtained her AA degree, but what is clear is that she just "disappeared." She ceased to write to her family back on Namoluk, and she did not engage in the widespread telephone conversations with friends and relatives in the States as did most of her peers. Her family has made efforts to track her down via the FSM Embassy in New York, thus far to no avail. Once or twice over the years, snippets of information about Roxanne have entered the Namoluk gossip chain. Apparently, she is married to an American and has several children. Supposedly, she moved from Florida to Georgia, where she has lived for many years. Certainly, she is unusual in the degree to which she has cut herself off from her Namoluk kin.

Kurt.   Kurt's case is somewhat more typical than the two above. He moved to Oregon for college in 1983 and attended Western Oregon University for a couple of years, although he has yet to finish his bachelor's degree. While in school he met and married his American wife, from whom he is now separated and by whom he has a son and a daughter. Neither she nor either of his children has ever visited Namoluk or Chuuk, and none of them has any facility in his native language. Except for a two-month hiatus in 1994—after eleven years in the States—when he returned to Namoluk and Wééné for a visit, Kurt has lived and worked in Oregon. In June 2002, when I stopped in at his apartment, he told me he never plans to do more than visit the islands because his children and his job are in the States. At the time of my visit, he shared a large apartment with a younger brother, his elderly mother, another brother's junior high–aged daughter, and a sister's fifteen-year-old son. His mother had come several times for visits, when a significant health problem and the need for good medical care led her to remain. His niece and nephew illustrate an ever-more-common phenomenon. Where thirty-five years ago a few Namoluk students were sponsored by American families for their senior year of high school in the United States, now Namoluk people "sponsor" their own relatives. Kids are sent, often when still in grade school, to live with their relatives on Guam or in the States where they can obtain a better education and improve their English-language skills and future job prospects. This "sponsorship" will receive further attention in Chapters 7 and 8.

With the exception of Roxanne, all of Namoluk's "long-timers" have kept in regular contact with their relatives via letters, phone calls, and in more recent years the Internet. Most of them visit other Namoluk people who live somewhat near them, and in some cases they travel over long distances for reunions with kin who reside elsewhere in the States (e.g., Trina's case above). They remain committed to the broader Namoluk community and eagerly share or ask for news about others. Namoluk as a place—as their "source"—continues to figure importantly in their self-conceptions.

Isolates, Clusters, and Networks

Namoluk migrants have not formed nucleated communities away from the atoll, even on Wééné, where they reside in seven of that island's nine traditional districts. Instead, they either live as isolates—like Moses in Cedar Falls, Iowa—or in small clusters—like that in Eureka, California, to be discussed in Chapter 8. Even so, the Namoluk community remains linked in a remarkably strong network that is bound together by face-to-face visits, telephone calls, shared video- and audio-tapes, digitized photographs, e-mail messages, and letters. As noted above when discussing the ICC congregation in Portland, Oregon, dispersed quasi-communities have formed around Chuukese-language churches, not only in Portland, but also in Guam and Honolulu. These networks involve at least weekly face-to-face meetings during Sunday services as well as a fair amount of socializing outside of church events themselves. Small groups of Namoluk people often live in different units of the same apartment complex or else in housing that is within walking distance of each other. This promotes informal visits, shared resources, and mutual use of vehicles, computers, and telephones.

Many of the clusters of Namoluk people are integrated with people from other island communities in the Mortlocks or from elsewhere in Chuuk State, for as I pointed out in Chapters 1 and 2, Namoluk is merely one community in a larger Mortlockese society. That larger society operates in the migration context just as it does back home, but it has been strengthened by many more intermarriages in recent years. With thirty years of a decided Namoluk presence on Wééné, and a greater number of marriages between *chon* Namoluk and people from Chuuk Lagoon than ever before, it is no stretch to see the Mortlocks (including Namoluk) as simply one component of a "greater Chuukese society."

This takes on special meaning in the context of overseas migration, and it relates importantly to matters of place and ethnic identity to which we will return in Chapter 9.

Notes

1. See Watson (2000, 127–129) for a discussion of McDonald's as a target for the ire of anti-American demonstrators in more than fifty different countries.

2. The dangerous and problematic nature of work in the meatpacking industry has been critically studied and eloquently presented by anthropologist Deborah Fink (1998), based upon her firsthand fieldwork in an IBP plant in Iowa.

3. One of the men who later worked for IBP spent the better part of a year in 1999–2000 employed by a chicken processing plant in Charles City, Iowa.

4. Much of the information I present in this section is drawn from a series of newspaper articles by investigative reporters Walter F. Roche Jr. and Willoughby Mariano. These articles appeared in mid-September 2002 in the *Baltimore Sun* and the *Orlando Sentinel* under the general title "Indentured in America."

5. Although I am not a *chon* Namoluk, they have plugged me into this communication network to some degree. I message and talk by phone with various community members regularly, and I visit with them occasionally if I'm near where they live (or vice versa). Computers also make it possible to quickly distribute digitized photographs, such as those I received of a funeral held on Wééné in April 2003.

7

Reef Crossings

. . . the funniest thing was she was using her full name as
her chatroom nickname. . . . I kept on trying to get her
attention and even threw at her my real name and still she
won't respond, and after that I signed out and changed
my nick again to another nick. . . . Oh, I also chatted
with Herman (Olofat), Mary (My-Star), and Toshiro
(Pinkaweiwei). It is so much fun to meet my family on
mecha and speak to them in pichin Chuukese language,
and now I'm back as a Chuukese person again, I speak a
lot better because I spent most of my time in chatroom
and learn. There were many of the chatters that already
got so huffy with me said that since I was from Chuuk why
not speak Chuukese, and when they said that I got so mad
with them.

(E-mail from Kaylee, 28 December 2000; pseudonyms
substituted)

MIGRANTS: THE NEW NAMOLUK

Kaylee, and the many others like her, represent "the new Namoluk"—the 60 percent of the community's members who have crossed the reef and who are now
dispersed in multiple sites across thousands of miles. When they can't manage
face-to-face visits away from the atoll, these migrants remain connected via the
telephone and the Internet. There they "meet" and "speak together" in "pidgin

Chuukese"—a mixture of their own language and American English—sharing news and gossip about their friends and relatives. In this chapter and the next one we will examine more closely those people who have moved away from Namoluk, even as they remain ineradicably tied to it.

Members of all twenty-six of Namoluk's lineages have participated in the exodus from the atoll, but they show different migration patterns. For example, in July 2001, five lineages retained half or more of their members on Namoluk, whereas 80 percent or more of another five had moved away from the island. Half or more of the members of four lineages lived on Wééné, and the same proportion of another four Namoluk lineages resided on Guam. At least 20 percent of yet another four lineages resided in Hawai'i or on the U.S. mainland in July 2001. In other words, there was no single template for emigration from the atoll. Different hopes for different folks.

To study the new Namoluk is to study continuous movement and flux, an ongoing, unfolding migration process. I offer here a typical example of such movement to underline this point: on July 2, 2001, the *Eekmwar* arrived on Wééné with eleven passengers from Namoluk.[1] She sailed back down to the Mortlocks the next morning carrying sixteen people bound for Namoluk. On July 9, the *Eekmwar* returned with twenty-four passengers from Namoluk. They included two *chon* Namoluk whose primary residence is the U.S. mainland, one who has lived on Pohnpei for the past twenty years, and four who've resided on Guam since the early 1990s. All of these people had been home for a visit and were in the process of returning to their places of residence and work. The ship also carried a Namoluk man in his forties who flew on the Island Hopper to Hawai'i for the first time a couple of days later. Back when the *Eekmwar* arrived on July 2, her Namoluk passengers included yet another man who has lived on the U.S. mainland for a dozen years who accompanied his teenaged niece. By the end of the month, the two of them flew from Chuuk to Portland, Oregon, for him to return to work and for her to enroll in junior high school.

Such access to more frequent interisland transportation makes the regular circular movement of people almost routine now. And this links Namoluk and the *chon* Namoluk resident on Wééné much more closely together than in previous years. These small private ships also make it possible to travel directly from Namoluk to the Lower Mortlocks without having to pass through the urban center, thus strengthening intercommunity bonds that date to precolonial times. There is now a regular ebb and flow of Namoluk people to and from their atoll and the new places they have colonized.

MIGRATION PATTERNS

Certain general migration patterns exist for *chon* Namoluk. In the past three decades, these reef crossings—migrations away from Namoluk—have expanded and repositioned where members of the community reside. The new Namoluk is a multisited, transnational community.

As we saw in Chapters 3 and 5, beginning in the early 1970s, migration outside of Chuuk State by members of the fifth and sixth waves was motivated primarily by a search for college education. Few of those who attended a year or more of college—particularly those who obtained a four-year college degree, or especially a graduate degree—have returned to live on Namoluk. A few examples will illustrate why.

A member of the fifth wave, Molly graduated from high school in 1972, left Chuuk a few months later for San Diego, and was the first Namoluk woman to earn a four-year college degree. With hard work and good focus, she completed a bachelor's degree in education at U.S. International University (USIU) and then returned to Chuuk, where she married a man from Satawan and began teaching at the junior high school located there. She has lived and worked on Satawan ever since.

Lincoln, another fifth waver, graduated from Xavier High School in 1971, earned an associate's degree at Maui Community College, and then completed a bachelor's degree and a master's in business administration in 1976 at USIU. After working for the FSM government on Pohnpei, he moved to the private sector in the early 1990s to work for the Bank of Guam. First he managed the Chuuk branch, then the Ebeye branch in the RMI, and finally the Palau branch on Koror. At the end of the 1990s, he began to work for the Chuuk State Government—taking several business trips to Hawai'i and the U.S. mainland—endeavoring to help get the state's financial house in order. In spring 2001, he became administrator of a joint UOG-Chuuk State Government project on Wééné designed to teach small business skills of bookkeeping and financial management. Over lunch during my 2001 stay on Wééné, he told me that his Mortlockese wife and their children were in Honolulu so that the kids could enroll in school there.

Lindsey is a sixth waver who graduated from Truk High School in 1977. As with most in his age cohort, he went off to the States for college—in his case a community college in Texas—which he attended with a Namoluk classmate to whom he was related on his father's side. Texas didn't appeal, and after a semester there, he transferred to Honolulu Community College. He attended that school for awhile, living with some other Namoluk young men, working in a store, and soaking up the polyglot multicultural Hawai'i experience. Although Lindsey accumulated quite a few credits, he never received an AA degree. Instead, he returned to Chuuk, graduated from a special fire prevention school on the U.S. mainland and the Micronesian Public Safety Academy in Palau (a part of MOC), and became a state police officer in the 1980s. He married a Mortlockese woman from a politically important family, established a home on Wééné, and has risen to the position of state fire chief.

Last, Lurline left Chuuk after high school to pursue a college education, studied at the University of Hawai'i–Mānoa, and finished a bachelor of science in nursing there in the mid– to late–1980s. Wishing to contribute to her home islands, she went back to Chuuk to work at the state's hospital. Unfortunately, Chuukese gender role expectations collided with Lurline's knowledge and ability, and she found herself marginalized and often frustrated at work. Eventually, she decided to move to Honolulu, where she has lived for the last eight years, working as a nurse in a large urban hospital. Lurline has traveled around the U.S. mainland, and her household in Hawai'i is full of younger relatives there to attend public schools or college.

From the late 1980s onward, the main stimulus for migration off the atoll and outside of Chuuk State has been primarily to find wage employment, and secondarily for healthcare or to visit kin who have moved away from Chuuk. As the above examples show, many of those from the fifth and sixth waves who went away for college were able to obtain work—usually a government job—in Chuuk State or in the national capital on Pohnpei. But those who came late in the sixth wave, or in the seventh or subsequent waves, have had few employment opportunities in the FSM, and consequently more and more of these young adults have moved away.

Markita is a case in point. She and her Namoluk husband established themselves on Guam in the late 1980s, and all five of their children were born there. Both spouses had well-paying jobs, and other members of her lineage resided with them to go to school or when visiting from Chuuk. But Guam's economy soured in the late 1990s, and so did the relationship between Markita and her husband. They separated, and he moved to Honolulu in search of work. Not long thereafter, she moved to Missouri and took a CNA job. Soon after that, her mother brought Markita's children and joined her in 2002. Grandma and the kids arrived in St. Louis with only a single suitcase and the clothes on their backs.

Starting in the mid– to late–1960s, Namoluk people began to settle and marry on Wééné. As some *chon* Namoluk came back from college and found jobs there, a community began to form in the urban center. By 2003, Wééné had become a "second home" for Namoluk people: just as every lineage is still represented by members living on the atoll, every lineage also has members who reside in the urban center. Luanne is a good example of this. She finished high school in 1975 and joined her older sister at Suomi College in Michigan, which she attended, but never finished her degree. She married a man from Chuuk Lagoon whom she met in the States, and they moved to Oregon, where they remained until the end of 1978. The next year they returned to Wééné, where she worked in a store until the mid–1980s when she landed a state government job, a source of employment that has continued. She and her husband have had six children and have made Wééné their home.

Others who have settled in the urban center include Butch and Kendrick. A fifth waver, Butch began at Maui Community College, and then transferred to Kapi'olani Community College and on to Chaminade University in Honolulu, where he earned his bachelor's degree. He married a woman from Losap, returned to Wééné, graduated at the top of his class from the Micronesian Public Safety Academy, and rose to the position of deputy chief of the Chuuk State Police. On the side, Butch began a small security business with one of his Namoluk cousins, and subsequently he has entered the business world full-time. He has traveled widely around the U.S. mainland, to Guam, Japan, and elsewhere.

Kendrick began college in a small town in Alabama, and not long afterward he transferred to Western Michigan University in Kalamazoo, a school that enrolled numerous *chon* Chuuk at that time. He accumulated quite a few college credits, and had many good times, but he received no degree. After several years in the States, he returned home with an American bride. She didn't last long, after which he married his Namoluk cross-cousin and kicked around between the atoll and Wééné, somewhat bored and underemployed. Fortuitously, the Pacific Basin Medical Officers Training Program (PBMOTP) was begun on Pohnpei, cosponsored by the University of Hawai'i and the University of the South Pacific. Kendrick's father, Sergio, had been the health aide on Namoluk, and Kendrick had worked at that job for awhile after he returned from the States. Seizing the opportunity, he entered the PBMOTP, graduated, and returned to begin work at Chuuk State Hospital. In 2001, he was the head of Primary Health Care for the state.

Most, but not all, Namoluk families have established family enclaves on Guam, and increasingly on Hawai'i and the U.S. mainland. Although Namoluk people may be said to comprise a loose-knit community on Guam, elsewhere Namoluk migrants live in small clusters, or even as isolates, and network with each other via telephone and the Internet. As is typical of younger generations from Namoluk, only one of Lindsey's six siblings has remained on the atoll. His three sisters live outside of Chuuk—one on Pohnpei (where she taught school and married a member of the Pohnpei Mortlockese community);[2] one in Portland, Oregon (where she works at a Wal-Mart and took computer classes); and one who very recently moved to Honolulu (after she married a Euro-American whom she met on Guam while he was stationed there in the Marine Corps). This last sister's husband was sent to Iraq in early 2003, so she flew from Wisconsin to Honolulu and moved in with an older female cousin. Both of them worked and shared living expenses while she waited for her husband to return from the war. Two of Lindsey's three brothers, Evan and Richard, graduated from high school on Chuuk and then moved to Eureka, California, to attend community college. Now some years later both have jobs in Eureka; are married; and, with their Mortlockese spouses (one of whom is from Namoluk), share a house together (see Chapter 8 for more details).

After she graduated from high school in 1976, Oprah, a sixth waver, spent a semester at a community college in Portland, Oregon. That did not work out, and she returned to Wééné and married a guy from Kuttu. That didn't work out either. A couple of years later she married a Kosraen she met on Guam in the early 1990s, where she had moved to work. Her firstborn, a daughter, married a man from Chuuk Lagoon, and by July 2001, that couple had had three children, all born and living on Guam.

Kaylee, also from the sixth wave, finished high school on Chuuk in 1979, boarded the Island Hopper, and flew all the way to a community college campus in North Carolina. She attended that school for a year, during which time she met and married a Euro-American, by whom she had a daughter and a son. They lived in North Carolina, but difficulties arose in the marriage, and she and the children moved out. His parents, eager to maintain a link to their grandchildren, helped support her while she took some business school classes and taught aerobics. She then met and married another Euro-American, and they moved just across the state line to a tiny town in Virginia. When Kaylee speaks English, it is with a decided southern drawl. Homesick for her family in Chuuk, Kaylee convinced her second husband to fly to Wééné for a visit. They arrived with their kids, a suitcase full of gifts, and Kaylee full of excitement. But the trip didn't turn out quite as she had hoped. During a 1995 visit to their house in Virginia, I asked her kids what they remembered of their trip. Their response was twofold: "The food was yukky, and there was no McDonald's"; and "Everybody was always touching me." Clearly, these were *chon* Namoluk of a new sort, an issue to be addressed in Chapter 9.

Today, a growing number of *chon* Namoluk are born and raised away from their home island, and in recent years this has meant outside of Chuuk State as well. Concurrently, an ever-greater number have a father who is *not* from Namoluk. In some instances, the combination of these things makes it difficult for the children to feel that they are a part of the Namoluk community (see Chapter 9). For instance, Kaylee's half Euro-American children grew up and graduated from high school in Virginia. Her daughter is employed in Columbus, Ohio, and her son lives with his father, works, and attends college part-time in Norfolk. Neither speaks Mortlockese nor identifies with Namoluk.

Nothing stays the same; no one stays put. In the two years since my July 2001 census of the full Namoluk population, some people have made bold migration moves. Laurel is a case in point. Born on Wééné, Laurel lived and attended school in Chuuk's urban center until she was fourteen. In 1995, she went to stay with her mother's younger sister and family, who had established themselves on Guam quite a few years before. Laurel was sent so she could get a better high school education than was available to her on Chuuk; she graduated from George Washington High School in 1999. After attending UOG for a year, she joined her mother in Honolulu and enrolled at Kapi'olani Community College for approximately another year. Then, in March 2002, she traveled to join her Namoluk husband-to-be in Eureka, California, where she was living when I visited there in June 2002 (see Chapter 8).

Laurel illustrates a recent trend to send children to live with kin who have migrated to Guam or the States to attend school there. In Honolulu, Lurline, the graduate nurse who had migrated to Hawai'i, provided a home for three of her sisters' children while they attended school there in 2001. The hope is that the kids will develop greater facility in English and acquire a superior education than they would if they remained in Chuuk State. An unexamined consequence of the practice is that many of these children are "seduced" by American life and do not wish to return to their island home (see Chapter 9).

Crusoe may represent this risk. As with many others, in 1986 he went to live with a relative so he could obtain a solid education in the United States. Although he lettered in wrestling at his North Carolina high school, once he graduated, he fell in with a bad crowd, and his life became troubled and complex. In 1990, he returned for a visit to Wééné, and then went back to Virginia. He got a job there for a couple of years, and bought a car, but the quality of his friends didn't improve, and his problems continued. One day he simply packed up and left his relative's house, without word or warning. They discovered that he'd sold his car for cash when they saw it in a local used car lot. Although no one in the family knew for sure, it appeared that he had set out for Florida where another relative was then living. That turned out to be the case, and by August 1992, he had a job there. But his problems continued, and late one night in 1993, while intoxicated, Crusoe had an encounter with a locomotive. He lost. Papers on his body led the authorities to notify family members back home, and he was flown to Chuuk, taken down to Namoluk, and buried on his ancestral land.

Starting in the 1990s, travel outside of Chuuk State began to cut across all Namoluk age groups. Young and middle-aged adults traveled in search of work or school. Teenagers and young children either accompanied their parents in migration or were sent to live with relatives abroad. Seniors traveled to visit their children and grandchildren. A retired school teacher named Ledyard provides a classic instance of this. He has visited Guam, Pohnpei, Hawai'i, California, and Oregon on his journeys. Even though he has been to Hawai'i and the U.S. mainland to see several of his children and other members of his lineage family who reside there, Ledyard has spent much of the past six years in Honolulu in order to obtain medical treatment for hypertension and related ailments. In April 2003, he flew from Honolulu to Chuuk so that he could go down to the atoll because he wanted to eat traditional food at Namoluk's Easter feast. A member of his family told me on the phone that when Ledyard returned in June, he would bring his eighteen-year-old granddaughter with him to Eureka, California, where she would enroll in school.

We turn now, in Chapter 8, to look at some of the communities where the migration patterns discussed above have played out.

Notes

1. Another Namoluk man joined the journey to Chuuk when the *Eekmwar* called at Moch.

2. Her husband is Molly's husband's brother, hence two "sisters" married two "brothers" in sibling-set marriage.

8

Four Locations
Beyond the Reef

Ledyard just went there [Eureka, California] last summer, 2000 to go and visit his sons. He is retired and is
roaming the globe. About one month later, Hyacinth,
one of his daughters sent for Janelle. And so Lobelia accompanied Janelle to Honolulu to baby-sit Hyacinth's
baby while she goes back to work. Yes, lots of Namolukese
are all over, large number of them is also in Honolulu.

(E-mail message from Maiyumi, 31 October 2000;
pseudonyms substituted)

ROAMING THE GLOBE

Material presented in earlier chapters shows that—taken collectively—members
of the post–World War II populace of Namoluk Atoll truly *have* begun to roam
the globe. At least one person from the island has been to Australia, East and
Southeast Asia, Europe, the Middle East, North America, the Caribbean, and all
over the Pacific Islands, including New Zealand. The only inhabited continents
not visited by *chon* Namoluk by the spring of 2003 were Africa and South
America. But although globe-trotting has not yet become the norm for Namoluk
people, travel to certain specific destinations has now become a normal part of
the contemporary life of community members of all ages. These destinations

have been mentioned in earlier chapters, as waves of people have spread out from "the lagoon in the middle." Four of these locations are highlighted below, along with a discussion of who is there, when they arrived, and what sort of life they live in their new surroundings. *Chon* Namoluk are on Wééné and Guam in sufficient numbers to form true migrant communities; in Hawai'i and Eureka, California, they live in clusters, and their numbers are not yet high enough to constitute actual expatriate Namoluk communities. We will see, however, that more encompassing identities than simply being a Namoluk person operate in such locales.

WÉÉNÉ: THE FIRST STEP

Other than a visit elsewhere in the Mortlocks, the only place one can reach by ship from Namoluk is the urban center on Wééné in Chuuk Lagoon. Even though its demographic numbers are quite small by international standards, with its urban lifestyle and Pacific port town characteristics, Wééné is a world apart in scale and modernity from a rural outer island such as Namoluk. Just as it was for Maiyumi in the story with which this book begins, Wééné is the first big step and the first main stop beyond the reef. Between 1958 and 1989, the town's population nearly quadrupled from 4,367 to 15,622 (Gorenflo 1995, 64), and it rose slightly again to 16,121 by the time of the 1994 national census (FSM 1996, 2). Few Namoluk people were there in 1958, but in the mid–1990s approximately 200 of them resided in the urban center. This was not much more than 1 percent of Wééné's overall population at that time, but it constituted more than 25 percent of Namoluk's people, and it was the largest concentration anywhere of *chon* Namoluk, other than those still resident on the atoll (see Table 3.1). With an FSM population in 1994 of 105,506 (FSM 1996, 1), Wééné had 15 percent of the total national population, and nearly a third that of Chuuk State, which in turn claimed half of all FSM citizens. So everything is relative, and Wééné is a "big place" among Micronesia's "little islands."

For *chon* Namoluk Wééné served as both a window on modernity and a jumping-off point for travels abroad. A few people from the atoll lived there during the 1960s, but the development of Wééné as *chon* Namoluk's second home took place during the 1970s and early 1980s. Table 3.1 shows that the number of *chon* Namoluk located there grew from 69 at the beginning of 1971 to 213 a little over thirty years later. That table also shows that since the mid–1970s, approximately one-fourth of Namoluk's total population has been in the urban center. During these three decades, a number of Namoluk people have managed to acquire land on which to erect homes on Wééné. In some cases they have been able to purchase it, while in others they have gained access via marriage to a spouse from that island. There are now several places where numerous *chon* Namoluk live within a few minutes' walk of each other, or right next door on occasion.

Chon Namoluk Outside One of Their Homes in
Iras Village on Wééné, July 2001

Although Namoluk people on Wééné were second in number only to those
who remained on the atoll, not all age groups were represented equally in town.
In July 2001, the number between the ages of 40–49 and 50–59 was higher on
Wééné than anywhere else, reflecting the state government employment found
by many of those in the fifth and sixth waves when they returned from college.
The urban center ranked second to Namoluk in the number of persons in the
10–19, 20–29, and 60–69 age groups, and it was essentially tied with Guam for
second place among those aged 30–39 (see Table 4.1).

Those *chon* Namoluk who are located on Wééné at any moment are of three
sorts: those who live and work there more or less permanently; those who are visiting from the atoll to see kin, seek medical care at the hospital, or just to sample
the "bright lights"; and those who have come back for a visit from abroad. Often,
when someone plans a short visit from the U.S. mainland, for example, her relatives on the atoll will ride the ship to Wééné, have their reunion, and then return
home after she flies off again to the United States.

Chon Namoluk on Wééné reflect the nascent social class divisions that were
mentioned in Chapter 4. Quite a few people from the island have had the talent,
education, and good fortune to occupy responsible, well-paying jobs in the state

government for years, and in many cases their spouse also is employed. The result is that they have enough money to purchase land and build a home; to own a car or a small pickup truck; to have a range of modern conveniences such as a telephone, a TV, and a VCR; and to afford the tuition and fees necessary to enroll their children in private church-sponsored schools. The greater resources that these new elite have also permit them and their children to buy expensive tickets for travel outside of Chuuk. It is also these people who take vacations or shopping trips to Guam or Honolulu, or even Bali, in one case. And many of them, of course, travel at government expense on business and are able to combine business with pleasure.

It was noted in Chapters 1 and 2 that one of the bigger "pull" factors that drew Namoluk people to Wééné was secondary school. This continues to be the case. Even with the development of the junior high school for ninth and tenth grades on Satawan, Namoluk young people must travel to Chuuk to complete their high school education. The mixing and meeting with students from other parts of Chuuk State that occurs during high school and at an age of sexual awakening has contributed to the significantly higher number of marriages between *chon* Namoluk and spouses from Chuuk Lagoon during the past thirty years. In the great majority of such marriages, the couples either reside on Wééné, elsewhere in the Lagoon, or abroad; rarely do they move to Namoluk for more than a brief while, if at all.

To be on Wééné is to walk to two rhythms at once. The slow, steady pace of island life continues—especially in the outlying districts of the island such as Wiichap or Sópúúk—even as it is crosscut by a more frenetic imported beat. People pick breadfruit, weed taro plots, and fish the adjacent reefs while they also buy bags of rice, shop in grocery stores, and purchase frozen chickens. Some Western Islanders visiting the town may wear traditional wraparound skirts and go topless while other Chuukese women home from Kansas City or Seattle may wear tight jeans, sandals with inch-high heels, and a bare midriff top. Young men in church may sport Chicago Bulls T-shirts and wear Tevas instead of a white shirt and zori. The local radio station plays Chuukese music, but it also plays rap tunes, reggae, and country western songs. Groups of foreigners arrive at the airport to scuba dive on World War II Japanese shipwrecks; they have virtually no contact with local people. Groups of local people depart from the airport to go live on Guam, attend college in West Virginia, or seek their fortune in Honolulu or Corsicana. Wééné is a fascinating perpetual bundle of contradictions.

One such contradiction in the 1990s was that it was a center without a core. Among Wééné's problems was a worsening government financial crisis and an insufficient number of jobs for its young and burgeoning populace. Out-migration from Chuuk to Guam began in earnest as Chuuk State's economy began to hemorrhage in the 1990s. Larry J. Gorenflo reported that wages in Chuuk were "markedly lower than elsewhere in the federation, exacerbated by 23 percent unemployment in the early 1990s" (1995, 103–104). This was made worse by the step-down in U.S. Compact funding to the FSM in 1996, which put the FSM's economy "into a sharp decline," and "the last five years [1996–2001] saw business expansion come to a halt" (Hezel 2003, 3). Heavy migration in search of wage work from Chuuk to Guam continued through the mid– to late–1990s, at which point tourism and business on Guam also took a turn in the wrong direction.

CHON GUAMOLUK:
LIVING WHERE AMERICA'S DAY BEGINS

Guam bills itself as "the place where America's day begins," a way of emphasizing that it has been a U.S. possession since it was wrested from Spain during the Spanish-American War in 1898. Save for a short three-year interlude from 1941–1944, following the Japanese invasion at the onset of World War II, Guam has remained connected to the United States ever since. The island was administered by the U.S. Navy prior to World War II, and this was continued once the Japanese were defeated there in 1944. When it became a U.S. territory with passage of the Organic Act in 1950, "the island government's responsibilities expanded to correspond approximately to those of a tiny U.S. state with direct civilian links to the Congress and the executive branch" (Rogers 1995, 224). By 2003, in a "white paper" designed to lure greater military presence and investment, the chair of the Guam Chamber of Commerce, Carl Peterson, could claim that "Guam has an English-speaking, fast-food and shopping-mall culture familiar to U.S. military personnel" (Brooke 2003, A14). When McDonald's and the Micronesia Mall open in Dededo, America's day truly begins.

With 150,000 people on a land mass of 209 square miles, Guam dwarfs all other islands in the Micronesian region. With a climate much less pleasant than Hawai'i's, and located in an area subject to frequent damaging typhoons, Guam is an odd mix of a Third World country and a southern California suburb. Larry Mayo (1992) notes that the military is responsible for the island's modern infrastructure, and much of its employment, but even the U.S. military can't keep the power on all the time or prevent the traffic gridlock on Marine Drive. For at least a dozen years beginning around 1984, Guam's economy "took off." Japan's and other Asian economies were thriving then, and millions of yen were invested in upscale tourist facilities, ranging from first-class hotels and duty-free shops to sophisticated restaurants and affordable golf courses. It was during this time that the "fast-food and shopping-mall culture" really embedded itself on Guam. Although this growth provided abundant employment, it also led to protests by some Chamorro rights activists against the military's size and control over land because tourism appeared to offer an economic alternative.[1] But as the Asian economies faltered in the late 1990s, fewer new tourist facilities were built, and fewer new tourists arrived from Japan, Taiwan, and South Korea. By 2002, according to James Brooke (2003), Guam's hotel occupancies were down to 55 percent of capacity, and Guam's government began to actively court the military once again to increase its presence.

Prior to and throughout the unfolding of these events on Guam, the island's social mix more and more began to resemble Hawai'i's ethnic potpourri. In 1940, there were 22,290 people on Guam, 90 percent of whom were indigenous Chamorros (Mayo 1992, 234). Although the raw number of Chamorros grew to an estimated 55,000 by 1986, at that time they comprised only 46 percent of the island's 120,000 people. The remainder of the population included approximately 30,000 "Statesiders" (principally Euro-Americans), 25,000 Filipinos (many originally imported to work for the military), 3,000 Chinese, 3,000 South Koreans, 3,000 "Micronesians" (including people from Palau, the FSM, and the RMI), and 1,000 Japanese (Mayo 1992, 235). It was into this polyglot and polyethnic collage that *chon* Namoluk began to move shortly after the formal approval of the Compact of Free Association between the USA and the FSM.

For many *chon* Namoluk, Guam was their first exposure to the positive and negative aspects of American culture. They sampled (and worked for) KFC and Little Caesar's Pizza. They went to the sleazy strip joints that catered to Asian male tourists and horny, homesick sailors. They shopped at K-Mart and watched the races at Guam's Greyhound Park. Along with Tony Roma's ribs, they tasted Japanese and Korean food. Some learned to chew betel the Chamorro way. A few drank at Planet Hollywood in Tumon Bay. And, of course, cable TV carried advertisements urging viewers to patronize places such as the Micronesia Mall, which Brooke (2003) called "a turquoise-colored temple of American consumerism." At least one Namoluk woman even took a job there.

Following the signing of the Compact of Free Association by the USA in 1986, many FSM citizens—and especially people from Chuuk State—moved to Guam in search of work. Even though at that time the FSM's economy was still growing by more than 4 percent per year (Hezel 2003, 3), work was difficult to come by, and wages paid on Guam were far above what could be earned in Pohnpei or Chuuk. Upon finding work in Guam's then-thriving economy, the young men (and some young women) who were the first to arrive soon attracted other family members, and migrant communities began to form. The number of FSM citizens resident on Guam increased nearly threefold from September 1988 to September 1992, with the number from Chuuk State more than tripling during those four years (Hezel and Levin 1996, 93).

More pertinent to our concerns, Chuuk State citizens made up close to three-fourths of the nearly 5,000 FSM nationals living on Guam in 1992. Among these Chuuk State citizens on Guam were *chon* Namoluk, many of whom were seventh wavers. By April 1995, Guam had the third largest concentration of *chon* Namoluk, after the atoll and Wééné. I refer to them as *chon* Guamoluk (Marshall 1996). By the summer of 2001, almost one-fifth of Namoluk's *de jure* population resided on Guam (see Table 3.1). This section chronicles the growth of the

Chon Guamoluk in an Apartment on Guam, May 1995

Guamoluk community since 1986 and notes how it has also served as an incubator or way-station for many who subsequently have moved to Hawai'i or the U.S. mainland.

Some members of this community began to marry on Guam, in a few cases to non-Chuukese spouses; give birth to their children there (thereby giving them the option of U.S. citizenship when they reach the age of majority); and send their school-aged children to Guam's heavily Americanized public schools. There have been a total of fifty-two marriages among the *chon* Namoluk who have been or are a part of the Guamoluk migrant community.[2] Almost half of these (N=24) were with spouses from islands in Chuuk Lagoon, nine were with people from elsewhere in Chuuk State (eight from the Mortlocks), and only five were between two Namoluk people. So nearly three-fourths of these marriages have been with other "Chuukese." At the same time, from another perspective, one in four of these marriages has been with a foreigner: six with Chamorros; two with Kosraens; and one each with spouses from the Marshall Islands, Palau, Pingelap, Pohnpei, the Philippines, and Ulithi. And from yet a different point of view, less than one in ten of the marriages made by *chon* Guamoluk were with someone from their own island. It seems, then, that Guam provides a more diverse pool of potential marriage partners, and/or it attracts people from Chuuk State who have married outside their own communities of origin.

Guam is not just a destination for migrants from Namoluk; it is now the birthplace of at least 8 percent of the members of Namoluk's 2001 *de jure* population. My count, which may be a slight *under*count, showed that by mid–July 2001, at least seventy-one Namoluk young people had been born on Guam.[3] The great majority of them were also being raised there. The earliest birth among these children of which I have a record was in January 1985, and sixteen had been born there by the end of 1990. As of the summer of 2001, I had records of at least seven *chon* Namoluk who had graduated from Guam high schools. This number will grow markedly over the coming years as the many Guamoluk children now in elementary school and junior high complete their high school educations.

It is also instructive to look at the demographic profile of the Guamoluk community in comparison to the number of *chon* Namoluk located on the atoll, on Wééné, and in the United States. Guam had the second largest number of 0–9 year olds after the atoll, the third largest number of 10–19 year olds and 60–69 year olds after the atoll and Wééné, and was nearly tied for the second largest number of 30–39 year olds with Wééné (Namoluk had the most; see Table 4.1). The two cohorts that were notably small on Guam, when compared to the other locations of Namoluk people, were the 40–49 year olds and 50–59 year olds. In both of these cases, the greatest number were on Wééné. For the 20–29 year olds, more were in the United States in July 2001 than were on Guam (N=31 versus N=26), although slightly higher numbers of this age group were on the atoll and on Wééné. What this reveals is that the Guamoluk community is composed mainly of adults in their twenties and thirties in 2001 (seventh and eighth wavers) and their young children, many of whom were born on Guam.

The Guamoluk community numbered 155 persons in July 2001, and it was a strikingly young bunch. Eighty-seven percent were under age forty. Fifty-nine percent were under age twenty-five; 45 percent—nearly half—were younger than fifteen years of age. Of those aged fifty-five or older, eight of nine were women. This reflects both women's greater longevity and also older women's economic usefulness as babysitters for their grandchildren. Guam is an extremely expensive place to live, and few Namoluk couples could survive there comfortably without jobs for both spouses. Thus grandmothers were essential to household economic success in many cases.

When *chon* Namoluk first began to move to Guam, its population was ten times more than Wééné's, and this offered the lure of urban anonymity. For a few Namoluk women who were somewhat marginalized and impoverished on the atoll, because they had several children to support and no husband, Guam presented an attractive place to begin again, without the negative aura that surrounded them back home. This had not dawned on me until I carried out my fieldwork with *chon* Guamoluk in 1995, at which point I observed that nearly all such women had moved from the atoll to Guam. While a couple of them picked up a husband on Wééné en route, most vaulted from the atoll all the way to Guam with but a brief interlude in Chuuk's urban center. In most cases they followed their young adult children, who had preceded them in search of work. Even though such "movin' out" didn't mean they had cut their ties to Namoluk, it did suggest that Guam provided a new freedom to these women.

I found one of them—a fourth waver named Erewhon—who as a divorcée and single mother had been hard-pressed to feed and clothe her kids on Namoluk, living a life of comparative luxury when I interviewed her in 1995. She had followed her sixth-wave son and seventh-wave daughter (the eldest and the youngest of her four children) to "the place where America's day begins," and a new day truly had begun for her. Living in an upscale apartment in Yigo with her daughter and her daughter's Chamorro husband,[4] Erewhon cared for their two toddlers and two other children whom she had adopted and brought to Guam for schooling.[5] Her daughter and son-in-law both had good jobs (as a saleswoman in a duty-free shop and as a cook at a hotel), and their combined income allowed them to pay the rent of nearly $1,000/month plus other living expenses. The apartment was filled with nice furniture and appliances, and it was a far cry, indeed, from Erewhon's typhoon house and earth oven back on Namoluk. Erewhon said that she felt fulfilled and supported by children and grandchildren on Guam. In addition to her daughter with whom she lived in 1995, her son and daughter-in-law (from Namoluk) had been there since 1986 and 1987, and all three of their children at that time were born on Guam. Moreover, her "brother's" eldest daughter, and this woman's Chuuk Lagoon husband, had lived on Guam since 1990. All three of their children also were born on Guam, and Erewhon had stayed with them in Dededo to baby-sit when she first arrived. Only one of her four natural children was on Namoluk in 1995, so if she wanted to be with most of her family, Erewhon needed to be on Guam. Escaping from relative poverty and stigma was an added bonus.

The rapid migration of FSM citizens to Guam—particularly those from Chuuk—produced a culture-clash and a certain amount of strain on Guam's social services. This became known as the "Compact impact," and Guam's representatives in Washington argued strongly for federal assistance to pay for the additional financial load. This political brouhaha led a number of social scientists to focus on both the Compact impact and the prejudice of some people on Guam toward *chon* Chuuk (e.g., Dobbin and Hezel 1996). Despite the heated rhetoric and unfair stereotypes surrounding this issue, I discovered in my short field trip during May 1995 that a majority of Namoluk adults on Guam were gainfully employed. My information about *chon* Guamoluk led me to conclude that if they were "at all typical of other FSM migrants, then the presumed Compact impact is largely a myth. Only one Guamoluk family received regular public assistance, and this was to help care for a young disabled child born on Guam prematurely who required special breathing equipment and other medical assistance. One other *chon* Guamoluk was on regular dialysis at Guam Memorial Hospital for late-stage diabetes mellitus. Twenty-two Guamoluk children attended the public schools, but the costs of their education were more than offset by the taxes and other contributions their parents and kin made to Guam's economy" (Marshall 1996, 10–11). The persistence and greater integration of the Guamoluk community in the years since my 1995 visit suggest that most of these people have quietly gone about their work and lives, contributing positively to Guam's economy and rich cultural mixture.

Part of Guam's attraction for FSM migrants is its proximity. Chuuk is but an hour away by jet, and this allows for a lot of visiting and for circular migration. People from Chuuk, including *chon* Namoluk, now take short vacations on Guam or go there for Christmas shopping. The airfare is not prohibitive, and they have kin with whom they can stay for free once they arrive. Guam's proximity means that Wééné is to Guam as Namoluk is to Wééné, that is, the Guamoluk community has in some senses become an extension of the Namoluk communities on the atoll and in Chuuk's urban center. In the 1960s there was considerable movement between Namoluk and Wééné, but not much beyond Chuuk. Beginning with the Compact in 1986, considerable movement began among people on Namoluk and their relatives on Guam, as well as on Wééné. To take but one example, Sabrina, a fourth waver, now routinely moves among these three venues. One of her daughters told me on the phone that, "Going to Guam for Mama now was just like going to Amwes [across Namoluk's lagoon] before." Sabrina comes and goes, but here are a few time and place markers of her movements: In April 1995, she was on Wééné; in July 1999, she was back home on Namoluk; in April 2000, she went to Oneop for Easter; two years later she was on Wééné again, and she sailed down to Namoluk while I was in Chuuk; in November 2002, she was on Guam, where she stayed until April 2003, when she flew back to Wééné to help care for her eldest daughter, who was ill. In all of these places she visits and stays with her children and grandchildren.

As early as the mid–1990s, and then increasingly by 2003, Guam's economy peaked and then began to struggle. As this occurred, some *chon* Guamoluk decided to strike out for greener pastures in Hawai'i or on the U.S. mainland. The job skills, savvy about American life, and facility in English they'd acquired on Guam stood them in good stead as they moved farther away from home. Hawai'i—especially Honolulu—has taken on a particular attraction of late. But even so, the bittersweetness of moving ever farther from "the lagoon in the middle" is captured in what Seraphim told me when we met on Guam in 1995: "I don't like Guam, but there was no work in Chuuk and I came here to provide my kids with better schools and to make a living. I get homesick for Namoluk, and think about going fishing, but my kids probably would never be happy down there because they're being raised on Guam."

WILL DREAMS COME TRUE IN BLUE HAWAI'I?

Seraphim has since separated from his wife, left Guam, and moved to Honolulu; his wife and kids also have left Guam to try a new life in the American Midwest.

Feeling somewhat blue, he hopes, as the song has it, that his dream of better times will come true "in blue Hawai'i." Before people like Seraphim came to "the islands," Namoluk people first began to spend time in Hawai'i around 1970, although there was never more than a handful of them there at any one time until the late 1990s. Back in the beginning, those who came arrived for one of two reasons: either to go to college or to receive medical care. Although a dozen or more *chon* Namoluk attended community colleges on Maui and O'ahu, and later at several of Hawai'i's four-year institutions, at least as many came to Hawai'i in search of better healthcare. Kula Sanitarium. Straub Clinic. Queen's Hospital. Tripler Army Medical Center. These were the places to which *chon* Namoluk were referred for treatments that they could not get from the hospital on Wééné.

Table 3.1 shows just how recent the migration of Namoluk people to Hawai'i has been: in April 1995, only seven of them were there; by July 2001, this had ballooned to forty-five.[6] Five of the seven who were in Hawai'i in 1995 were still there in 2001, and they lived in several clusters scattered around Honolulu and its suburbs. Many of the migrants who came during that six-year period were related to them and joined these clusters. For instance, by 2001, Lurline's household (she was all by herself in 1995) included six others: her sister's son in his early twenties; her brother's twelve-year-old daughter; two of her sisters' daughters (one in her late teens and one a grade-schooler); and two young women in their twenties, both of whom were her mother's "brother's" son's daughters.

As with *chon* Guamoluk, those who were in Hawai'i in 2001 were on the young side. Eighty-seven percent were under age forty-five, 76 percent were under age thirty-five, and just over half (23/45) were between fifteen and thirty-four years old. Perhaps because the move to Hawai'i had been so recent, there only had been two births to Namoluk women there at the time of my 2001 census, a number that doubtless will grow in the years to come. All five people over age fifty were there to visit their children or to help care for their grandchildren. By spring 2003, at least three more seniors were there in this role.

It's interesting to examine where those who moved to Hawai'i between 1995 and 2001 were in 1995. The largest number (fourteen) were then on Namoluk, another eleven were in Chuuk Lagoon, seven were on Guam, and three were on Pohnpei. One each was on the U.S. mainland and in Sāmoa. Of course, five of the forty-five were already in Hawai'i, and three of those in Hawai'i in 2001 were as yet unborn in 1995 (one was born on Guam in 1998, and two in Honolulu in 2000 and 2001). Of the fourteen who were located on Namoluk in 1995, five went to Hawai'i explicitly to live with relatives and to attend school there (including college). Two more went to Honolulu primarily for medical care for themselves or a child (a third person accompanied his mother as a companion). Three seniors were in Hawai'i visiting children and grandchildren. The remaining three people who had been on Namoluk in 1995 were all working or looking for work in Honolulu in 2001.

Those eleven who were located in Chuuk Lagoon in 1995 represented the same range of reasons for moving to Hawai'i: to attend school, to seek treatment for a health problem, to accompany parents who moved, to visit children and grandchildren, and to find employment. Four of the seven who had been on Guam, including Seraphim, found better job prospects in the Aloha State; one of the other three came for college, one married an American in Hawai'i, and the last accompanied his mother. All three who were on Pohnpei in 1995 had gone there for school: two at COM–Pohnpei, and the other at the Pohnpei Agricultural and Technical School (PATS), run by the Catholic Church. The former two completed their associate's degrees on Pohnpei and transferred to Hawai'i to work on their bachelor's degrees. The one who was at PATS entered the Job Corps training program in Hawai'i, from which he graduated by 2001. A woman who was on the U.S. mainland for college in 1995 moved with her husband to Hawai'i by 2001; a man who attended the University of the South Pacific extension campus in Sāmoa in 1995 relocated to Honolulu by 2001.

I know of at least ten more *chon* Namoluk who were in Hawai'i in April 2003. Four of them were on Guam in 1995, three on Namoluk, two on Wééné, and one on the U.S. mainland. Three of the ten are in their mid- to late sixties and were in Honolulu to be with their adult children, although one of them, Ledyard, also was there due to a chronic health condition. The other seven were all between twenty-seven and forty-one years old, and all came to find jobs.[7] Six of them joined existing households comprised of other Namoluk people, but the others established their own. In at least one case, where the Namoluk man's wife is from Chuuk Lagoon, members of her family also moved to Honolulu and shared that household.

Namoluk people in Honolulu have begun to name these household clusters after places on their own island. For instance, one is called Lemaur, another is known as Somas, and still a third is identified as Urowa. "Home place" thus is mapped onto "new place" in a manner analogous to the way immigrants bestowed place-names on the United States derived from Mother England or continental Europe (e.g., Birmingham and Cambridge). To name a place, what Keith Basso (1996, 5) calls "place-making," even if it's a rented venue, is to invoke a kind of "cultural possession" over it and implies an intention to remain and put down roots. This process also is a way for "identity-making," as "Deliberately and otherwise, people are forever presenting each other with culturally mediated images of where and how they dwell. In large ways and small, they are forever performing acts that reproduce and express their own sense of place—and also, inextricably, their own understandings of who and what they are" (Basso 1996, 110). By naming household clusters in Honolulu, *chon* Namoluk "localize" a foreign place, thus reproducing and expressing "culturally mediated images" of home.

Whether named or not, the various Namoluk household clusters are in fairly regular communication among themselves, and many of their members get together for church services or for weekend recreation. When they do so, the services, cookouts, and games frequently include other Mortlockese or people from elsewhere in Chuuk State. There are many more persons in Hawai'i from Ettal than from Namoluk, for example, and the close ties between these two communities have been reinforced in Honolulu. Some of the early Namoluk migrants lived with people from Ettal, and at least one Namoluk-Ettal marriage has resulted from such arrangements. *Chon* Namoluk in Hawai'i are not known as such, nor are they known as Mortlockese. Instead, in Hawai'i's complex ethnic declension, they are labeled either as "Micronesians" or as "Chuukese." These more encompassing identities also operate on the U.S. mainland, as we'll see in the next section, and they are important for comprehending Namoluk people's changing senses of personal and cultural identity in the twenty-first century—a matter to which we'll return in Chapter 9.

Hawai'i is a crossroads, a transit point between the U.S. mainland and the islands further west, whether Guam, Pohnpei, or those of Chuuk State. As *chon* Namoluk who reside on the mainland pass through Honolulu coming and going, they are now met by their kin or fellow islanders at the airport (see Chapter 3). Some who've lived and worked in Hawai'i for awhile have used it as a springboard to migrate to the mainland. For example, one unmarried seventh wave woman from the Katamak clan moved to Hawai'i in 1994, accompanied by Malcolm, her father, who had attended university there years before. After several years of work in Honolulu, she moved to Portland, Oregon, where she got an apartment near her lineage brother, Jasper, and his Mortlockese wife. There she rooms with two other Mortlockese women, all of whom are employed. Others use Hawai'i as a place to meet with family members, as is true of the grandparents from Namoluk who come for visits with their kids and grandchildren.

Among local people who live in Hawai'i, O'ahu is known as "the gathering place," and it has become that for *chon* Namoluk too. Members of the Wáánikar–2 subclan illustrate this "coming together" on O'ahu. In the fall of 1994, Horatio and his wife were in Honolulu, visiting from Pohnpei, where they both worked. While there, they got together for Thanksgiving dinner with their two daughters (then in school in Hawai'i); Horatio's sister Dominique's son, Oliver (then a student at the University of Hawai'i–Hilo campus); and Horatio's sister Janelle's son, Oscar (who flew out for the holiday reunion from his workplace in Eureka, California). Other kinds of gatherings occur among Namoluk people in Honolulu as well. On an invitation from some members of the Hawai'i contingent, Harold (a member of the Wáánikar–1 subclan) flew there from Los Angeles to celebrate Easter 2003 with a group of Namoluk Protestants who live in the various household clusters and worship together on Sundays. O'ahu: the gathering place.

Another gathering place of a quite different sort lies 2,700 miles further to the east, along the rocky northern coast of California. Where Honolulu is tropical and balmy, Eureka is temperate and foggy. Where Honolulu has four or five dozen *chon* Namoluk, Eureka had only half a dozen of them when I visited there in June 2002. But other Namoluk people had lived there, some quite recently; other *chon Morschlok* made up part of Eureka's cluster; and still others from Namoluk had visited there over the years. Eureka offers a good example of the sorts of living situations in which *chon* Namoluk find themselves on the U.S. mainland.

EUREKA! I'VE FOUND IT![8]

Namoluk's "Eureka moment" began in August 1985 when Rex, an eighteen-year-old high school graduate and seventh waver, arrived by himself to attend the College of the Redwoods (COR), a community college located on the southern outskirts of Eureka, California. The spacious modern campus lies opposite the Humboldt Bay National Wildlife Refuge in the heart of northern California's redwood country.[9] Over the ensuing eighteen years, as of this writing, a cluster of Namoluk residents has formed and been sustained in Eureka, even as some have come and gone. Although it is a bit off the beaten path, the Eureka cluster has had its share of Namoluk visitors over the years, and the Eureka bunch themselves make periodic trips to see relatives up north in Portland and Salem, Oregon. When family members fly in from Chuuk or Honolulu for a visit, Namoluk's "Eurekans" wind their way down the 300 miles of Highway 101 by car to the airport in San Francisco or Oakland, meet their plane, and drive them back up the coast.

Less than a year after Rex arrived, one of Namoluk's Xavier graduates, Wilbur, followed him to COR. They took a short trip to Texas that summer to visit Wilbur's brother, one of Namoluk's "long-timers" who'd moved there in 1977 and had not returned to Chuuk even once as of 2002. Upon their return to Eureka, both applied themselves to their studies, and each eventually received an associate's degree. At that point Rex transferred to Humboldt State University (HSU), just up the road in Arcata, and Wilbur went to work in the construction industry for five or six years "when [he] just burned out." A Palauan friend,[10] also resident in Eureka, told him of an opening at a big lumber mill in Scotia, and he hired on there for three years until the mill experienced a series of layoffs. He then got a good job with full benefits at another smaller lumber company, located in Arcata. Earning between $25,000 and $30,000 a year at the mill, Wilbur also managed the twelve-unit apartment building in which he lived, which added further to his income. At the time I interviewed him in 2002, Wilbur hadn't returned to Wééné or Namoluk for a visit in the sixteen years since he moved to Eureka.[11]

Rex followed a different path. In a phone conversation we had in March 2003, he told me that "I really wanted my degree," and so he persevered in his studies. When he transferred to HSU, he worked construction jobs during the summers to help pay for tuition, and he joined the Apostolic Faith Church, where he met a young woman whose father was the minister there. In 1990, Rex received a BS in finance from HSU and married the preacher's daughter. After a trip back to

Wééné by himself in 1991, the young couple moved to Honolulu in 1992, where Rex went to work for an insurance company and enrolled as a part-time graduate student at the University of Hawai'i's Mānoa campus. Of his visit home, he told me in a December 1991 phone conversation that it was "hard when I went back—it was too slow—I'm more used to the fast-paced life." However, when I casually asked him whether he found it difficult to readjust to Chuukese food again, he replied, "Oh, no! That was the best part! I ate fish every day until I was almost sick." Rex and his wife had a baby in Honolulu, and in 1994, they moved back to the west coast, first to Sacramento, and then up to Salem, Oregon. They remained there until late summer 2001, when they and their three children moved to Wééné for Rex to take up a special position with the state government. This was the first time that his Euro-American wife and their kids had been there, so there were many adjustments to be made and many relatives to meet. The family remained on Wééné for approximately a year, and then all five of them relocated to Honolulu in October 2002, joining the growing Namoluk contingent that has assembled there.

At Rex's encouragement, Evan arrived in Eureka in the fall of 1987, and like his predecessors, enrolled at COR. Also like them, he finished an associate's degree there. But while he has taken some classes at HSU in the years since, he found a good job with UPS and settled into a comfortable lifestyle in Eureka. In the fall of 1991, his younger brother, Richard, also a member of the Katamak clan, was the fourth *chon* Namoluk to join the growing cluster. Richard spent two semesters at COR while he also worked full-time at Pacific Choice Seafood down on Eureka's waterfront. All of this proved too much to handle, and since he had bills to pay, he quit school and began a series of jobs in lumber mills that eventually led to his working in the same Arcata mill that hired Wilbur. In 2002, Wilbur was without a vehicle, and so the two of them rode together back and forth to work in Richard's 1992 Mazda pickup. After he'd been in Eureka for a couple of years, Richard returned for a two-week visit to Wééné in 1993; since then, he hasn't gone home. However, he did travel all the way back to upstate New York in the summer of 2001 to be present when his younger sister married an American marine whom she had met on Guam. Interestingly, it was at that function that he first encountered his fellow *chon* Namoluk, Steemer—Steemer had left Chuuk for school in Hawai'i the same year that Richard was born (see Chapter 3).

By 1991, then, the Eureka cluster was made up of four young men, all seventh wavers. Soon thereafter, Rex and his wife moved to Honolulu, and no one else arrived in Eureka until Oscar showed up in January 1994, having moved there from Portland, where he'd worked for the previous two years.[12] Oscar immediately found a job as a board grader in a different lumber yard from where Wilbur and Richard worked, and he has stayed at that company ever since. In November 2001 he married Gwynne, a young woman from Losap, at ICC in Portland, which is where they first met, and she moved to Eureka with him.[13]

In September 1996, after Rex and his wife and Horatio's daughter all had left, and before Oscar got married, Oscar's younger brother, Gawain—also from the Wáánikar–2 subclan—arrived in Eureka, bringing the number of then-resident *chon* Namoluk to five. An eighth waver, Gawain graduated from high school on Wééné in 1995 and attended COM-Pohnpei during the next academic year. When he got to Eureka, he enrolled at COR, but they would not accept many of the COM credits that he sought to transfer, and he essentially had to start all over again on his degree objective. He continued in school for three semesters until financial obligations overwhelmed him, so with five semesters of college work and no degree to show for it, he went to work full-time. Initially, he found employment at Pacific Choice Seafood, but he then switched to a cafeteria job, where he worked for $7.50/hour and no benefits when I saw him in June 2002. While on a trip to Portland for the big Easter fete at ICC in spring of 2000, he finally met in person a young woman from Kuttu with whom he first became acquainted on coconutchat. Kara had been recruited from Chuuk as a CNA and worked in a nursing home in Maryland before she "escaped" and went all the way across country to Portland. Immediately after the ICC Easter service, Kara moved to Eureka to be with Gawain, and they share a two-bedroom apartment with Oscar and Gwynne.

Before either Oscar or Gawain got married and brought their Mortlockese wives to Eureka, another Namoluk person, Helen, arrived to attend COR in 1999. She was Wilbur's sister's daughter and also related to Oscar and Gawain as members of the same subclan. From the eighth wave, born on Wééné and a graduate of Berea High School, Helen spent three semesters at COR without finishing a degree. During part of that time, she lived in an apartment in the building managed by Wilbur, although later she moved in with a Marshallese boyfriend. In March 2002, Helen traveled from Eureka to Florida—the same month that Laurel arrived from Honolulu to stay with Richard, her husband-to-be.[14] She worked in Florida briefly as a CNA and most recently popped up in western Iowa, living with a Namoluk boyfriend.

While Helen still lived in Eureka, and before Laurel joined the others there, yet another Namoluk person came and went. From the Wáánikar–2 subclan, like Richard and Oscar, Tamara was already something of a wanderer. A member of the seventh wave, she spent her early years on the atoll, lived a number of years on Wééné, and then by 1990 moved to Guam. There she married a man from Chuuk Lagoon with whom she had three children, all born on Guam, and from whom she divorced. She next married a Pohnpeian on Guam and had a daughter by him. Tamara next surfaced in my fieldnotes in October 1999, at which time she lived in Honolulu with lineage mates there. In June 2000, she came to Eureka, where she held various jobs as a housekeeper, a CNA, and a counter person at Burger King. In January 2002, Tamara headed for Georgia to stay with another subclan "sister" there who had married an African American and had had a young baby. Most recently, Tamara drifted from Georgia to Louisville, Kentucky, where she stayed near an older subclan "sister" and her husband and children who had moved there from Guam in 2002.

Thus the Eureka cluster has grown and shrunk over the past eighteen years, reaching its maximum number of six *chon* Namoluk between 2000 and 2002. But the cluster included more than just *chon* Namoluk: by June 2002, it also included four other Mortlockese (one of them from Namoluk), all married to Namoluk men. In addition to Gwynne, Kara, and Laurel, Evan had married a woman from Moch named Sylvia, and their daughter was born in Eureka at the end of 2001. These people live in three separate households: Wilbur lives alone; Evan and Sylvia and their baby share a small house with Richard and Laurel; and Oscar and Gwynne live together with Gawain and Kara.

Two Members of the Namoluk Contingent in Eureka, California, Outside Their House, July 2002

Even though Eureka is not the most accessible community in America, the Namoluk Eurekans are hardly cut off from other *chon* Namoluk. In addition to their access to virtual kinship, they travel the seven and a half hours via Crescent City, over to Grants Pass, and then up I–5 to Portland-Salem several times per year. They have also had quite a few guests over the years. The first visitor was Malcolm,[15] Evan and Richard's father, who spent a month with Evan, Rex, and Wilbur during the summer of 1991. Within the next year, Nathan—then a theology student in Los Angeles—rented a car and drove up to see the sights and to "play" with his Namoluk age-mates. Soon thereafter, Ross, from the Wáánikar–1 subclan and also a student in Los Angeles, also drove up to Eureka. He and Evan then drove on to Portland, where they took the elderly Kenneth (see Chapter 3) through downtown Portland and to see the Clackamas Mall. Evan said that "his eyes got big," and, "It was really fun for me to do that and watch his reaction." The year 1997 saw many Namoluk visitors to Eureka. Richard and Evan's parents both came all the way from Namoluk, and so did Gawain and Oscar's lineage "brother," Oliver, from Hawai'i. The next year—accompanied by his wife— Richard and Evan's older brother, Lindsey, flew from Wééné to San Francisco and spent a month in Eureka. During that time, they drove up to see Jasper in Portland. In 1999, a different lineage brother of Oscar and Gawain's, Kendrick, passed through for a few days while he was in the States on business, and Richard and Evan's parents returned for another visit. This time they, too, drove up to Portland to visit Jasper and their daughter who lived there. As the epigraph to this chapter indicates, while "roaming the globe," Ledyard stopped through to visit in the late summer of 2000.[16] Less than a year later, Oscar and Gawain's mother— then living with their sister Hyacinth and her family in Honolulu—caught a flight to San Francisco, got to walk across the Golden Gate Bridge, and then spent nearly three months with her sons before returning to Hawai'i. Kurt and his entourage from Salem, Oregon (including his elderly mother, Micky, his younger brother, and two still younger kin), also drove to Eureka for a visit in 2001. Then in March 2003, Malcolm, who had gone back to Namoluk from Portland for a visit, landed in Oakland, was met by his sons, and went up the coast to Eureka to see everyone there.[17]

Today, Eureka has so entered *chon* Namoluk's collective cultural consciousness that a Namoluk couple resident on Wééné, who had never been to California, named their daughter "Eureka." They've got it! The new world inhabited by *chon* Namoluk extends all the way to the North American continent. Who knows? Perhaps fifteen years from now Eureka from Namoluk Atoll will enroll in college in Eureka, California. And the question as to what the identity of such young women as Eureka might then be is the matter to which we turn in the final chapter.

Notes

1. Chamorro are the indigenous people of Guam (Guahan) and the other Marianas Islands, and during the 1990s, activists among them initiated a Chamorro rights movement, modeled somewhat on the Native Hawaiian sovereignty movement. Land alienation was a key issue in the Chamorro rights movement, and because the U.S. military is the largest landholder on Guam, protestors urged that the military presence on the island be reduced. They justified the inevitable loss of jobs such a reduction would produce by pointing to the robust tourist economy.

2. This includes marriages that subsequently ended in divorce.

3. Of the wave that washed from Namoluk to Guam, we certainly can say that it was *popo*, "pregnant"!

4. Reflecting Guam's ethnic diversity, this man's father was a Filipino and his mother was a Chamorra with a German father. Thus, genetically, his children by his Namoluk wife are a cosmopolitan mixture reminiscent of many people in Hawai'i who are the product of multiple ethnic intermarriages.

5. One was her six-year-old granddaughter by a daughter who remained in Chuuk, and the other was her "brother's" eighteen-year-old daughter whom she brought to Guam from Wééné in 1994 to finish high school on Guam.

6. Incomplete data that I have acquired via telephone calls and e-mail correspondence in the spring of 2003 suggest that the number of *chon* Namoluk in Hawai'i by then probably exceeded sixty.

7. One moved to Honolulu to resume college, having begun but not completed his studies at COM. He dropped out of Kapi'olani Community College after one semester to take a job at a Burger King.

8. "The Greek expression for 'I have found it,' associated with the great geometrician, Archimedes, has common currency in Western civilization. As a geographical term it apparently originated in California. . . . The motto became popular after the California constitutional convention on October 2, 1849, approved the great seal of the state, with the inscription 'Eureka'" (Gudde 1969, 105).

9. Eureka has a population of 26,000, but it is just a few minutes by car to Arcata, which has 17,000 people. Adding in those who live in smaller towns nearby, the area has about 60,000 residents.

10. A number of Palauans, a Pohnpeian, and several "Hawaiians" resided in Eureka, many of whom worked in the lumber mills, and some of whom play basketball every week with a few of the *chon* Namoluk. Given the place-name Sāmoa on the barrier island across Humboldt Bay from Eureka, it is fitting that there also are Sāmoans living and working in Eureka. One or two other students from Chuuk State, and at least one from the RMI, also came to the College of the Redwoods and Humboldt State after 1986, obtained degrees, and then moved elsewhere.

11. I learned in July 2003 that he finally returned home for a visit in June of that year, after seventeen years away.

12. In August 1993, Horatio's daughter—herself a *chon* Lukunoch—arrived and attended COR for a semester and a half. Evan, Richard, and Wilbur, then in Eureka, were all

related to her father. While she was in Portland over Christmas 1993, she convinced her cross-cousin, Oscar, to accompany her back to Eureka, which he did. She left Eureka in spring 1994 to attend her mother's brother's funeral on Wééné, after which she relocated to Hawai'i and enrolled at Honolulu Community College. Horatio told me that the main reason she didn't continue her schooling at COR was that it simply required more money than he could afford.

13. Although Losap is Gwynne's home island, her life path mirrors that of many younger *chon* Namoluk. Born and raised on Wééné, she has only been to Losap for short visits. At age sixteen she went to stay with relatives on Maui, from whence she moved to Honolulu and graduated from Roosevelt High School there in the early 1990s. She lived in Honolulu for several years, and then in 1997 flew to Las Vegas to stay with a sister. After six months in Vegas, she shifted to Portland, Oregon, where her father was a pastor at ICC and where she took a job at Wal-Mart. Gwynne and Oscar met each other at ICC.

14. Laurel is a member of the Souwon clan and is profiled in Chapter 7.

15. Evan and Richard's father, Malcolm, retired and moved around among his Katamak clan children, most of whom live away from the atoll. He stayed with his sons in Eureka on several occasions and drove down from Portland (where he stayed with another son and his wife and a daughter) for Father's Day 2002. He brought with him a video of the Namoluk Protestant Church jubilee—held in August 2001.

16. Ledyard is Oscar and Gawain's father and Evan and Richard's mother's "brother"; he is also related to Wilbur somewhat more distantly.

17. Sadly, Malcolm passed away just a couple of months later in 2003.

9
Closings: Points of Departure

... sense of place roots individuals in the social and cultural soils from which they have sprung together, holding
them there in the grip of a shared identity, a localized
version of selfhood.

Keith H. Basso (1996, 146)

The phrase "point of departure" has special significance
in islands with deep and active seafaring traditions. It
refers to both metaphorical and physical spaces from
which seafarers launch their journeys. In Chuukese traditions of seafaring, this point of departure is called
"Muir," steering point, and also connotes "home" or "island." Travellers set their course by using the point of
departure, or the home/island, as a guiding point.

Joakim Peter (2000, 255)

NO ISLAND IS AN ISLAND

The author of the second epigraph above, Joakim "Jojo" Peter, is president of the
COM–Chuuk campus, a *chon* Ettal with graduate degrees in Pacific history and
Pacific Islands Studies from the University of Hawai'i, a professional colleague,

and a personal friend. His sister is married to a *chon* Namoluk, and she, her husband, and their children have lived and worked on Guam for at least the past decade. Jojo himself is a traveler to Guam, having completed his undergraduate studies at UOG once he graduated from Xavier High School. He knows intimately about points of departure and about how it is to be a *chon* Ettal in the Mortlocks, a Mortlockese in Chuuk, a Chuukese on Guam, a Micronesian in Hawai'i, and a Pacific Islander scholar among his international academic colleagues. Points of departure and shifting identities are among the topics I will address in this final chapter.

Also to be discussed is the matter of place, as we have encountered it in the form of a small, outer island atoll community in Chuuk State, FSM. This place, Namoluk, is very clearly illustrative of "the local" when set against "the global" in the debates that have gripped scholars during the past fifteen years. Namoluk is an island community, to be sure, but as the preceding chapters show, in the year 2003 the Namoluk community is no longer just located on an island. Paraphrasing poet John Donne,[1] "no island is an island," a fact that Namoluk exemplifies well. But if Namoluk has never been only an island, the atoll provides the essential material for what Harri Englund calls "emplacement:" "*Emplacement* refers to a perspective in which the subject is inextricably *situated* in a historically and existentially specific condition, defined, for brevity, as a 'place'" (2002, 267; italics in original). From this perspective, at the beginning of the twenty-first century, *chon* Namoluk find themselves situated in specific historical circumstances "that are as much embodied as they are discursively imagined" (Englund 2002, 263). Their personal identities derive from a collective community identity that is rooted in a place: their island home. They carry Namoluk with them when they move—wherever they move.

This relationship between person and community, identity and local place, is widespread, even in a world overtaken by global flows and transnational migration. Englund (2002) documents it for Malawi in southern Africa. Joe Jorgensen (1990; cited in Sahlins 1999, viii) reports it for an Eskimo village in the far north of Alaska. Edward M. Bruner (1999) discusses it for the Toba Batak of Sumatra, Indonesia. James L. Watson describes it for the members of a Chinese lineage from the New Territories (lecture presented at the University of Iowa, November 12, 2002).[2] And whether they remain on their own land or migrate overseas, the literature insists that local places play a particularly important role in identity formation for Pacific Islanders (e.g., Diaz and Kauanui 2001; Howard 1999; Howard and Rensel 2001; Linnekin and Poyer 1990a; Spickard et al. 2002; Wilson 2000). This emphasis on the centrality of place poses a challenge to those who argue that place is relatively unimportant or even that it no longer matters in a deterritorialized, postlocal world of diasporas and transnational population flows. What can *chon* Namoluk who have moved "beyond the reef" teach us about this? And how does the Namoluk case fit in with other material about the importance of place for Pacific Islanders?

POINTS OF ORIGIN

As explained in Chapter 1, *chon* means "a person or citizen of"; hence, *chon* Namoluk refers to the people or citizens of the Namoluk community. In preceding chapters we have seen that for the past thirty years, members of this once largely endogamous community increasingly have married *outside* the *chon* Namoluk category. Although this has made the Namoluk population more diverse, it also provides an opportunity to rehearse what is known of the historical heterogeneity of this community and the variety of ways by which people have become *chon* Namoluk.

That place matters to Pacific Islanders has been known for a very long time. Indeed, notions of kinship that are widespread in Oceania are predicated as much on shared land rights in a particular place as they are on shared biogenetic substance. Elsewhere, this linkage of person (as kin) and place (as land) has been discussed for Micronesian societies at some length (Marshall 1999, 121–125). Suffice it to emphasize here that people's most intimate personal identities concurrently involve relationships to those who produced them (their "blood" relatives) and that which sustains them all (their land, from which they obtain food) (see Chapter 1). People are not only related to each other, but they are also related to their land—their place. This is summed up beautifully by the Indo-Fijian Pacific historian Brij V. Lal: "Place matters. It gives us identity, shapes our imagination and experience and informs our understanding of the world around us. It is both matter as well as metaphor, a source of material as well as of cultural and spiritual sustenance. It can be 'home' or 'away'" (in press). Whether they be at home on their little atoll in the wide sea, or away on larger islands or distant continents in a wide world, *chon* Namoluk are who they are because of where they are from.

Members of the eight clans represented on the atoll in 1969 (see Table 2.1 and footnote) immigrated to Namoluk from at least ten other islands: seven in the Mortlocks, two in Chuuk Lagoon, and Polowat Atoll. This diversity of background is typical of Carolinian atoll communities and is hardly unique to Namoluk. The crucial issue for an immigrant clan is access to land—without land rights on the atoll, they cannot claim to be *chon* Namoluk. Land is the fundamental basis of the *chon* Namoluk identity. Unless. . . The "unless" is equally important in the decisions people make concerning whether someone else is or isn't a *chon* Namoluk. Here is how it was taught to me: "The concept of 'Namoluk citizen' is a complex of factors that includes birth, residence, land rights, marriage, clientship, adoption, and, sometimes, official government registration and employment" (Marshall 1975a, 172). Let's explore this concept in greater detail.

First, birth. *Where* one is born geographically is of little consequence, but in keeping with matrilineal kinship, if one's mother is a *chon* Namoluk, one is a member of a Namoluk matrilineage by birth and thereby a Namoluk person. If one's father is a *chon* Namoluk, and one's mother is from another island in

Chuuk State, one usually will become a "citizen" of their mother's home island.[3] When one's mother is from someplace outside the compass of Chuuk's clan system, one is more likely to be considered beyond the pale, and this clearly is what has occurred for most of the children that Namoluk men have sired by American women (see "Your Place or Mine?" below). Nevertheless, at least in theory, if such children received a gift of land on the atoll from their father, and someday decided to move to Namoluk and live on their land, the *potential* exists for them to be incorporated as *chon* Namoluk.

In most cases, if either of one's parents is from Namoluk, one will inherit rights to land on the atoll, and this is another way to distinguish "Namoluk citizens" from noncitizens. As noted above, those who inherit such property matrilineally are automatically *chon* Namoluk by birth because they belong to a localized matrilineage. If one has land rights on Namoluk from one's father, however, in and of itself this isn't sufficient to count oneself a Namoluk person. Only when such land combines with lengthy residence on the atoll might one thereby become a *chon* Namoluk, but this does not commonly happen.

Some people become *chon* Namoluk through marriage to a Namoluk person and subsequent long-term residence on the atoll. This is by no means a given, "and a spouse from another island may never consider himself a 'Namoluk citizen' in spite of years of residence on the atoll. Likewise, some 'Namoluk citizens' may refer to such a spouse as a 'Namoluk citizen' whereas others may not. Normally in such situations, however, outside spouses are converted to the 'Namoluk citizen' category" (Marshall 1975a, 173). In-marrying spouses typically become client members of a Namoluk lineage.[4]

Adoption offers another path by which a person might become a *chon* Namoluk. Most adoptions are by relatives—usually aunts, uncles, and grandparents—and so the child is likely to already be a member of the Namoluk community. But occasionally a child born as a citizen of another island is adopted by *chon* Namoluk and becomes a "Namoluk citizen" that way.

For governmental purposes, the island on which one pays taxes and votes in local elections is one's "home island." It is possible to alter one's home island by changing one's official tax and voting registration, and this is often done when one's affiliation already has been altered by one of the means discussed above (e.g., marriage to a *chon* Namoluk and long-term residence there).

The last way to become a "Namoluk citizen" is by way of employment. The only instance of this known to me concerned the former Protestant minister (from Piis-Emmwar) and his family (from Wééné). They are considered *chon* Namoluk even though they didn't become client members of a Namoluk lineage and only acquired limited landholdings on the atoll. Long-term residence of close to twenty years, and a strong commitment to the local community, seemed crucial in this case. It may be significant that only the minister's five younger children are referred to as *chon* Namoluk. The five older ones never moved to the atoll with their parents and don't consider themselves to be "Namoluk citizens," nor are they so viewed by Namoluk people.

NESTED IDENTITIES

Namoluk people evince a phenomenon that is widespread in many parts of the world: their identities shift from very narrowly focused to broader, more inclusive categories, depending upon the situation and setting in which they find themselves. I alluded to this at the beginning of this chapter in regards to Joakim Peter. Namoluk has three named villages, and when *chon* Namoluk are on their home island, they identify themselves by the village in which they live and with which they're affiliated. Hence, *on the atoll,* people may identify as *chon* Pukos, *chon* Lukelap, or *chon* Sópwonewel. In relation to people from the other communities that comprise the Mortlocks, they are *chon* Namoluk, and this is a self-identity that they claim and retain wherever they go in Chuuk State. In most situations in Chuuk State, Namoluk is a known place; however, for some specific purposes in relation to other collectivities that make up this political jurisdiction, *chon* Namoluk may self-identify or be lumped together with their neighbors as *chon* Morschlok, or "Mortlockese" (see Chapters 1 and 2).[5] Generally, when people from Chuuk State, including those from Namoluk, move outside of that state's borders, they identify and are identified by others as *chon* Chuuk, or "Chuukese." This is definitely the case elsewhere in the FSM; in the RMI, CNMI, and Palau; on Guam; and to some degree in Hawai'i. It is more likely in Hawai'i, however, that someone from Chuuk (including *chon* Namoluk) would identify as "Micronesian," and this identity is widely understood there to include all of the inhabitants of the former USTTPI.

On the U.S. mainland, matters become more complex. Most people there are quite poorly informed about "the Pacific," and very few know where Chuuk is (although the older generation who lived through World War II as adults certainly have heard of Truk!). *Chon* Namoluk who've lived on the mainland and confronted this problem give me a variety of answers to the question of how they present themselves to others in terms of identity. Some say, "I'm from the Pacific Islands." Others respond, "I'm from the Micronesian Islands." But even these general labels don't always work, and sometimes in frustration they'll just tell their questioner, "I'm from Hawai'i." That usually works since most people on the mainland know about Hawai'i nowadays.[6] This is similar to what Alan Howard and Jan Rensel (2001) report for Rotuman migrants to Australia and New Zealand. Because others in those countries didn't know the category "Rotuman," the islanders generally identified themselves as Fijian or Polynesian.

Shifting identities are understood by and affect people located on the atoll. As noted in Chapter 7, young children may be taken by their relatives directly from Namoluk to such places as Guam, Hawai'i, Kentucky, or Oregon to enroll in school there. These kids are almost immediately confronted with having to "redefine" themselves for others. And many people who reside on the atoll have spent considerable time—sometimes years—abroad, during which they've become familiar with identities necessitated by and created as a consequence of their emplacement in new situations and conditions. The point is that the continuing flow of people to and from Namoluk implicates the atoll's residents in the nested identities that may develop far beyond the reef.

Depending on *where* Namoluk people end up on the mainland, however, others may ascribe an inappropriate identity to them based on assumptions about their appearance. Some in North Carolina or who live in the Southwest are misidentified as Native Americans. Others find themselves being addressed in Spanish by Mexican Americans in California or by Hispanics in Florida. One trashed a bar in Alabama when a white guy called him by the "N" word. Through all of these locations and all of these episodes, however, *chon* Namoluk are very clear that they are "the people or citizens of Namoluk Atoll." Problems arise only when their personal identity lies beyond the ken of some of those with whom they must interact when far away from their island home.

Matters of ethnic, cultural, and individual identities for Pacific Islands migrants to New Zealand have received much greater attention than for islander migrants to the United States. Contributors to a recent collection edited by Cluny Macpherson, Paul Spoonley, and Melani Anae (2001a) address a host of identity issues that have arisen in New Zealand that may presage the future for *chon* Namoluk and other Pacific peoples in America. Pacific Islanders are much more "visible" in New Zealand, making up close to 6 percent of that country's population of about 3.3 million people (Cook, Didham, and Khawaja 2001, 45), whereas such immigrants comprise about 1.5 percent of the USA's 275 million people. New Zealand's islander migrants moved there mainly in the 1970s, but they have now matured such that a majority who were recorded in the 1996 census had been born in New Zealand (Bedford and Didham 2001). As discussed in Chapters 3 and 5–8 above, the migration of *chon* Namoluk to the United States commenced in the 1970s for educational reasons, but the overwhelming majority of those fifth and sixth wavers returned to Chuuk State after a few years away. Only with the leap to Guam beginning in the late 1980s did substantial numbers of Namoluk people begin to take up residence outside of the FSM, and the moves to Hawai'i and the U.S. mainland have for most people been more recent still (see Chapters 7 and 8). Thus as of 2003, relatively few *chon* Namoluk had been born in the United States, although their number continues to grow.

Macpherson, Spoonley, and Anae (2001b) focus on the formation of "transnational island societies," some members of whom have never left their home islands, whereas others have never been in them. They are concerned with the "process in which a given 'cultural identity' no longer rests on a more or less homogeneous set of shared social experiences in a single location," and explore "the diverse identities that result from being a Pacific person in the many places in which Pacific peoples are now found" (2001b, 13). They also give attention to the "new identity options, and issues" for those who have mixed ancestry (2001b, 14). They and their contributors discover a set of emergent identities among young Pacific Islanders born and raised in New Zealand that cut across but do not elide ethnic categories. For these young people, "Their knowledge and understanding of the worldviews, lifestyles and languages of their ancestral homes will vary greatly as will their commitment to them. Just as their knowledge of their ancestral 'culture' and language varies, so too will their associated identities" (2001b, 13).

All of these circumstances obtain for *chon* Namoluk as well. There are many who have not yet left Chuuk State, and there are some who have yet to visit those islands. The children of *chon* Namoluk on Guam, in Hawai'i, or on the U.S. mainland are learning what it means to be "a Micronesian" or "a Pacific person" in these new settings, and their identities will vary accordingly. The influence of public schools, peer groups, television, and myriad other experiences make their socialization very different from their kin who are still reared on the atoll. Those of mixed ancestry, those who only speak English, those who know little or nothing about Chuukese society and culture must forge new identities in the United States, comparable to what their Pacific Islander counterparts have created in New Zealand. It may come to pass for *chon* Namoluk in the United States, as Macpherson argues it has for Sāmoans and Tongans in New Zealand, that various and divergent identities will result, "in turn nested within an emerging Pacific identity which embodies certain common experiences of growing up as a person of Pacific descent" (2001, 67). Indeed, Anae shows that the "PI" (Pacific Islander) identity is claimed mostly by young, New Zealand–born Pacific Islanders not fluent in a Pacific language, who find that it offers a broader identification than, for example, Tokelauan, and a larger peer group with whom to interact. It seems more likely to me that a "PI" identity might develop among islander youth on the U.S. mainland rather than in Hawai'i or on Guam, but only time will tell.

POINTS OF ENTANGLEMENT

All of this notwithstanding, with only a handful of exceptions discussed in Chapters 5 and 6, Namoluk people remain heavily entangled in one another's lives. They are in regular communication with each other through a variety of different media; when they are far apart, they often go out of their way to arrange face-to-face visits; and if they live near each other, they stop off frequently to chat or eat. Even among the few exceptions to this pattern, only Roxanne has truly "disentangled" from the Namoluk network (see Chapter 6). Other long-timers keep in touch with Namoluk kin and friends, even if they stay away from Wééné and Namoluk for years and years. And, sooner or later, most of these folks return for a visit (e.g., Steemer in Chapter 3 and Kaylee in Chapter 7). Like the huge *apeipei*, "drift logs," carried by currents from Oregon and California to lodge on

Micronesian reefs, these people eventually find their way home to the lagoon of Nomoilam. But they "drift" home on a stretch–737 and a small interisland ship like the *Eekmwar.*

Namoluk people are entangled in each other's lives, regardless of where they are located, but they are also increasingly entangled in the lives of people from elsewhere in the Mortlocks and Chuuk Lagoon. This is an old pattern for the Mortlocks, but much newer for Chuuk proper (see Chapters 2, 7, and 8). As more marriages with people from other communities in Chuuk State occur, and as more people from Chuuk State live near each other and worship together away from Chuuk, these entanglements serve to strengthen more inclusive emergent identities as "Mortlockese" or "Chuukese" (see Chapter 6).

I am always astonished when I speak with *chon* Namoluk on the phone by how quickly news spreads among them. When an adult from the community dies, the "coconut wireless" hums. When someone moves from Guam to Kentucky or Missouri, other community members learn that within days or weeks. Word travels like people: If Ledyard visits Eureka, that becomes known to *chon* Namoluk in Tennessee, on Guam, in Honolulu, and in Portland. Although there is no Namoluk website comparable to the one that Alan Howard (1999) helped establish for Rotumans, *chon* Namoluk now inhabit the same sort of "virtual community" as Rotumans. Of the latter, Howard writes that "it now transcends national boundaries and has become increasingly diffuse," but that "it is a community whose focal point is the island itself, in which membership depends on. . . an interest in Rotuman history, language, and culture. More important, it is a community defined by a common interest in one another's lives by virtue of kinship, marriage, friendship, or shared experience" (1999, 171). Chapters 2–8 above document a similar set of links, processes, and ideas for the Namoluk community, even as it is now dispersed in multiple sites across thousands of miles.

Nearly fifteen years ago, in a widely cited volume, Jocelyn Linnekin and Lin Poyer suggested Westerners' and Pacific Islanders' "views are characterized by fundamentally different theories about the determination of identity," and they proposed "an Oceanic theory of cultural identity that privileges environment, behavior, and situational flexibility over descent, innate characteristics, and unchanging boundaries" (1990b, 6). As an important corollary, they noted of Oceanic groups that "their theories of affiliation consistently emphasize context, situation, performance, and place over biological descent" (1990b, 11). Place rears its head once again. More recently, the literary and cultural studies scholar Rob Wilson, focusing especially on Hawai'i, sought "to understand these localist drives and place-based orientations as part of a complex Pacific and Asian affiliation that does not fully fit the Eurocentric. . . model" (2000, ix). As his book unfolded, he examined "the cultural dynamic, within the Asia-Pacific, to reclaim place and locality as basis of subnational identity" (2000, 104). Place again!

The drum beat about place in the Pacific goes on. In a recent collection it receives particularly eloquent expression from David Welchman Gegeo, the

Solomon Islander scholar. Writing about his home place, Kwara'ae, Malaita, Gegeo delineates nine aspects of place that, taken together, mark indigeneity: "for us, Indigenous encompasses the place from which we see the world, interact with it, and interpret social reality" (2001, 493). Gegeo goes on to distinguish place from space, and he defines the latter as having "to do with the *location* where a Kwara'ae person may be at any given time as necessitated by contemporary conditions (such as going to an urban area to get a job to meet basic needs, or going overseas in pursuit of an education)" (2001, 494; italics in original). From this distinction he argues that "because of the possibility of space, a person can be anywhere and still be inextricably tied to place. Place is portable" (2001, 495). Following Gegeo, I maintain that Namoluk identity also is portable. *Chon* Namoluk may live in a space far from home, but their place-based identity travels there with them. So long as they continue to interact with other community members meaningfully, in the sense of shared interpretations of reality, they remain *chon* Namoluk. But this view of place and identity poses a dilemma.

YOUR PLACE OR MINE?

The dilemma is a consequence of greater out-marriage from the community, which combined with greater residence off-island poses identity conflicts (or options) for the progeny of these marriages. If Mom is from Namoluk, Dad is from Toon, and junior grows up in Kansas City, junior may be more likely to identify as *chon* Chuuk than anything else. Of course, if he was born in the United States, barely speaks Chuukese, and has never visited those islands, he may think of himself as an "American," too. And at age eighteen he could claim American citizenship by virtue of his birthplace (Russell 1993). But the dilemma of place and identity is heightened and literally embodied by those children and young adults born and raised in the United States to a Namoluk mother and an American father.

When I've asked Namoluk people whether or not they consider such children to be *chon* Namoluk, the answer is always an emphatic "Yes." But when I have spoken with these young people about *their* identity, none of them thinks of themselves as "a Namoluk person"; instead, they say they are "Americans." Even though they are aware of their island heritage, and most of them have met a few of their Namoluk relatives in the United States, they have been socialized and enculturated as Americans. None of them speaks and understands Mortlockese, and most of them only know a handful of words, if that. Many of them have never been to Wééné, let alone the atoll (see Chapter 7). Returning to Gegeo's analysis of the links among place, identity, and "indigeneity," these young people lack a crucial component of his definition of place: "place means knowing cultural models, and having a Kwara'ae cultural framework such that even if one is born and raised in another space, on going to Malaita one can quickly make sense of and acquire depth in aspects of Kwara'ae cultural knowledge that one previously did not know" (2001, 494). Although these young people are *genetically* connected to Namoluk's matrilineages via their mother, they are minimally connected to the atoll *socially, culturally, and linguistically.*

We should not be surprised that these children reared far away from Namoluk in a different sociocultural system do not identify as *chon* Namoluk.[7] If we employ the "Oceanic theory of cultural identity" discussed by Linnekin and Poyer (1990b), none of the important Oceanic criteria for theories of affiliation—context, place, situation, performance, and behavior—is met. All that's left is biological descent. What Keith H. Basso calls "sense of place" as a crucial component of personal identity is "locked within the mental horizons of those who give it life," and it "issues in a stream of symbolically drawn particulars—the visible particulars of local topographies, the personal particulars of biographical associations, and the notional particulars of socially given systems of thought" (1996, 144). Without these particulars about Namoluk as a physical place, Namoluk as a kin-community, and Namoluk as one part of a broader Mortlockese or Chuukese culture, people don't think of themselves as *chon* Namoluk.

This issue of place and identity is also manifest in the numerous offspring Namoluk men have produced in the United States, in and out of marriage. In all but one or two cases of divorce that have resulted in a joint custody arrangement, these children have remained with and have been reared by their American mothers. A couple of them have accompanied their fathers to Chuuk for a brief visit, and a few more have met some Namoluk relatives in the States. But the overwhelming majority of these young people—especially those born out of wedlock—have Namoluk genes, but nothing else. They do not identify as *chon* Namoluk and in fact know next to nothing about their father's homeland. But when Namoluk people discuss these children, they think of them as *chon* Namoluk, at least somehow. The rub is in the "somehow." Like the children of mixed marriages with Namoluk mothers discussed above, biological descent provides the only link. And biology is not enough.

A canoe that breaks its moorings and is carried off by wind and current is said to *waapas*, "to drift away." The increased number of marriages and relationships resulting in children between *chon* Namoluk and non-Chuuk State persons has produced a group of people who have drifted away. Potential members of the Namoluk community by virtue of their birth, the great majority of them drift away, instead identifying as Marshallese, American, or something else. In these situations, the anchor that is missing is place. Lacking knowledge of the atoll's physical environment, lacking involvement in ongoing Namoluk relationships, lacking facility in the Mortlockese language, and lacking a "Chuukese cultural framework" by which to understand the world, these young people have no mooring that ties them to the atoll community, let alone Chuuk more broadly construed. And so they drift away: *waasééla*, "drift voyagers."[8]

THE PERSPECTIVE OF FOLKS ON THE SHORE

Nearly twenty years ago, Sherry Ortner wrote that "the attempt to view other systems from ground level is the basis. . . of anthropology's distinctive contribution to the human sciences. It is our capacity, largely developed in fieldwork, to take the perspective of the folks on the shore, that allows us to learn anything at all—even in our own culture—beyond what we already know. . . . Further, it is our location 'on the ground' that puts us in a position to see people not simply as passive reactors to and enactors of some 'system,' but as active agents and subjects in their own history" (1984, 143). This book has been an effort to look at the Namoluk community in this way, presenting as best I can in a "101st account" "the perspective of the folks on the shore." In this case, the shore certainly includes Pieman and Namoluk's other sandy beaches, but Namoluk folks stand on other shores as well. They visit the beach at Newúwé on Wééné. They work and gain perspective on the shore of Guam's hotel-lined Tumon Bay. They swim and picnic at Ala Moana Beach Park in Honolulu. And there are many shores on the U.S. mainland, even including some where Pacific Islanders meet the Atlantic Ocean. No matter what shore they stand on, *chon* Namoluk are active agents in their own unfolding history.

Namoluk people today form part of what Marshall Sahlins calls a "translocal community": "symbolically focused on the homeland, whence its members derive their identity and their destiny, the translocal community is strategically dependent on its urban outliers for material wherewithal. The rural order extends itself into the city, inasmuch as the migrant folk are transitively associated with each other on the bases of their relationships at home" (1999, xix). But unlike many other translocal Pacific Islander communities in the United States, New Zealand, or Australia (e.g., the Tongans and Sāmoans, whom Sahlins clearly has in mind), *chon* Namoluk do not send large remittances home on a regular basis. In this respect they more resemble migrants from the RMI who also settled in the USA following the Compact of Free Association in 1986 (Hess et al. 2001). The main reason for a lack of remittances is the high cost of living in places like Hawai'i and California, and the same applies to Guam. By the time they've paid rent, bought food, purchased gasoline for their car, covered their utility bills, picked up some occasional new clothes, and saved a modest amount for recreation, there's nothing left for the migrants to send home. This is doubly so for those who are employed in the "unheralded, largely forgotten jobs" discussed in Chapter 6.

For centuries Westerners have romanticized and imagined Pacific Islands as "paradise," and images of paradise have been exploited to market destinations like Hawai'i, Tahiti, and Fiji to wealthy tourists from First World countries. Although Chuuk only recently appeared on tourist maps, Micronesian islands conform to the Western myth of paradise: palm trees, sandy beaches, warm breezes, dazzling coral reefs swarming with polychrome fish, and friendly people. As such images are marketed to potential visitors, those visitors often fail to comprehend why any islander would want to move away from paradise on earth. But island peoples have their own reasons and their own myths.

This became clear as I chatted with Lindsey one afternoon inside a neighborhood store near his modern home on Wééné. I mused about why *chon* Namoluk seemed so attracted to places beyond the reef, and he didn't hesitate a moment in providing a response: "We think of Guam, Hawai'i, and the mainland as cleaner and more beautiful than Chuuk. We think of them as paradise, just as *re-won*, "foreigners," think of our islands as paradise." Dreams of cleanliness, beauty, opportunity, excitement, adventure—dreams of paradise—continue to pull Namoluk people beyond the reef toward an unknown future. As *chon* Namoluk make themselves and their own history through these twenty-first century journeys, they indulge in an ancient Micronesian curiosity to explore what lies over the horizon. And who knows? Maybe they'll actually find paradise there.

CODA

Who are you? Where are you from? In spite of the recent academic maelstrom over globalization, transnationalism, deterritorialization, postcommunities, and the like, for the overwhelming majority of the world's inhabitants the fundamental link between answers to these two questions remains basic to their sense of self and how they live their lives. People still identify themselves and think of themselves as attached to places, emotionally and imaginatively, if not always physically. But people also adopt new locales as their own—what I've called "colonizing" in Chapters 1 and 3—as their personal biography is woven into new places (see Chapter 8). Of course, adopting new locales as their own is something *chon* Namoluk and other Carolinian atoll dwellers have always done, as the discussion about "Points of Origin" earlier in this chapter makes clear. Atoll communities have what might be called an "absorptive quality," taking in new members via several possible means.

As Namoluk people have moved to new homes in new lands, they've retained a certainty about who they are and where they're from, but they've also carried with them a flexibility and openness. This has aided them in developing broader, more inclusive identities as warranted, identities such as "Mortlockese," "Chuukese," "Micronesian," "Pacific Islander," or even for a very few "American." These nested identities in varied circumstances are not mutually exclusive or incompatible with each other, and they have implications for all of us who live in an increasingly fluid and interconnected world. They underscore the point that while our identities may shift over our lifetime, or according to where we live, few, if any, of us are "rootless."

My own case may serve as an example: my father immigrated to America from the United Kingdom, so I have a "Scottish" component to my personal identity to mix with the English, Scottish, and French "blood" from my mother's side. At a distant remove, these countries—especially Scotland—form a part of my idea of who I am. Born and reared (mostly) in the United States, I'm an "American" by birth and citizenship. Born in San Francisco, I'm a "Californian," and that's the place where I own property and intend to retire. Within the United States, my parents' families settled in Indiana and Illinois, and these were places we visited regularly as I grew up, to see grandparents, aunts, uncles, cousins, and other acquaintances. I went to college in Iowa and returned to Iowa after graduate school, where I've taught for thirty-one years, so the Hawkeye State is a part of me too. Thus I have multiple "Midwestern" roots. At age eight I moved with my family to Hawai'i, where my family put down mangrove-like roots: "even though right now none of us actually resides in the islands, Hawai'i is my family's emotional home. Our roots in Hawai'i's lateritic soil nourished my childhood love affair with islands until that affair sprouted in college and eventually grew into a career that carried me much farther into the Pacific" (Marshall, in press). So my identity is linked to multiple places: Scotland, the United States, the Midwest, California, and Hawai'i. Each of these places means something special to me; I've visited all of them and have lived in all of them but Scotland. So how does this relate to Namoluk people "beyond the reef?"

The ways Namoluk people historically have absorbed new members into their community, and the ways that today they take on new identities in new places, all illustrate what Harri Englund calls "emplacement": "Rather than heralding a return to place-bound ethnography, emplacement provides a perspective in which current analytical insights into a global space are enhanced by the postglobalist realization that globalism itself hinges on specific circumstances. A key analytical consequence is the realization that the widespread ethnographic doubt about local-global distinctions may indicate the futility of disconnecting culture from place. Emplacement defines the human condition in which globalism has its permutations" (2002, 276). Edward Bruner (1999, 475) comments that Batak village members identify themselves as such, even in cases where they were born elsewhere and have never actually been to the village. Helen Morton (2002) emphasizes that diasporic Tongans still identify as having ties to Tonga as a cultural island home. I suggest that these Batak and Tongan connections are similar to my own felt connection to Scotland as a place: distant but definite. Like Pukueu, we humans will continue to move about, to relocate, to seek the satisfaction of "opening up those dark seas." As we do so, our canoes will be launched from known points of departure—from a home—and these home places, wherever they may be, will continue to hold us "in the grip of a shared identity." People are no longer bound to places, but they are still bound up in them.

Notes

1. "No man is an island, entire of itself" (Donne 1624, *Devotions* XVII).

2. Guest lectures by Watson were sponsored by the Center for Asian and Pacific Studies at the University of Iowa during November 2002. On November 12th he spoke on "Tracking a post-modern diaspora: The Man lineage in Hong Kong, London, and beyond."

3. Only if such children took up long-term residence on Namoluk or met some of the other criteria for Namoluk citizenship to be discussed would they become *chon* Namoluk.

4. Goodenough (1951) called people counted among a lineage's members who were neither born nor adopted into it as children "client members," and this language has been adopted by other anthropologists who've worked in Chuuk State. For more information about clientship, see Marshall (1977).

5. This is an identity that also is used on Pohnpei and throughout Pohnpei State as a consequence of the now-sizeable Mortlockese community that first was established there during the German colonial period following a severe typhoon that struck the Lower Mortlocks in 1907. The Germans relocated several hundred people to Pohnpei who otherwise would likely have perished for want of food and water, and these people eventually acquired land rights in Sokehs.

6. When I was fourteen years old, my family and I moved from Hawai'i to Michigan. Soon thereafter we drove through Indiana, headed for my mother's hometown in southern Indiana for a family reunion. En route we stopped at a gas station in a small town, and the attendant kept looking at the Hawai'i plates on our car, and then at us. Finally, he screwed up his courage and asked my father, "Where's that there aloha Hawaya?" That was two years before statehood and many years before *Hawai'i-Five-O*.

7. There are, of course, "in-between" cases. In one, the children of a Namoluk man who lives on Pohnpei have visited the atoll nearly every summer, and they understand Mortlockese quite well. They identify with Kosrae, their mother's island, but they are definitely aware of their ties to Namoluk and are familiar with the place and its people. In another, the daughter of an American man and a Namoluk woman grew up in Yap, raised by her mother and her Yapese stepfather. She, too, speaks a modicum of Mortlockese and is acquainted with her Namoluk kin, but when I asked her how she self-identifies, without hesitation she said, "Yapese."

8. Although it is not about contemporary travelers, Goodenough (1988) has published a poem by this title, written in both Chuukese and English.

Glossary

afakúr
    descendants of the men of a matrilineage or matriclan.

afakúran eu ainang
    co-descendants of one matrilineage or matriclan.

ainang
    clan.

akkapwas
    a shout used to announce the presence of a canoe, ship, or airplane, similar to "Sail ho!" Also a shout indicating anger, often uttered by intoxicated men.

alillis ffengen
    cooperate (literally, "help together").

aluel
    young man approximately between the ages of fifteen and thirty-five.

amoleset
    a beach strand tree that may grow to 10 meters in height; *Tournefortia argentea L.*

angarap
    skipjack tuna, called *aku* in Hawaiian.

apeipei
    drift log.

asipwar
    nephew.

benunu
    the soft, gelatinous flesh found inside the kernel of green or drinking coconuts.

bwang
    an indigenous martial arts tradition of the Caroline Islands.

chielap
    an elderly person.

chin
    one of two traditional alliances in the Mortlock Islands, including Kuttu, Lukunoch, Satawan, and Ta.

chon	person or citizen of.
fáál	canoe house.
fanu	dry land; also used in reference to an island.
holokū	a Hawaiian dress, like a long, fitted *mu'umu'u*.
ichich	a jack fish.
kansopa	a copra-drying oven.
katekista	a catechist in the Catholic Church (a lay leader).
kul	a beach strand tree with many uses; *Barringtonia asiatica* (L.) Kurz.
likapich	spearfishing.
likeriker	long-nosed butterfly fish.
mae	stone fish weir built into the reef flat.
makal	atoll chief.
marau	one of two traditional alliances in the Mortlock Islands, including Ettal, Moch, Namoluk, and Oneop.
mataw	open sea; deep ocean beyond the reef.
mei	breadfruit tree; breadfruit.
meyi iwi	greasy, oily.
mon	a species of reef fish.
Morschlok	Mortlocks, the Mortlock Islands.
mosoro	cookhouse.
muuti	to adopt.
mwáán	an adult man, typically over age thirty-five.
mwaramwar	a lei; a garland of flowers and other sweet-smelling things.
mwéngé	food; to eat; also used in reference to land and related resources that can be used to produce food.
ngel	a big game fish called wahoo in English and *ono* in Hawaiian.
nom	lagoon.

nóó popo	a large, rounded ocean swell or wave; literally, "pregnant wave."
nu	a coconut palm; a coconut.
palu	navigator.
póllai	yellowtail.
pwá	a swarming, circling dense flock of seabirds feeding on minnows; used by fishermen to locate schools of tuna and other game fish.
pwiipwi	created sibling; friend.
pwól	taro swamp; taro plot.
rewon	non-Micronesian foreigner.
samol an ainang	traditional clan chief.
serau	barracuda.
set	named, owned sections of the reef flat.
takou	yellowfin tuna, called *ahi* in Hawaiian.
tetel en aramas	descent line; literally, "a line of people."
til	minnows; small fry.
tipeuo ffengen	agree, be of one mind; literally, "agree together."
tola	all [the rest].
ttong	love; pity.
tumwunuu ffengen	take care of or look after one another; literally, "nurture together."
waafatil	paddling canoe.
waapas	to drift away.
waasééla	drift voyager.
waaserik	sailing canoe; open-ocean voyaging canoe.
yiis	alcoholic home brew produced from baker's yeast, sugar, and water.

Suggestions for Further Reading

A number of recent books examine contemporary Oceanic societies, particularly as they are engaged and intertwined with such places as Australia, New Zealand, and the United States. In this regard, see Vicente M. Diaz and J. Kēhaulani Kauanui (2001); Cluny MacPherson, Paul Spoonley, and Melani Anae (2001); and Paul Spickard, Joanne L. Rondilla, and Debbie Wright (2002), all of which are cited in the reference list. In addition, the following three volumes are highly informative: David Hanlon and Geoffrey M. White, eds. (2000), *Voyaging Through the Contemporary Pacific* (Lanham, Md.: Rowman & Littlefield); Victoria S. Lockwood, Thomas G. Harding, and Ben J. Wallace, eds. (1993), *Contemporary Pacific Societies: Studies in Development and Change* (Englewood Cliffs, N.J.: Prentice-Hall); and Victoria S. Lockwood, ed. (2004), *Globalization and Culture Change in the Pacific Islands* (Englewood Cliffs, N.J.: Prentice-Hall).

There are several good overviews of the contemporary situation in Micronesia from the perspectives of both anthropology and history. Volumes by David Hanlon (1998) and Francis X. Hezel (2001) are cited in the reference list. To these must be added an anthropological stock-taking of post–World War II research in Micronesia: Robert C. Kiste and Mac Marshall, eds. (1999), *American Anthropology in Micronesia: An Assessment* (Honolulu: University of Hawai'i Press).

Finally, there are two good case studies of Pacific Islander migrants to the United States. The first is a study of Sāmoans in California—Craig R. Janes (1990), *Migration, Social Change, and Health: A Samoan Community in Urban California* (Stanford: Stanford University Press)—and the second is a study of Tongans in the United States—Cathy A. Small (1997), *Voyages: From Tongan Villages to American Suburbs* (Ithaca, N.Y.: Cornell University Press).

References

Allen, Linda. 2002. Maintaining Marshallese fundamentals with Christian fundamentalism. In *Constructing Moral Communities: Pacific Islander Strategies for Settling in New Places*, ed. Judith S. Modell. Special Issue of *Pacific Studies* 25(1&2):95–116.

Anae, Melani. 2001. The new "Vikings of the sunrise": New Zealand-borns in the information age. In *Tangata O Te Moana Nui: The Evolving Identities of Pacific Peoples in Aotearoa/New Zealand*, eds. Cluny Macpherson, Paul Spoonley, and Melani Anae. pp. 101–121. Palmerston North, New Zealand: Dunmore Press.

Anderson, Benedict. 1983. *Imagined Communities: Reflections on the Origin and Spread of Nationalism*. London: Verso.

Appadurai, Arjun. 1988. Introduction: Place and voice in anthropological theory. *Cultural Anthropology* 3(1):16–20.

Ashby, Gene, and Giff Johnson. 2001. Internet explosion in FSM, Marshalls. *Pacific Magazine* 26(1):27.

Basso, Keith H. 1996. *Wisdom Sits in Places: Landscape and Language Among the Western Apache*. Albuquerque: University of New Mexico Press.

Bedford, Richard, and Robert Didham. 2001. Who are the "Pacific peoples"? Ethnic identification and the New Zealand census. In *Tangata O Te Moana Nui: The Evolving Identities of Pacific Peoples in Aotearoa/New Zealand*, eds. Cluny Macpherson, Paul Spoonley, and Melani Anae. pp. 21–43. Palmerston North, New Zealand: Dunmore Press.

Brady, Ivan A., ed. 1976. *Transactions in Kinship: Adoption and Fosterage in Oceania*. ASAO Monograph No. 4. Honolulu: University Press of Hawai'i.

Brooke, James. 2003. Guam, hurt by slump, hopes for economic help from military. *The New York Times* 10 March:A14.

Bruner, Edward M. 1999. Return to Sumatra: 1957, 1997. *American Ethnologist* 26(2):461–477.

Carroll, Vern, ed. 1970. *Adoption in Eastern Oceania*. ASAO Monograph No. 1. Honolulu: University of Hawai'i Press.

Cheyne, Andrew. 1852. *A Description of Islands in the Western Pacific Ocean.* . . . London: J. D. Potter.

Clifford, James. 2001. Indigenous articulations. In *Native Pacific Cultural Studies on the Edge,* eds. Vicente M. Diaz and J. Kēhaulani Kauanui. Special Issue of *The Contemporary Pacific: A Journal of Island Affairs* 13(2):468–490.

Cook, Len, Robert Didham, and Mansoor Khawaja. 2001. The shape of the future: On the demography of Pacific people. In *Tangata O Te Moana Nui: The Evolving Identities of Pacific Peoples in Aotearoa/New Zealand,* eds. Cluny Macpherson, Paul Spoonley, and Melani Anae. pp. 44–65. Palmerston North, New Zealand: Dunmore Press.

Davis, George. 1959. *Truk Agricultural Information Booklet.* Moen, Truk, Eastern Caroline Islands: Department of Agriculture.

Day, A. Grove. 1966. *Explorers of the Pacific.* New York: Duell, Sloan and Pearce.

Diaz, Vicente M., and J. Kēhaulani Kauanui, eds. 2001. *Native Pacific Cultural Studies on the Edge.* Special Issue of *The Contemporary Pacific: A Journal of Island Affairs* 13(2).

Doane, E. T. 1874. The Caroline Islands. *The Geographical Magazine* pp. 203–205. [Manuscript examined at the Gregg Sinclair Library, University of Hawai'i–Mānoa.]

Dobbin, Jay, and Francis X. Hezel, eds. 1996. Micronesian migration since World War II. In *The Micronesian Counselor* Series 2, Number 2. Pohnpei: The Micronesian Seminar.

Englund, Harri. 2002. Ethnography after globalism: Migration and emplacement in Malawi. *American Ethnologist* 29(2):261–286.

Fink, Deborah. 1998. *Cutting into the Meatpacking Line: Workers and Change in the Rural Midwest.* Chapel Hill, N.C.: University of North Carolina Press.

Finney, Ben R. 1979. *Hōkūle'a: The Way to Tahiti.* New York: Dodd, Mead.

FSM [Federated States of Micronesia]. 1996. *1994 FSM Census of Population and Housing. National Detailed Tables.* Palikir, Pohnpei: Office of Planning and Statistics, FSM National Government.

Geertz, Clifford. 2000. The uses of diversity. In *Available Light: Anthropological Reflections on Philosophical Topics,* by Clifford Geertz. pp. 68–88. Princeton: Princeton University Press.

Gegeo, David Welchman. 2001. Cultural rupture and indigeneity: The challenge of (re)visioning "place" in the Pacific. In *Native Pacific Cultural Studies on the Edge,* eds. Vicente M. Diaz and J. Kēhaulani Kauanui. Special Issue of *The Contemporary Pacific: A Journal of Island Affairs* 13(2):491–507.

Girschner, Max. 1912. Die Karolineninsul Namoluk und ihre Bewohner. *Baessler-Archiv* 2:123–215.

Gladwin, Thomas. 1970. *East Is a Big Bird: Navigation and Logic on Puluwat Atoll.* Cambridge, Mass.: Harvard University Press.

Goodenough, Ward H. 1951. *Property, Kin, and Community on Truk.* Yale University Publications in Anthropology Number 46. New Haven: Yale University Press.

———. 1988. *Waasééna* "Drift Voyager." *Anthropology and Humanism Quarterly* 13(1):26–27.

————. 2002. *Under Heaven's Brow: Pre-Christian Religious Tradition in Chuuk.* Memoirs of the American Philosophical Society Volume 246. Philadelphia: American Philosophical Society.

Goodenough, Ward H., and Hiroshi Sugita. 1980. *Trukese-English Dictionary.* Memoirs of the American Philosophical Society Volume 141. Philadelphia: American Philosophical Society.

Gorenflo, Larry J. 1995. Regional demographic change in Chuuk State, Federated States of Micronesia. *Pacific Studies* 18(3):47–118.

Greenhouse, Steven. 2002. Where hands still labor. *The New York Times* 1 September:3.

Gudde, Erwin G. 1969. *California Place Names. The Origin and Etymology of Current Geographical Names.* 3rd ed. Berkeley: University of California Press.

Gulick, Reverend Luther H. 1862. Micronesia—of the Pacific Ocean. *The Nautical Magazine and Naval Chronicle* 31:169–182, 237–245, 298–308, 358–363, 408–417.

Gupta, Akhil, and James Ferguson. 1997a. Beyond "culture": Space, identity, and the politics of difference. In *Culture, Power, Place: Explorations in Critical Anthropology,* eds. Akhil Gupta and James Ferguson. pp. 33–51. Durham, N.C.: Duke University Press.

————. 1997b. Discipline and practice: "The field" as site, method, and location in anthropology. In *Anthropological Locations: Boundaries and Grounds of a Field Science,* eds. Akhil Gupta and James Ferguson. pp. 1–46. Berkeley: University of California Press.

Hanlon, David. 1998. *Remaking Micronesia: Discourses over Development in a Pacific Territory 1944–1982.* Honolulu: University of Hawai'i Press.

Hess, Jim, Karen L. Nero, and Michael L. Burton. 2001. Creating options: Forming a Marshallese community in Orange County, California. *The Contemporary Pacific: A Journal of Island Affairs* 13(1):89–121.

Hezel, Francis X. 1973. The beginnings of foreign contact with Truk. *Journal of Pacific History* 8:51–73.

————. 1979. The education explosion in Truk. *Pacific Studies* 2(2):167–185.

————. 1983. *The First Taint of Civilization: A History of the Caroline and Marshall Islands in Pre-Colonial Days, 1521–1885.* Pacific Islands Monograph Series 1. Honolulu: University of Hawai'i Press.

————. 1991. *The Catholic Church in Micronesia: Historical Essays on the Catholic Church in the Caroline-Marshall Islands.* Chicago: Loyola University Press.

————. 1995. *Strangers in Their Own Land: A Century of Colonial Rule in the Caroline and Marshall Islands.* Pacific Islands Monograph Series 13. Honolulu: University of Hawai'i Press.

————. 2001. *The New Shape of Old Island Cultures: A Half Century of Social Change in Micronesia.* Honolulu: University of Hawai'i Press.

————. 2003. Rough seas ahead: The FSM economy during Compact II. *Micronesian Counselor* Issue 44. Pohnpei: Micronesian Seminar.

Hezel, Francis X., and Michael J. Levin. 1996. New trends in Micronesian migration: FSM migration to Guam and the Marianas, 1990–1993. *Pacific Studies* 19(1):91–114.

Hezel, Francis X., and Thomas B. McGrath. 1989. The great flight northward: FSM migration to Guam and the Northern Mariana Islands. *Pacific Studies* 13(1):47–64.

Howard, Alan. 1999. Pacific-based virtual communities: Rotuma on the World Wide Web. *The Contemporary Pacific: A Journal of Island Affairs* 11(1):160–175.

Howard, Alan, and Jan Rensel. 2001. Where has Rotuman culture gone? And what is it doing there? *Pacific Studies* 24(1&2):63–88.

Janes, Craig. 1990. *Migration, Social Change, and Health: A Samoan Community in Urban California.* Stanford: Stanford University Press.

Jervis, Lori L. 2001. The pollution of incontinence and the dirty work of caregiving in a U.S. nursing home. *Medical Anthropology Quarterly* 15(1):84–99.

Jorgensen, Joseph G. 1990. *Oil Age Eskimos.* Berkeley: University of California Press.

Kohl, Manfred Waldemar. 1971. *Lagoon in the Pacific: The Story of Truk.* Schooley's Mountain, N.J.: Liebenzell Mission U.S.A.

Krämer, A. 1935. Inseln um Truk. (Zentralkarolinen Ost, Lukunor, Namoluk, Losap, Nama, Lemarafat, Namonuito, Pollap-Tamatam). In *Ergebnisse der Südsee-Expedition, 1908–1910,* ed. G. Thilenius. Series 2, Volume 6. Hamburg: Friederichsen, DeGruyter & Co.

Kubary, Jan S. 1880. Die Bewohner der Mortlock-Inseln. *Geographischen Gesellschaft in Hamburg. Mitteilungen* 1878–1879:224–299.

Lal, Brij V. in press. Introduction: Place and person. In *Pacific Places, Pacific History: Essays in Honour of Robert C. Kiste,* ed. Brij V. Lal. Honolulu: University of Hawai'i Press.

Larson, Robert Bruce. 1989. Sojourning and personhood: College students return to Truk, Federated States of Micronesia. Ph.D. dissertation, University of Hawai'i.

Lessa, William A. 1964. The social effects of Typhoon Ophelia (1960) on Ulithi. *Micronesica* 1:1–48.

Lessa, William A., and Carlos G. Velez-I. 1978. *Bwang,* a martial art of the Caroline Islands. *Micronesica* 14(2):139–176.

Linnekin, Jocelyn, and Lin Poyer, eds. 1990a. *Cultural Identity and Ethnicity in the Pacific.* Honolulu: University of Hawai'i Press.

———. 1990b. Introduction. In *Cultural Identity and Ethnicity in the Pacific.* pp. 1–16. Honolulu: University of Hawai'i Press.

Lütke, Par Frédéric. 1835. *Voyage Autour Du Monde, Exécuté par Ordre De Sa Majesté L'Empereur Nicholas Ier, Sue la Corvette Le Séniavine dans les années 1826, 1827, 1828 et 1829.* Vol. 2. Paris: Didot Freres.

Macpherson, Cluny. 2001. One trunk sends out many branches: Pacific cultures and cultural identities. In *Tangata O Te Moana Nui: The Evolving Identities of Pacific Peoples in Aotearoa/New Zealand,* eds. Cluny Macpherson, Paul Spoonley, and Melani Anae. pp. 66–80. Palmerston North, New Zealand: Dunmore Press.

Macpherson, Cluny, Paul Spoonley, and Melani Anae, eds. 2001a. *Tangata O Te Moana Nui: The Evolving Identities of Pacific Peoples in Aotearoa/New Zealand.* Palmerston North, New Zealand: Dunmore Press.

———. 2001b. Pacific peoples in Aotearoa: An introduction. In *Tangata O Te Moana Nui: The Evolving Identities of Pacific Peoples in Aotearoa/New Zealand,* eds. Cluny Macpherson, Paul Spoonley, and Melani Anae. pp. 11–15. Palmerston North, New Zealand: Dunmore Press.

Manchester, Curtis A., Jr. 1951. The Caroline Islands. In *Geography of the Pacific,* ed. Otis W. Freeman. pp. 236-269. New York: Wiley.

Marcus, George E. 1998. Ethnography in/of the world system: The emergence of multi-sited ethnography. In *Ethnography Through Thick and Thin,* by George E. Marcus. pp. 79–104. Princeton: Princeton University Press.

Marshall, Mac [Keith]. 1972. The structure of solidarity and alliance on Namoluk Atoll. Ph.D. dissertation, University of Washington.

———. 1975a. Changing patterns of marriage and migration on Namoluk Atoll. In *Pacific Atoll Populations,* ed. Vern Carroll. ASAO Monograph Number 3. pp. 160–211. Honolulu: University Press of Hawai'i.

———. 1975b. The politics of prohibition on Namoluk Atoll. *Journal of Studies on Alcohol* 36(5):597–610.

———. 1976. Solidarity or sterility? Adoption and fosterage on Namoluk Atoll. In *Transactions in Kinship: Adoption and Fosterage in Oceania,* ed. Ivan Brady. ASAO Monograph Number 4. pp. 28–50. Honolulu: University Press of Hawai'i.

———. 1977. The nature of nurture. *American Ethnologist* 4(4):643–662.

———. 1979a. *Weekend Warriors: Alcohol in a Micronesian Culture.* Explorations in World Ethnology Series. Palo Alto, Calif.: Mayfield Publishing.

———. 1979b. Natural and unnatural disaster in the Mortlock Islands of Micronesia. *Human Organization* 38(3):265–272.

———. 1981. Sibling sets as building blocks in Greater Trukese Society. In *Siblingship in Oceania: Studies in the Meaning of Kin Relations,* ed. Mac Marshall. ASAO Monograph Number 8. pp. 201–224. Ann Arbor: University of Michigan Press.

———. 1990a. Two tales from the Trukese taproom. In *The Humbled Anthropologist: Tales from the Pacific,* ed. Philip DeVita. pp. 12–17. Belmont, Calif.: Wadsworth Publishing.

———. 1990b. Combining insights from epidemiological and ethnographic data to investigate substance use in Truk, Federated States of Micronesia. *British Journal of Addiction* 85:1457–1468.

———. 1990c. "Problem deflation" and the ethnographic record: Interpretation and introspection in anthropological studies of alcohol. *Journal of Substance Abuse* 2(3):353–367.

———. 1996. *Chon* Guamoluk: Namoluk people on Guam, 1995. Paper presented at the 25th Annual Meeting of the Association for Social Anthropology in Oceania, 7–11 February, Kailua-Kona, Hawai'i. [An abbreviated version of this paper appeared in Dobbin and Hezel (1996:33–36).]

———. 1999. "Partial connections": Kinship and social organization in Micronesia. In *American Anthropology in Micronesia: An Assessment,* eds. Robert C. Kiste and Mac Marshall. pp. 107–143. Honolulu: University of Hawai'i Press.

————. in press. Imagining islands. In *Pacific Places, Pacific History: Essays in Honour of Robert C. Kiste*, ed. Brij V. Lal. Honolulu: University of Hawai'i Press.

Marshall, Mac, and Leslie B. Marshall. 1990. *Silent Voices Speak: Women and Prohibition in Truk*. Belmont, Calif.: Wadsworth Publishing.

Marshall, Mac, and Mark Borthwick. 1974. Consensus, dissensus, and Guttman scales: The Namoluk case. *Journal of Anthropological Research* 30(4):252–270.

Marshall, Mac, Larry Gabriel, and Joakim Manniwel Peter. 1998. Chuuk. In *Australia and the Pacific Islands*, eds. Adrienne L. Kaeppler and J. W. Love. The Garland Encyclopedia of World Music Volume 9. pp. 733–737. New York: Garland Publishing.

Mayo, Larry W. 1992. The militarization of Guamanian society. In *Social Change in the Pacific Islands*, ed. Albert B. Robillard. pp. 220–240. London: Kegan Paul International.

Missionary Herald. (A periodical published by the American Board of Commissioners for Foreign Missions, Cambridge, Mass.: The Riverside Press.).

————. 1876. Letters from the missions. Micronesia Mission. 72(10):308–311.

————. 1879. Letters from the missions. Micronesia Mission. 75(6):216–221.

————. 1880a. Letters from the missions. Micronesia Mission. 76(5):175–178.

————. 1880b. Letters from the missions. Micronesia Mission. 76(7):264–265.

————. 1881a. Letters from the missions. Micronesia Mission. 77(1):16–19.

————. 1881b. Letters from the missions. Micronesia Mission. 77(7):269–272.

————. 1882. Letters from the missions. Micronesia Mission. 78(6):220–222.

————. 1886a. Letters from the missions. Micronesia Mission. 82(8):308–311.

————. 1886b. A visit to Micronesia (by Charles H. Wetmore, M.D.). 82(9):333–339.

————. 1888. Letters from the missions. Micronesia Mission. 84(7):300–304.

————. 1891. Letters from the missions. Micronesia Mission. 87(9):369–372.

————. 1901. Letters from the missions. Micronesia Mission. 97(9):413–416.

————. 1903. Letters from the missions. Micronesia Mission. 99(4):157–159.

Moore, Henrietta L. 1999. Anthropological theory at the turn of the century. In *Anthropological Theory Today*, ed. Henrietta L. Moore. pp. 1–23. Cambridge: Polity Press.

Morrell, Captain Benjamin. 1832. *A Narrative of Four Voyages to the South Sea, North and South Pacific Oceans, Chinese Sea, Ethiopic and Southern Atlantic Ocean, Indian and Antarctic Ocean from the Year 1822 to 1831*. New York: J & J Harper.

Morton, Helen. 2002. Creating their own culture: Diasporic Tongans. In *Pacific Diaspora: Island Peoples in the United States and Across the Pacific*, eds. Paul Spickard, Joanne L. Rondilla, and Debbie Hippolite Wright. pp. 135–149. Honolulu: University of Hawai'i Press.

Namoluk Constitution. 1991. *Muun Namoluk, Chuuk State, Federated States of Micronesia. Aewan Chulapan Alluk noun Muun Namoluk*. Namoluk Constitutional Convention, 9 December 1991.

Nason, James D. 1970. Clan and copra: Modernization on Etal Island, Eastern Caroline Islands. Ph.D. dissertation, University of Washington.

Ortner, Sherry B. 1984. Theory in anthropology since the sixties. *Comparative Study of Society and History* 26(1):126–166.

Pelto, Pertti J. 1973. *The Snowmobile Revolution: Technology and Social Change in the Arctic.* Menlo Park, Calif.: Cummings Publishing.

Peter, Joakim. 2000. Chuukese travellers and the idea of horizon. *Asia Pacific Viewpoint* 41(3):253–267.

Quackenbush, Edward M. 1968. From Sonsorol to Truk: A dialect chain. Ph.D. dissertation, University of Michigan, Ann Arbor.

Reuney, Theophil Saret. 1994. The pulling of Olap's canoe. *Boundary 2: An International Journal of Literature and Culture* 21(1):254–258.

Richards, Dorothy E. 1957. *United States Naval Administration of the Trust Territory of the Pacific Islands* Volume 2. Washington, D.C.: Office of the Chief of Naval Operations.

Riesenberg, Saul H. 1965. Table of voyages affecting Micronesian islands. *Oceania* 36:155–170.

Roche, Walter F., Jr. 2003. Marshall Islands agrees to set regulations for "body brokers." *Orlando Sentinel* 3 April. http://www.orlandosentinel.com/news/nationworld/orl-asecbrokers03040303apr03,0,3046972.story?coll+orl%2Dhome%2Dheadlines.

Roche, Walter F., Jr., and Willoughby Mariano. 2002a. Indentured in America: A ray of hope in Springdale. A series in the *Baltimore Sun* and *Orlando Sentinel* 15–17 September. http://pidp.eastwestcenter.org/pireport/2002/September/09–19–02.htm.

———. 2002b. Indentured in America: Trapped in servitude far from their homes. A series in the *Baltimore Sun* and *Orlando Sentinel* 15–17 September. http://www.sunspot.net/bal-te.indent15sep15story.

Rodman, Margaret C. 1992. Empowering place: Multilocality and multivocality. *American Anthropologist* 94(3):640–656.

Rogers, Robert F. 1995. *Destiny's Landfall: A History of Guam.* Honolulu: University of Hawai'i Press.

Ruben, Kino S. 1973. [No title.] In *Micronesia: Island Wilderness,* by Kenneth Brower; photographs and an introduction by Robert Wenkam. New York: Seabury Press for Friends of the Earth, San Francisco.

Russell, Alison. 1993. Born in the U.S.A. *Guam Business News* 11(5):20–22, 24, 26, 28, 30.

Sahlins, Marshall D. 1999. What is anthropological enlightenment? Some lessons of the twentieth century. *Annual Review of Anthropology* 28:i–xxiii.

Schlosser, Eric. 2002. *Fast Food Nation. The Dark Side of the All-American Meal.* New York: Perennial/HarperCollins.

Schneider, David M. 1968. *American Kinship: A Cultural Account.* Englewood Cliffs, N.J.: Prentice-Hall.

Sharp, Andrew. 1960. *The Discovery of the Pacific Islands.* Oxford: Clarendon Press.

Slusser, R. C., and R. E. Hughes. 1970. Letters and photocopies of printed information relating to Typhoon Phyllis, 1958, on file at the Joint Typhoon Warning Center, U.S. Fleet Weather Central, Guam.

Spickard, Paul, Joanne L. Rondilla, and Debbie Hippolite Wright, eds. 2002. *Pacific Diaspora: Island Peoples in the United States and Across the Pacific.* Honolulu: University of Hawai'i Press.

Ulin, Robert C. 2001. *Understanding Cultures: Perspectives in Anthropology and Social Theory.* 2nd ed. Oxford: Blackwell Publishers.

Ward, R. Gerard, ed. 1967. *American Activities in the Central Pacific, 1790–1870* Volume 5. Ridgewood, N.J.: Gregg Press.

Warner Pacific College. 2001. *Warner Pacific College 2001–2002 Catalog.* Portland, Oreg.: Warner Pacific College.

Watson, James L., ed. 1997. *Golden Arches East: McDonald's in East Asia.* Stanford: Stanford University Press.

———. 2000. China's Big Mac attack. *Foreign Affairs* 79(3):120–134.

———. 2002. Globalization and culture. *Encyclopedia Britannica.* revised 15th ed. pp. 133–137.

Wendel, John. 1998. That all may be one: Negotiating personhood and modernity at a boarding school in Micronesia. Ph.D. dissertation, University of Rochester.

Wolf, Margery. 1992. *A Thrice Told Tale: Feminism, Postmodernism, and Ethnographic Responsibility.* Stanford: Stanford University Press.

WHO [World Health Organization]. 2001. *Mid-level and Nurse Practitioners in the Pacific: Models and Issues.* Manila: World Health Organization, Western Pacific Region.

Wilson, Rob. 2000. *Reimagining the American Pacific: From South Pacific to Bamboo Ridge and Beyond.* Durham, N.C.: Duke University Press.

Index

Adoption, 14, 36, 39, 41 (n19), 52, 121,
    135–136, 146 (n4), 148
Africa, 134
Agriculture/Agriculture
    Department/agricultural agent,
    26–27, 34, 47, 69
Airfield/airport/airstrip, 3, 25, 43, 50, 68,
    77–78, 90, 116, 125–126
Aircraft/airplane/jet, 25, 34, 43, 47, 55, 58,
    73, 77–79, 98, 122, 126, 140, 147
Akin, David, xv
Ala Moana Beach Park, 143
Alabama, 109, 138
Alaska, 134
Alcohol/alcoholic beverages, 32, 57–58, 60
    (n14), 149
    beer, 55, 57–58, 84
    drinking/drunkenness/inebriated/intoxi
    cated, 32, 57–58, 60 (n13, n15), 85,
    111, 118, 147
    vodka, 20
    yeast, 33, 57, 149
Allen, Linda, 96
America. *See* United States of America
American/Americans, 5, 8, 21, 25, 27, 32,
    34, 39–40 (n11), 44, 50–51, 54, 56, 58,
    76, 81, 85–86, 91, 93, 99–103 (n1),
    109, 111, 118–119, 122, 124, 127, 136,
    141–142, 144–146 (n7)
    African American, 128
    Euro-American, 109–110, 118, 127
    Mexican American, 138
    Native American, 138
American Board of Commissioners for
    Foreign Missions (ABCFM), 22–24,
    40 (n16)
Amwes Islet, 9 (map), 25–26, 65, 68, 76
    (n2), 122
Anae, Melani, 138–139, 151
Andaman Islands, 8
Anderson, Benedict, 11
Angaur Island, 3–4 (map), 23–24, 45
Antarctic, 20
Apartment, 82, 86, 94–95, 101–102, 119,
    121, 125–126, 128
Appadurai, Arjun, 10
Arcata, California, 126–127, 131 (n9)
Armed forces/military, 2–3, 25, 40 (n11),
    45, 54, 59 (n8), 81, 95, 117–118, 131
    (n1)
    U.S. Army, 49–50, 95
    U.S. Marine Corps, 59 (n8), 109, 127
    U.S. Navy, 26, 47, 51, 54–55, 95, 117
Ashburn, Georgia, 93

Ashby, Gene, 87
Asian, 117–118, 140
Association for Social Anthropology in
    Oceania (ASAO), 59 (n8)
Asterion, 2
Atlantic Ocean, 83, 143
Aunt, 39, 52, 71, 76, 136, 145
Aurora, Oregon, 98
Australia, 21, 48, 51, 80, 113, 137,
    143, 151

Bali, 116
Bananas, 28, 55, 65
Bangkok, 101
Bank of Guam, 49, 107
Barnwell, Jane, xv
Basso, Keith, 10, 13, 124, 133, 142
Bay
    Humboldt Bay, 126, 131 (n10)
    Tumon Bay, 94, 118, 143
Beach/beaches, 15, 68, 70–71, 100, 143,
    147–148
Berea High School, 128
Betel, 118
Big Island, 54
Bilateral, 35
Bingo, 33, 71
Bishop Museum, 14
Blackbirder/blackbirding, 22
Blue Mountains, 83
Body brokers, 92–93
Borthwick, Mark, 32
Brady, Ivan A., 39
Brain drain, 69
Breadfruit, 20–21, 26, 28, 32, 38, 41 (n20),
    56, 65, 68, 71, 116, 148
Britannia, 39 (n2)
Brooke, James, 117–118
Brother, 36–37, 40 (n19), 41 (n19), 81, 101,
    109, 111 (n2), 121, 123, 125–128,
    130–131 (n5), 132 (n12, n16)
Bruner, Edward M., 134, 145

California, xv, 50, 56, 76 (n5), 88 (n3), 99,
    101, 111, 117, 125–126, 130–131
    (n8), 138–139, 143, 151
California Maritime Academy (CMA), 54
Canned meat, 27–28, 56, 66
Canoe house, 25, 30, 32–33, 46, 63, 71, 148
Canoe, 20, 22, 26, 30, 33, 142, 145, 147
    paddling, 28, 61, 149
    sailing, 3, 6, 8, 19, 24–25, 27–28, 30, 45,
        61–65, 70, 149
Capuchins, 24
Car/automobile, 34, 59, 73, 97, 100, 102,
    111, 116, 126, 131 (n9)
Carl, 22
Caroline Islands/Carolines, 4 (map), 9–10,
    16 (n1), 22–23, 27, 45, 73, 147
Carolinian, 8, 18, 43, 59 (n8), 88 (n3), 135,
    144
Carroll, Vern, 39
Carucci, Laurence M., 60 (n9)
Cash economy/wage economy. *See also*
    Wage employment, 24, 26–27, 31, 34,
    48, 52
Catechist, 24, 73, 148
Catholic Church. *See* Churches
Cedar Falls, Iowa, 12, 85–86, 91, 102
Cedar Rapids, Iowa, 77–79
Cell phone, 100
Cement house, 14, 30, 67, 69
Census. *See also De facto* population; *De
    jure* population, 52–53, 59 (n7), 74,
    114, 123, 138
Certified nursing assistant (CNA), 90,
    92–93, 98, 108, 128
Chaminade University, 108
Chamorro/Chamorros, 117–119, 121, 131
    (n1, n4)
Charles City, Iowa, 103 (n3)
Charleston, South Carolina, 83
Chat room, 54, 87–88, 105
Chen, 73
Cheyne, Andrew, 21–22
Chicken, 30, 71, 103 (n3), 116

Chief, 32, 36, 148–149
Child/children, 2, 8, 15, 30–32, 34, 37, 39,
    44, 46, 48, 51–54, 68–71, 73–74, 76,
    82, 84, 91, 93, 97–98, 101, 107–108,
    110–111, 116, 119–124, 127–129, 131
    (n4)–132 (n15), 134, 136–137, 139,
    141–142, 146 (n3, n4, n7)
China/Chinese, 50, 85, 118, 134
Christian/Christianity, 23, 26, 28, 71–72,
    96
Christmas, 132 (n12)
Churches
    Apostolic Faith Church, 126
    Baptist Church, 85
    Berea Evangelical Church, 96
    Catholic Church/Catholic Mission, 24,
        26, 29–30, 40 (n7, n8), 72–73, 96,
        124, 148
    Church of God, 96
    Congregational Church, 2, 22, 40 (n16)
    Island Community Church (ICC),
        96–98, 102, 127–128, 132 (n13)
    Liebenzell Mission, 24, 96
    Missionary Memorial Church Beyond
        the Reef, 98
    Namoluk Protestant Church, 23–24,
        29–31, 39 (n3), 40 (n8, n17), 72, 132
        (n15)
    Protestant Church/Protestant Mission,
        2, 22, 24, 34, 47, 51, 96, 125
    Seventh-Day Adventist, 40 (n8)
    United Church of Christ, 34, 40 (n16)
Chuuk/Truk (as a place), 2–3, 6–7, 9–11,
    14–16, 18–20, 24–26, 28–29, 31–32,
    34, 38–39 (n1, n5), 40 (n8, n10, n13,
    n15), 43, 45, 48–49, 51, 54–55, 57–59
    (n4), 64–65, 67, 70, 72, 77–79, 81–82,
    84–85, 88 (n4), 93, 96, 98–101,
    105–111, 116, 118, 120–122, 126, 128,
    131 (n5), 134, 136–137, 140–144
Chuuk/Truk High School, 6, 34, 76 (n3),
    107

Chuuk Lagoon (as a place), 2–3, 5 (map),
    16 (n2), 18, 23, 26, 38, 44, 64, 73, 75,
    82, 86, 88 (n6), 98, 102, 108, 110, 114,
    116, 119, 121, 123–124, 128, 135, 140
Chuuk State, 4 (map), 5 (map)–9, 12, 16
    (n1), 19, 24, 28, 34–35, 40 (n13), 43,
    45, 47–50, 52–53 (table), 55, 58, 60
    (n13), 68–69, 74–76 (n3), 80, 82–83,
    86, 96–99, 102, 107–108, 110–111,
    114, 116, 118–119, 125, 131 (n10),
    134, 136–140, 142, 146 (n4)
    government of, 32, 48–49, 51, 79, 85
Chuuk State Hospital, 48–49, 51–52,
    108–109, 115, 123
Chuukese language, xvi–xvii, 16 (n3), 18,
    44, 54, 102, 105–106, 141, 146 (n8)
Chuukese people/ethnicity, 7, 14, 32, 40
    (n13), 55, 59 (n8), 60 (n13), 73, 87,
    96, 105, 108–109, 116, 119, 125, 134,
    137, 139–140, 142, 144
Cigarettes, 20, 31, 34, 57
Clans, 14, 30, 32, 35–37 (table), 41 (n19),
    135–136, 147, 149
    Fáánimey, 36–37 (table)
    Imwo, 36–37 (table), 40 (n17)
    Inemaraw, 36–37 (table), 40 (n17)
    Katamak, 36–37 (table), 40 (n17), 125,
        127, 132 (n15)
    Sópwunipi, 36–37 (table)
    Sór, 14, 36–37 (table)
    Souwon, 36–37 (table), 132 (n14)
    Tum, 40 (n17)
    Wáánikar, 14, 36–37 (table), 125, 128,
        130
Cleveland State University, 85
Clientship/client members, 135–136, 146
    (n4)
Clifford, James, 14, 16
Cluster, 93, 96, 102, 109, 114, 123–127, 129
Coconut wireless, 86, 140
Coconut, 2, 19–21, 26, 28, 31–32, 38–39
    (n6), 40 (n14), 41 (n20), 46, 65, 68,
    71, 87, 147, 149

Coconutchat, 54, 87–88, 128

Collage, 89–90, 92–93, 95–96, 118

College degrees, 5, 47, 49, 52, 80, 90, 95
  Associate, 47, 49, 51, 69, 79–80, 83–84, 86, 95, 101, 107, 124, 126–127
  Bachelor's, 47, 49, 51–52, 55, 72, 79–80, 82–84, 86, 88 (n1), 95, 101, 107–108, 124, 126
  Master's, 49, 51–52, 80, 82, 86, 95, 107

College of Micronesia-Chuuk Campus (COM), 49, 65, 80, 99, 131 (n7), 133

College of Micronesia-Pohnpei Campus (COM), 51, 80, 84, 124, 128

College of the Redwoods (COR), 126–128, 131 (n10, n12), 132 (n12)

Colonial eras/periods/governments, 28
  German, 3, 23–24, 45, 146 (n5)
  Japanese, 3, 6, 24–26, 32, 45, 56, 72
  Spanish, 23
  U.S./American, 3, 17, 26, 47–48

Colonized/colonizing, 23, 53–54, 106, 144

Columbus, Ohio, 110

Communicate/communication, 12–13, 15, 31, 67, 87, 98–100, 103 (n5), 124, 139

Community college, 76 (n5), 77, 80–81, 83–84, 93, 95, 101, 109–110, 123, 126

Commonwealth of the Northern Mariana Islands (CNMI), 4 (map), 7, 48, 75 (table), 80, 86, 137

Compact of Free Association/The Compact, 7–8, 52–53, 92, 117–118, 122, 143
  Compact impact, 121

Computer, 49, 79, 87, 99, 102–103 (n5), 109

Congregational. *See* Churches

Continental Air Micronesia/"Air Mike", 43, 95, 98

Cookhouse, 30–31, 148

Cook Islands, 48

Copra, 23, 25–26, 31–34, 148

Coronado, California, 12

Corsicana, Texas, 8, 84–85, 88 (n2), 116

Cousin. *See also* Cross-cousin, 39, 76, 86, 101, 109, 145

Crescent City, California, 130

Cross-cousin, 37, 72, 109, 132 (n12)

Cynthiana, Kentucky, 93

Dallas, Texas, 76

Daughter, 2, 14, 84, 101, 109–110, 113, 121–123, 125–126, 128–131 (n5, n12), 132 (n15), 146 (n7)

Davis, George, 26–27

Day, A. Grove, 19

Dededo. *See* Guam

De Facto population, 76 (n6)

De Jure population, 15, 36–37 (table), 53 (table), 74, 80, 118, 120

Department of the Interior, 47

Dernbach, Kate, xv

Des Moines, Iowa, 76, 78

Descent line/descent group, 25, 36, 149

Diabetes (NIDDM), 56–57, 60 (n12), 121

Diaspora, 99, 134, 146 (n2)

Diaz, Vicente, 134, 151

Diocese of the Caroline and Marshall Islands, 73

Dispensary, 14, 26, 31

District center. *See* Urban center

Divorce, 16, 54, 93, 121, 128, 131 (n2), 142

Doane, E.T., 22

Dobbin, Jay, 121

Donne, John, 134, 146 (n1)

Drift/drifting/drift voyager, 100, 139–140, 142, 147, 149

Earth oven, 30, 121

East-West Center, 47

Easter, 72, 100, 111, 122, 125, 128

Eastern Oregon State College (EOSC), 83–84

Ebeye, 107

Economy. *See* Cash economy; subsistence economy

Education. *See* School

Eekmwar, 106, 111 (n1), 140

Elderly/elders. *See* Senior citizen

Elementary school, 24, 46, 48, 50, 82, 120

Berea School, 96

Namoluk Elementary School, 14, 26, 29, 31, 48, 69, 80, 86

Elites, 69, 73, 116

E-mail, 15, 54, 60 (n9), 87, 99–100, 102, 105, 113, 131 (n6)

Emplacement, 134, 138, 145

Endogamy/endogamous/in-marriage, 37, 135

English language, xvi-xvii, 51, 54, 59, 76, 87, 92, 97, 102, 106, 110–111, 117, 122, 139, 146 (n8), 148

Englund, Harri, 134, 145

Epidemic, 25–26

Epidemiological transition, 56

Eskimo, 134

Ettal, 5 (map), 8, 12, 16 (n2)–20, 24–26, 45, 65, 125, 133–134, 148

Eureka, California, 11–12, 95, 102, 109–111, 113–114, 125–131 (n9, n10, n12), 132 (n12, n15), 140

Europe/European, 18, 20, 64

Exogamy/exogamous/out-marriage, 35, 38, 141

Extended family, 14, 27

Fais, 3, 4 (map), 45

Falgout, Suzanne, 60 (n9)

Fast food, 56, 76, 90–92, 98, 117

Burger King, 91, 128, 131 (n7)

Denny's, 91

Hardee's, 86, 91

Kentucky Fried Chicken (KFC), 56, 91, 118

Little Caesar's Pizza, 118

McDonald's, 13, 56, 90–91, 103 (n1), 110, 117

Pizza Hut, 91

Sizzler Steakhouse, 91

Tony Roma's, 118

Village Inn, 86, 91

Father, 15–16, 36–38, 40 (n19), 54, 58, 83, 107, 110, 125–126, 130–131 (n4), 132 (n12, n13, n15, n16), 135–136, 141–142, 145–146 (n6)

Father's Day, 132 (n15)

Federated States of Micronesia (FSM), 3–4 (map), 7, 9, 16 (n1), 19, 40 (n13), 48, 52–53, 59 (n4), 60 (n9), 67, 73, 75 (table), 84, 86–87, 90–93, 95, 107–108, 114, 117–118, 121–122, 134, 137–138

Congress of, 49, 73

Embassy of, 93, 95, 101

Ferguson, James, 10–11

Field-trip, 2, 6, 28, 31–32, 34, 62, 73, 121

Fiji/Fijian, 22, 48, 59 (n8), 80, 96, 137, 143

Filipino/Philippines, 34, 118–119, 131 (n4)

Fink, Deborah, 103 (n2)

Finney, Ben, 65

Firth, Raymond, 8

Fish/fishing, 17, 20, 28–29, 41 (n20), 55–56, 62, 70, 73, 91, 116, 122, 127, 144, 148–149

spearfishing, 29, 34, 71, 148

trolling, 28, 32, 62–63, 70–71

Flagstaff, Arizona, 95

Florida, 60 (n15), 101, 111, 128, 138

Flour, 26–28, 34, 66

Food. *See also* Fast food, 24–25, 27–28, 30, 32, 38, 56, 63, 65, 71, 78, 91, 94, 110–111, 118, 127, 135, 143, 146 (n5), 148

Foreign exchange student, 5, 79

Fosterage, 39, 52

Fourth of July, 84

Gabriel, Larry, xv, 40 (n15)

Garment factories, 7

Geertz, Clifford, 89–90

Gegeo, David Welchman, 140–141

Genealogies, 15, 38

Geneva, Switzerland, 101
George Washington High School (Guam), 110
Georgia, 101, 128
Germany/German. *See also* Colonial eras, German, 3, 23, 35, 45, 50, 81, 100, 131 (n4)
Girschner, Max, 18, 24, 39 (n1, n5), 40 (n17)
Gladwin, Thomas, 6
Globalism/globalization, 10, 13, 144–145
Golden Gate Bridge, 130
Gonzaga University, 80
Goodenough, Ward H., xvi, 18, 39 (n5), 146 (n4, n8)
Gorenflo, Larry, 114, 116
Grandchildren/granddaughter, 48, 58, 74, 98, 110–111, 120–125, 131 (n5)
Grandparent, 52, 98, 108, 125, 136, 145
Grants Pass, Oregon, 130
Great Smoky Mountains, 83
Greenhouse, Steven, 89–90
Grecian formula, 73
Greyhound bus, 85–86, 100
Guam, 4 (map)–5, 7–8, 11–12, 43–45, 47–48, 50–53 (table)–58, 60 (n15), 65, 67, 69, 73–76, 78, 80, 82, 84–87, 91–92, 94–96, 98–100, 102, 106, 108–111, 114–125, 127–129, 131, 134, 137–140, 143–144
    Guamoluk, 117–123
    Guam Memorial Hospital, 52, 121
    villages on Dededo, 117, 121
    Yigo, 121
Guano. *See* Phosphate
Gulick, Luther, 22
Gupta, Akhil, 10–11

Hanlon, David, 151
Harding, Thomas G., 151
Harwood, Captain, 21
Hashmy, 21

Hawai'i, xv, 5, 7–8, 12, 22, 44, 47–53 (table)–54, 56, 65, 69, 74–76, 78–79, 82, 84, 86–87, 94–95, 98, 100, 106–111, 114, 117–119, 122, 126–127, 130–131 (n4, n6)–132 (n12), 134, 137–140, 143–146 (n6)
Hawai'i Pacific College, 82
Hawai'i School of Business, 51
Hawaiian, 82, 131 (n1, n10), 147–148
Health aide/health assistant, 14, 26, 47, 59 (n4), 69, 109
Health care/medical care, 7, 34, 38, 60 (n12), 102, 108, 115, 121, 123–124
Health problem/ill health, 39 (n3), 56–57, 84, 93, 102, 124
Hess, James, 143
Hezel, Francis X., 6–7, 22–24, 34, 39 (n2, n4)–40 (n7), 77, 88 (n2), 117–118, 121, 151
High school/secondary school, 2, 5–7, 26, 34, 38, 47, 49, 51–52, 54, 67–69, 72–73, 77, 79–80, 82, 84, 87, 92–93, 102, 107–110, 116, 120, 126, 128, 131 (n5)
Hispanic, 138
HIV/AIDS, 60 (n10)
Hōkūle'a, 65
Holokū, 77, 79
Home/home place, 6, 8, 10–12, 15, 25, 34, 44, 52, 55–56, 58–59, 67, 78, 80, 82–84, 87, 90, 93, 97–98, 108, 110–111, 114, 120, 122, 124, 127, 132 (n13)–134, 136, 138–141, 143, 145
Honolulu, 8, 12, 15, 43–44, 58, 82, 91, 94–95, 98–102, 107–111, 113, 116, 122–128, 130–131 (n7), 132 (n13), 140, 143
Honolulu Community College, 5, 107, 132 (n12)
Hospital, 34, 52, 85–86, 108, 115
Hotel maid. *See* Housekeeping
Hotel, 7, 48, 89, 92, 94, 117–118, 121, 143

Household, 30, 39, 44, 69, 108, 120, 123–125, 129

Housekeeping, 48, 90, 92, 128

Howard, Alan, 134, 137, 140

Humboldt State University, 126–127, 131 (n10)

Husband, 5, 15, 32, 83–84, 93, 101, 108–109, 111 (n2), 120–121, 124, 128–129, 134

Identity/identities, xvii, 10–11, 13–14, 35, 55, 69, 86–87, 97, 103, 114, 125, 130, 133–135, 137–146 (n7)

Illinois, 53, 79, 145

Immigration and Naturalization Service, 92

Indiana, 145–146 (n6)

Internet, 12, 16, 54–55, 87–88, 93, 99, 102, 105, 109

Iowa, 77–78, 81, 99–100, 103 (n2), 128, 145

Iowa Beef Packers (IBP), 86, 91, 103 (n2, n3)

Iowa City, Iowa, 12, 83, 85

Iraq, 109

Iras, 78

Island Hopper, 43–44, 58, 84, 98, 106, 110

Israel, 48

Italy, 50

Jaluit Gesellschaft, 23

Janes, Craig R., 96, 151

Japan/Japanese. *See also* Colonial eras, Japanese, 3, 5–7, 20–21, 24–26, 29, 32, 34, 40 (n10, n11), 45–48, 50, 56, 64, 109, 116–118

Jervis, Lori, 92

Jesuits, 34, 86

Job Corps, 52, 124

Johnson, Giff, 87

Jorgensen, Joe, 134

Jubilee, 72, 132 (n15)

Junior high school, 7, 40 (n16), 47, 106–107, 116, 120

Kailua, Hawai'i, 12, 14, 78

Kalamazoo, Michigan, 109

Kansas City, 82, 116, 141

Kauanui, Kēhaulani, 134, 151

Kapingamarangi, 4 (map), 25, 47

Kapi'olani Community College, 108, 110, 131 (n7)

Keating, Elizabeth, xv

Keesing, Roger, 16 (n4)

Kennedy administration, 6, 34

Kentucky, 137, 140

Key West, Florida, 48

Kinship, 10, 14, 30, 35–36, 38–40 (n19), 54, 65, 98, 135, 140

Kiribati, 4 (map), 48

Kiste, Robert C., 151

K-Mart, 118

Kohl, Manfred, 24

Korea/Korean/South Korea, 29, 48, 50, 73, 88 (n3), 100, 117–118

Koror, 4 (map), 25, 51, 107

Kosrae/Kosraen/Kosrae State, 4 (map), 16 (n1), 43–44, 109, 119, 146 (n7)

Krämer, A., 24

Kubary, Jan, 18

Kula Sanitarium, 123

Kuttu, 5 (map), 8, 16 (n2), 18, 26, 65, 109, 128, 147

Kwajalein, 4 (map), 43

Kwara'ae, Malaita (Solomon Islands), 141–142

Lal, Brij V., 135

Land, 10–11, 14–15, 24, 36–39, 41 (n20), 44, 61, 68–69, 111, 114, 116–117, 131 (n1), 134–135, 146 (n5), 148

Larson, Bruce, 7

Las Vegas, Nevada, 132 (n13)

League of Nations, 46

Leor, 1, 33

Lessa, William A., 27, 88 (n3)

Levin, Michael, 118

Levirate, 38

Lincoln, Nebraska, 12, 95
Lineage, 8–9, 15, 35–36, 38–40 (n18)–41
    (n19), 106, 108, 111, 128, 134, 146
    (n2, n4)
    matrilineage/matrilineal, 14–15, 35–38,
    40 (n9), 135–136, 142, 147
Linnekin, Jocelyn, 134, 140, 142
Lockwood, Victoria S., 151
Long Beach, California, 76
Long-timers, 8, 100, 102, 126, 139
Los Angeles, California (LA), 78, 98, 100,
    125, 130
Losap, 2, 5 (map), 9, 16 (n2)–19, 24, 39
    (n1), 65, 108, 127, 132 (n13)
Louisville, Kentucky, 100, 128
Lukeisel. *See* Mortlock Islands
Lukelap, 29, 137
Luken Islet, 9 (map)
Lukunoch, 5 (map), 9, 16 (n2)–18, 20–24,
    26, 131 (n12), 147
Lumber/lumber mill/lumber yard, 25, 27,
    66–67, 95, 126–127, 131 (n10)
Lütke, Fedor, 19–21

Macpherson, Cluny, 138–139, 151
Macy, Captain Richard, 19
Maid. *See* Housekeeping
Mailo, Petrus, 26
Majuro, 43, 67
Malawi, 134
Mall, 94, 117–118, 130
Man/men, 3, 5, 15, 24, 26–27, 30, 32, 36, 40
    (n8), 41 (n19), 44–48, 52–53, 55,
    57–59 (n1, n2, n3, n5, n6), 60 (n10,
    n13, n14, n15)–64, 67, 69–71, 73,
    78–79, 88 (n3, n4), 89, 91–93, 95, 97,
    100, 103 (n3), 106–109, 111 (n1),
    116, 118, 124, 127, 129, 131 (n8), 136,
    142, 146 (n7), 148
Manchester, Curtis A., Jr., 19
Marcus, George, 12
Mariano, Willoughby, 92–93, 103 (n4)

Mariana Islands, 4 (map), 40 (n13), 131
    (n1)
Marriage/marry, 9, 35–38, 50–52, 54–55,
    69, 72–73, 75, 79–82, 86, 88, 93, 99,
    101, 107–110, 114, 116, 119, 124–126,
    128–129, 131 (n2, n4), 134–136, 140,
    142
Marshall Islands/Republic of the Marshall
    Islands (RMI)/Marshallese, 4 (map),
    40 (n13), 44, 48, 59 (n4), 60 (n9), 73,
    75 (table), 84, 86–87, 91–93, 96, 107,
    118–119, 128, 131 (n10), 137,
    142–143
Marshall, Leslie B., xv, 1–2, 14, 16, 27, 51,
    60, 73, 77–79, 83, 86
Martial arts, 51, 85, 88 (n3), 95, 147
    bwang, 88 (n3), 147
    judo, 85
    tae kwan do, 85, 88 (n3)
Maryland, 128
Masculinity, 63, 94
Mass, 24, 73
Matrilineage/matrilineal. *See* Lineage
Maui, 123, 132 (n13)
Maui Community College, 107–108, 123
Mayo, Larry, 117–118
McDonald's. *See* Fast food
McGrath, Thomas, 7
Medical treatment. *See* Healthcare
Meatpacking, 91, 103 (n2)
Medex, 49, 59 (n4)
Merika, 44, 53–54, 56, 78–79
Michigan, 77, 79, 83, 108, 146 (n6)
Micronesia (as a region), 3, 4 (map), 7, 11,
    14, 20, 23–24, 28, 34, 38, 40 (n16),
    44–51, 53 (table), 56, 58, 80, 84, 92,
    100, 114, 117, 135, 137, 140, 143, 151
Micronesian (as an identity), 3, 6–8,
    22–23, 44, 46–47, 49–51, 56–57,
    63–64, 82, 84, 87–88 (n2), 91–93,
    118, 125, 134, 137, 139, 144, 149
Micronesian archipelago, 8, 84, 93

Micronesian Occupational College (MOC), 49, 107
Micronesian Public Safety Academy, 107, 109
Migrant/migrate/migration, 5–7, 10–11, 16, 35, 38, 44–45, 50, 52, 54–55, 59–60 (n12), 62, 67, 69, 73–74, 86, 96, 100, 102–103, 105–108, 110, 114, 117, 120–123, 134, 143, 151
   emigration, 6, 34, 52, 67–68, 70, 106, 116
   immigration/immigrant, 7, 43, 89–92, 98, 124–125, 135, 138, 145
Military. *See* Armed forces
Minister, 23–24, 40 (n17), 51, 72, 96, 126, 132 (n13), 136
Minnesota, 79
Missionaries, 2, 22–23, 40 (n16)
Mission/missionization, 23–24, 26, 28, 39 (n3), 47, 62, 96
Missouri, 108, 140
Mizpah High School, 2, 14, 34, 40 (n16), 76 (n3)
Moch, 5 (map), 8, 16 (n2), 18, 24, 26, 73, 111 (n1), 129, 148
Modern/modernity, 63, 69, 114, 117, 144
Moen. *See* Wééné
Money, 62–63, 67, 69, 82, 116, 132 (n12)
Moore, Henrietta, 14
Morning Star, 22
Morrell, Captain Benjamin, 20–21
Mortlock Islands/the Mortlocks, 3–4 (map)–5 (map), 7, 9–11, 16 (n2)–18, 21, 23–24, 28, 31, 37–39 (n2)–40 (n16), 66, 98, 102, 106, 114, 119, 134–135, 137, 140, 147–148
   Lower Mortlocks/Nomoi, 17–19, 21–25, 35, 39 (n1), 65, 86, 106, 146 (n5)
   Upper Mortlocks/Lukeisel, 17, 19, 39 (n1), 65, 73, 96
Mortlockese
   communities, 9–10, 15, 18, 24, 35, 109, 146 (n5)

language, xvi-xvii, 18, 54, 97, 101, 110, 141–142, 146 (n7)
   people/ethnicity, 17–18, 35, 38, 55, 73, 82–83, 86–87, 96, 98, 101, 107, 109, 125–126, 128–129, 134, 137, 140, 142, 144
   society/culture, 13, 15, 102
Mortlock, Captain James, 17, 39 (n2)
Morton, Helen, 145
Mother, 2, 32, 37, 40 (n19), 71, 101, 108, 110, 121, 123–124, 130–131 (n4)–132 (n12, n16), 135–136, 141–142, 145–146 (n6, n7)
Motorboat, 1, 19, 28, 34, 61–64, 70, 73
Mountain, 2, 16 (n3), 58, 83
Multilocality, 10–11
Multisited, 12, 107
Music, 15, 32, 40 (n15), 44, 71, 97, 116
Mwáán, 40 (n13)

Nama, 2, 5 (map), 8, 16–19, 39 (n1)
Namoluk community, xvii, 6, 8, 11–16, 25–26, 28–31, 35–37, 61, 65, 68–69, 72–73, 80, 98, 102–103 (n5), 105, 107, 110, 113, 135, 140–143, 145
Namoluk Constitution/Constitutional convention, 18, 61, 72
Namoluk municipal government, 18, 26, 32–33
Nantakku, 2
Nantucket, Massachusetts, 19
Nanyō Bōeki Kaisha (NBK), 25, 40 (n10)
Nason, James D., xv, 25
Nauru, 3, 4 (map), 23, 45, 48
Navarro College, 84–85
Navigation/navigator, 3, 6, 18, 20, 43, 45, 63, 90, 149
Nedelic, Pierre, 23
Nero, Karen, 60 (n9)
Network, 5–6, 11, 15, 45, 55, 98, 102–103 (n5), 109, 139
New England, 2, 22
New York, 93, 95, 101, 127

New Zealand, 48, 59 (n8), 113, 137–139, 143, 151
Newúwé, 143
NIDDM. *See* Diabetes
Nomoi. *See* Mortlock Islands
Nomoilam, 18–19, 87, 100, 140
Norfolk, Virginia, 51, 110
North America, 130
North Carolina, 84, 93, 110–111, 138
Northeast Missouri State University, 85
Nukuoro, 4 (map), 19, 47
Nurse/nursing (as a profession), 47, 49, 59 (n4), 86, 92, 95, 108, 110
Nursing home, 92–93, 128

O'ahu, 14, 125
Oceania/Oceanic, 135, 140, 142, 151
Oakland, California, 126, 130
Okinawan, 40 (n10)
Old folks/old man/old people/old woman. *See* Senior citizen
Oleson, Alice, 60 (n9)
Oneop, 3, 5 (map), 8–9, 16, 18, 24, 26, 40 (n9), 45, 47, 72, 122, 148
Ono, Sarah, xv
Oregon, xv, 5, 49, 55, 58, 73, 79, 84, 86, 101, 108, 111, 137, 139
Organic Act, 117
Ortner, Sherry, 143
Outer island, 2, 6, 23, 26, 32, 35, 57–58, 68, 73, 114, 134
Ozark, 91

Pacific Basin Medical Officers Training Program (PBMOTP), 51, 109
Pacific Choice Seafood, 127–128
Pacific Islands/Pacific Islander/the Pacific, 1, 3, 13, 16 (n1), 19–20, 22, 28, 38–39, 48–49, 57, 80, 96, 98, 113, 133–135, 137–140, 143–145, 151
Pacific Islands Central School (PICS), 47
Pacific Northwest, 55

Palau/Palauan/Republic of Palau, 4 (map), 9, 25, 40 (n13), 45, 47–49, 51, 59 (n8), 60 (n9), 67, 75 (table), 84–86, 88 (n4), 107, 118–119, 126, 131 (n10), 139
Palau Community College, 51
Pandanus, 26, 28, 32, 62
Papua New Guinea, 50, 80, 82
Paradise, 143–144
Parent, 12, 14–15, 39, 52, 67. 69–70, 76, 78, 99, 110, 124, 130, 136–137, 145
Pastor. *See* Minister
Patrilateral, 36–37
Peace Corps/Peace Corps Volunteer (PCVs), 14, 34, 48, 50
Pelto, Pertti J., 76 (n1)
Peniyésene, 9, 78
Pensacola, Florida, 12
Peter, Joakim, xv, 40 (n15), 133, 137
Phosphate, 3, 23, 45
Pickup truck, 2–3, 116, 127
Pieman, 143
Pingelap, 4 (map), 39 (n3), 48, 119
Piis Emmwar, 5 (map), 16 (n2), 24, 136
Place, 5, 7–8, 10–13, 15, 32, 38, 53, 64, 76, 78, 86, 88–89, 102–103, 106, 114, 120, 123–124, 133–135, 138, 140–142, 144–146 (n7)
Planet Hollywood, 118
Pohnpei/Pohnpeian/Pohnpei State, FSM, 4 (map), 9, 12, 16 (n1), 19, 22–24, 35, 39 (n3), 40 (n13, n16), 43–45, 47–48, 52, 55, 58–59 (n8), 67, 73, 78, 84, 86–87, 93, 106–109, 111, 118–119, 123–125, 128, 131 (n10), 146 (n5, n7)
Pohnpei Agricultural and Technical School (PATS), 124
Polowat, 4 (map)–5 (map)–6, 9, 19, 65, 135
Polynesian, 137
Port town. *See* Urban center
Portland, Oregon, 8, 12, 55, 58, 91, 95–98, 100, 102, 106, 109, 125–128, 130, 132 (n12, n13, n15), 140

Poyer, Linette, 134, 140, 142
Priest, 24, 73
Principal (of a school), 48, 69, 96
Protestant. *See* Churches
Pull factors, 6, 34, 116, 144
Pukos, 29, 137
Pukueu, 1, 65, 145

Quackenbush, Edward, 9
Queens Hospital, 123

Radcliffe-Brown, A.R., 8
Radio, 31–32, 34, 47–48, 61, 67, 99
Rain/rainfall, 30, 65, 71, 76 (n4)
Raven, Captain, 39 (n2)
Red Cross, 66
Rensel, Jan, xv, 134, 137
Reuney, Theophil Saret, 1, 15, 43
Rice, 24, 26–28, 32, 34, 56, 66, 70, 97, 116
Richards, Dorothy E., 40 (n11)
Riesenberg, Saul H., 19
Roche, Walter F., Jr., 92–93, 103 (n4)
Rodman, Margaret, 10–11
Rogers, Robert F., 117
Rondilla, Joanne L., 151
Roosevelt High School (Honolulu), 132
    (n13)
Rotuman, 137, 140
Ruben, Kino S. 17, 28
Russia/Russian, 19–20

Sahlins, Marshall, 143
Saipan, 4 (map), 7, 45, 47, 49, 52, 67, 82, 84
Salem, Oregon, 8, 12, 55, 95, 97–99,
    126–127, 130
Sāmoa/Sāmoan, 48, 59 (n8), 80, 96,
    123–124, 131 (n10), 139, 143, 151
San Diego, California, 107
San Francisco, California, 126, 130, 145
Santa Rosa, California, 59 (n8)
Satawan, 5 (map), 7, 9, 16 (n2)–18, 21–23,
    26, 39, 45, 74, 107, 116, 147
Satawan Junior High School, 7, 107

Schlosser, Eric, 91
Schneider, David M., 36
School, 5, 34, 39 (n3), 46, 48, 54–55, 69, 71,
    74, 76, 79–80, 82–83, 88 (n3), 96, 101,
    107–111, 121–124, 127–128, 138
  church-based, 34, 69, 116
  public, 34, 76, 108, 119, 121, 139
Schoolteacher. *See* Teacher
Scotia, California, 126
Scotland, 145
Seawall, 68
Seattle, Washington, 1, 116
Security guard, 90, 93–94, 109
Senior citizen, 15–16, 31, 37, 40 (n18), 45,
    58–59, 63, 67, 71, 74, 91–92, 96, 98,
    111, 123, 130, 149
Sennit, 28, 40 (n14), 46, 71
Senyavin, 19
Severance, Craig, 59 (n8)
Sharp, Andrew, 19
Ship, 1–2, 6, 12, 20–26, 31–35, 40 (n10),
    45, 47, 55, 62, 73, 98, 106, 114–115,
    140, 147
Sibling/sibling set/siblingship, 14, 32,
    36–37, 39–40 (n19), 52, 67, 70, 87, 99,
    109, 149
  sibling-set marriage, 37, 111 (n2)
Sister, 32, 36–37, 41 (n19), 78, 81, 100,
    108–111 (n2), 123, 125, 127–130, 132
    (n13), 134
Slusser, R.C., 26
Small, Cathy A., 151
Social class, 68–69, 115
Sokehs, 146 (n5)
Solimeo, Samantha, xv
Solomon Islander, 141
Son, 14, 32, 36, 58, 83, 101, 110, 113, 121,
    123, 125, 130, 132 (n15)
Sópúúk, 116
Sópwonewel, 29, 137
Sororate, 38
Southeast Missouri State University, 85
Southwest Islands (of Palau), 9, 59 (n8)

Southwest (of USA), 138
Spain/Spanish. *See also* Colonial eras, Spanish, 3, 45, 85, 117, 138
Spickard, Paul, 134, 151
Sponsored, 55, 102
Spoonley, Paul, 138, 151
Springdale, Arkansas, 91
S.S. Monterey, 76 (n5)
Star of the Sea, 73
Stonington, Connecticut, 20
Store, 2, 27–28, 31, 56, 64, 94, 107–108, 144
Straub Clinic, 123
Subclan, 30, 35–36, 41 (n19), 125, 128–130
Subsistence economy, 31
Sugita, Hiroshi, xvi, 18
Sumatra, Indonesia, 134
Suomi College, 108
Switzerland, 50, 101

Ta, 5 (map), 16 (n2), 18, 147
Tahiti, 65, 143
Taiwan, 29, 56, 117
Taro
    as food, 26, 28, 32, 40 (n12), 56, 70
    plot/patch, 36, 41 (n20), 68, 71, 116, 149
    swamp, 25–26, 40 (n12), 41 (n20), 65, 68, 149
Teacher, 28, 39 (n3), 47–49, 51, 69, 71–72, 76 (n3), 81–82, 84, 86, 88 (n3), 95, 107, 109, 111
Telephone/phone, 12, 15–16, 73, 79, 82, 85–86, 93, 99–103 (n5), 105, 109, 116, 122, 126–127, 131 (n6), 140
Television/TV, 73, 76, 85, 116, 118, 139
Tennessee, 140
Texas, 51, 88 (n3), 95, 107, 126
Thailand, 50
Thanksgiving, 12, 85, 125
Thatch house, 30
The 101st account, 16, 143
Tikopia, 8
Tinned fish, 28, 56
Toba Batak, 134, 145

Tobacco. *See* Cigarettes
Toinom Islet, 9 (map), 32, 76 (n5)
Tokelauan, 139
Tokyo, 44
Tonga/Tongan, 48, 139, 143, 145, 151
Tonowas, 3, 5 (map), 24, 45, 47
Toon, 5 (map), 86, 141
Tourist/tourism, 7, 34, 43, 92, 94, 117–118, 131 (n1), 143
Trade/trader, 20–21, 23, 26, 28, 32, 55, 63
Translocal community, 143
Transnational/transnationalism, 10–11, 13, 64, 99, 107, 134, 138, 144
Transportation, 6, 13, 55, 62, 98, 106
Tripler Army Medical Center, 123
Truk District. *See* Chuuk State
Truk Islander, 2
Trust Territory. *See* U.S. Trust Territory of the Pacific Islands
Trust Territory School of Nursing, 49
Tuition, 34, 69, 116, 126
Tuna, 28, 32–33, 62–63, 70, 147, 149
Turkey tails, 55–57, 60 (n9)
Turkey tail disease, 57
Tuvalu, 48
Typhoon, 26–28, 35, 70, 117, 146 (n5)
    typhoon house, 29, 121
    Typhoon Pamela, 65–68
    Typhoon Phyllis, 26–30, 65–66, 69
Tyson Foods, 91

Ulithi, 4 (map), 27, 119
Ulin, Robert, 13
Umap Islet, 9 (map)
Uncle, 39, 52, 76, 136, 145
Unilineal, 35, 38
United Kingdom, 145
United Nations (UN), 5, 34
United Parcel Service (UPS), 95, 127
United States of America/ USA/ the States/America. *See also* American; Colonial eras, U.S.

as a country/place, 2–3, 7–8, 12, 15, 18,
    21, 26, 34–35, 44, 49, 51–54, 57, 60
    (n13), 64, 74–75, 78–88 (n3), 90–96,
    99–103 (n4), 109–111, 115, 117–121,
    124, 130, 138–139, 141–143, 145, 151
  government of, 5–6, 34, 49, 79
U.S. mainland, 7–8, 12, 44, 47–53
    (table)–54, 56, 58, 67, 69, 74–76, 79,
    84, 86–87, 98, 100, 106–109, 111, 115,
    119, 122–126, 137–139, 143–144
U.S. Trust Territory of the Pacific Islands
    (USTTPI), 3, 6–7, 26, 34, 40 (n13),
    47–48, 66, 74, 79, 86, 137
University of California, Berkeley, 80
University of Guam (UOG), 47, 51, 79, 82,
    107, 110, 134
University of Hawai'i, Hilo, 125
University of Hawai'i, Mānoa, 48, 54, 59
    (n4), 80, 82, 107, 109, 127, 133
University of Iowa, xv, 77, 80–81, 85–86,
    134, 146 (n2)
University of Northern Iowa (UNI), 85
University of the South Pacific, 109, 124
U.S. International University (USIU), 107
Urban center, 2, 6–7, 28, 34–35, 38, 40
    (n13), 56–57, 68, 73–74, 80, 99, 106,
    108, 110, 114–115, 120, 122
USSR. *See* Russia

Vacation, 67, 73, 116, 122
Valedictorian, 80, 86
Vehicle. *See* Car; Pickup truck
Velez-I, Carlos G., 88 (n3)
Videocassette/VCR, 99–100, 102, 116, 132
    (n15)
Village, 25, 29, 32, 40 (n13), 137
Virginia, 54, 110–111
Virtual community, 140
Virtual kinship, 98–99, 130
Visit/visiting/visitor, 12, 15, 18, 33, 52, 63,
    67, 73–74, 84–86, 98, 100, 102–103
    (n5), 105–106, 108, 115, 122, 125,

127, 130–131 (n11), 132 (n13), 139,
    142, 144–146 (n7)
Vladivostok, 20
Vocational training, 47, 49, 52, 69, 96
Voyage/voyaging, 2–3, 6, 18–19, 45, 63, 65,
    98, 149

Wage employment/wage job/wage work.
    See also Cash economy, 3, 6–7, 38, 45,
    48, 51–52, 67–69, 74, 80, 108, 115,
    117, 121
Wallace, Ben J., 151
Wal-Mart, 109, 132 (n13)
Warner Pacific College (WPC), 96
War
  Gulf War, 54–55
  Iraq War, 109
  Spanish-American War, 117
  World War I, 3, 46
  World War II, 3, 5–6, 17, 25–26, 38, 40
    (n11), 45–48, 113, 116–117, 137, 151
Ward, R. Gerard, 21
Washington, 83, 85–86, 121
Watson, James L., 13, 90, 103 (n1), 134,
    146 (n2)
Wééné, xv, 2–3, 5 (map)–7, 9, 12, 24, 26,
    32, 34, 38, 40 (n13, n17), 45, 47–48,
    50, 52–53 (table), 55–58, 67, 69,
    71–76, 78–80, 82–84, 86, 95–96,
    98–103 (n5), 106–111, 114–118, 120,
    122–124, 126–128, 130–131 (n5), 132
    (n12, n13), 136, 139, 141, 143–144
Wendel, John, 88 (n5)
West Virginia, 116
Western Apache, 13
Western Islands/Islanders (of Chuuk
    State), 5 (map), 6, 65, 116
Western Michigan University, 109
Western Oregon University, 101
Whaler, 19–21, 23, 28
White, Geoffrey M., 151

Wife, 40, 54, 58, 88 (n6), 101, 107, 122, 125, 127–128, 130–131 (n4), 132 (n15)

Wiichap, 116

Willamette Valley, 58

Wilson, Rob, 134, 140

Wisconsin, 79, 109

Woleai, 4 (map), 45

Wolf, Margery, xvi, 13

Woman/women, 1, 3, 5, 15, 24, 26–27, 30, 32, 36, 40 (n9), 44, 46–48, 50–52, 55–59 (n1, n2, n3, n5, n6), 67, 69, 71, 77–79, 82, 86, 88 (n3), 89, 92–93, 95, 97, 100–101, 107, 116, 118, 120–121, 123–130, 136, 146 (n7)

Wooden house, 29, 31, 67, 69

World Health Organization (WHO), xv, 59 (n4), 101

World Wide Web, 87, 99

Wright, Debbie H., 151

WSZC (radio station in Chuuk), 32, 71

Xavier High School, 34, 76 (n3), 81, 86, 88 (n5), 107, 126, 134

Yap/Yapese/Yap State, FSM, 4 (map), 6, 9, 16, 35, 40 (n13), 47, 58, 65, 67, 146 (n7)

Yigo. *See* Guam

Young William, 17, 39 (n2)